What do the Scriptures Say About the Last Days?

Now learn the parable of the fig tree... when the branches are yet tender, and it begins to put forth leaves you know that summer is at hand so likewise my elect who see all these things will know that He is near, even at the door.

Matthew 24:41, 42

Although the fig tree shall not blossom, neither shall fruit be in the vines; the labor of the olive shall fail, and the fields shall yield no meat; the flocks shall be cut off from the fold and there shall be no herd in the stalls.

Yet shall I rejoice in the Lord, I will Joy in the God of my salvation. The Lord God is my strength, and He will make my feet like hinds' feet, and He will make me to walk upon mine high places....

Habakkuk 3:17-19

What Do the Scriptures Say About the Last Days?

A Documentary of Scriptures
regarding The Last Days

by Jeanne Roberts
and RSBlain

What Do the Scriptures Say, About the Last Days?
Answers are taken from: The Inspired Version of the Bible, The Book
of Mormon, and The Doctrine and Covenants

iUniverse books may be ordered through booksellers or by contacting:

iUniverse
1663 Liberty Drive
Bloomington, IN 47403
www.iuniverse.com
1-800-Authors (1-800-288-4677)

ISBN: 978-1-4620-3117-7 (sc)
ISBN: 978-1-4620-3118-4 (e)

Printed in the United States of America

iUniverse rev. date: 11/17/2011

Dedication

This book is dedicated to **Jesus Christ** for whom it is written.

It is also dedicated to my friend and teacher, Brother Robert Bradford (formerly of the Reynoldsburg, Ohio congregation) whose personal study of scripture and the Last Days, and development of his own <u>Life After Death Chart</u>, inspired my interest in this subject.

I must also remember Brother Clark Hutchison (Reynoldsburg, Ohio congregation) whose criticism of my first completed writing attempt in 1998 or 99 made me realize that a successfully finished manuscript would take a whole lot more work.

Finally, this book is dedicated to my husband, the rest of my family, my church family and to all who choose to read, ponder and respond to the information provided. God bless you.

Contents

SIGN 5: False Christs
SIGN 6: Sin is rampant.
SIGN 7: Wars and Rumors of Wars
SIGN 8: Famines, Pestilences, and Earthquakes
SIGN 9: The Gospel is preached throughout the world.
SIGN 10: People cry "Peace, peace" but there will be no peace.
SIGN 11: People will run to and fro and knowledge will be increased but the wisdom of the wise will be confounded.
SIGN 12: People will reject the scriptures concerning the Last Days.
SIGN 13: Moral decay and corruption are widespread.
SIGN 14: There will be false teachers.

List of Illustrations

Book covers, front and back designed by RSBlain and Jeanne Roberts.
Interspersed Doves by Jeanne Roberts. Floral Photos and Floral Graphics by RSBlain.
Other art works are by Laura Roberts, Matt Jordon, and Matt Zelnick.

Acknowledgements

If it were not for the Lord, this book would not have been written. He insisted and I procrastinated (for two years). Finally, He let me know that if the project did not start soon, there would not be enough time to finish it. This could be interpreted in several ways, but not one of the options was appealing. With lots of foot-dragging, the task of writing began. Little did I know how long it would take! To say this has been an awesome, challenging, and ever-demanding task is an understatement. On numerous occasions I breathed a sigh of relief, thinking the book was finished. Then He would show me where more intensive work needed to be done. As years passed, I was genuinely unsure it would ever be completed. The Lord chose a truly fractured vessel for this assignment! However, He directed the content, located scripture references, and rearranged chapters. Any praise and honor belong to Him. He also provided the following people; each of them helped considerably and must be thanked.

Alvin Roberts, my dear husband and best friend for fifty years (our 50th wedding anniversary was June 11, 2010.) He searched for elusive scriptures, debated my theological concepts, read numerous manuscript pages, and gave me several sabbatical leaves free from cooking and housework. He tolerated years of neglect while I sat at the computer writing this manuscript. He also encouraged me to finish the project when the going got rough. I think his tolerance had something to do with receiving somewhat regular meals even though our house went to pot.

Brian and Laura Roberts, my techie son and daughter-in-law, provided the services of computer technicians, advisers, consultants, instructors, repairman and woman, keeping the equipment operational during endless months of writing, rewriting, correcting the manuscript, and tearing their hair over my woeful lack of computer skills.

My friend Andrea Clute is my excellent, long-suffering local editor. Her husband, Scott Clute also helped with graphics and computer issues.

An unnamed saint and brother in the Center Place worked on my fuzzy theological concepts until I finally got them right. He prefers to remain anonymous but is responsible for ideas in Chapter 2 in this book.

Illustrations are by RSBlain, Matt Jordan, Laura Roberts and Matt Zelnik.

Numerous people, unknown to me, wrote or contributed to the many reference books I've used continually. Without the compendiums, concordances, study Bibles, scripture reference books, and Book of Mormon RLDS LDS Conversion Table, this manuscript could not have been written.

Finally, I thank Skipper, my overgrown Catahoula dog who passed away during this project and Cappy, our ridiculous Labradoodle puppy. In addition, Ronan, a beautiful Akita pup who came to live with us by accident and Kat, our old alley cat who intimidates three very big dogs, wants regular meals and insists on outings, forcing me to leave the computer to care for his needs. Without their help, I would get no exercise at all. Every day and week and month and year this project continues, I am more and more thankful to everyone listed. Without them, I would have given up long ago.

The Book of Mormon makes a promise, appropriate here.

<u>Moroni 10:4-7</u>
When you receive these things, I exhort you to ask God, the eternal Father, in the name of Christ, whether these things are true. And, if you ask with a sincere heart and with real intent, having faith in Christ, He will manifest the truth of it to you by the power of the Holy Ghost; and by the power of the Holy Ghost you may know the truth of all things.

Whatever thing is good is also just and true. Therefore, nothing that is good denies the Christ, but acknowledges that He is. And, that you may know He is, by the power of the Holy Ghost, I would exhort you not to deny the power of God; for He works by power, according to the faith of the children of men, the same today and tomorrow and forever. Amen.

Readers
are encouraged to validate
the truthfulness
of concepts within this book
through personal study and prayer.

Preface
My Reasons for Writing This Book

I wrote this book out of concern that many of God's people are uninformed and ill prepared for the Second Coming of Jesus Christ. The fundamental belief expressed in this manuscript is, three sacred books, *(1) the Inspired Version of the Bible, (2)- the Book of Mormon, and (3)- the Doctrine and Covenants*, contain the Word of God, insofar as they are correctly translated. All three books contain emphatic warnings about the Last Days, indicating Christ's return is very near.

This book, "*What do the Scriptures Say About the Last Days*", has 3 Purposes, IDENTIFICATION, ORGANIZATION and PROVISION of SCRIPTURES so God's directions concerning the Last Days are gathered together into one place for comparisons and study.

1- Identification of:

- scriptural warning signs alerting Christians to the coming of the Great Tribulation and the return of Jesus Christ
- the current fulfillment of prophecy (See page 16.)

Specific clues in the Old and New Testament prophecies, which identify God's references to the Last Days are:

- Clue #1, the words 'at that day', 'at that time', 'in those days', 'in that day', and similar phrases found in scripture are good indicators that these verses refer to the end times. They separate prophetic verses for the future from prophecy already fulfilled. There may be exceptions but close examination reveals that most references using these phrases concern the Last Days.
- Clue #2, the phrase 'the day of the Lord' specifically refers to the second coming of Christ. Example, Joel 2:31, "the sun shall be turned into darkness and the moon into blood before the great and terrible day of the Lord."

2- Organization:

- Last Days scripture from all three books are organized so readers can follow one prophetic event to the next from the return of Christ's church in the 1830's to the final judgment.
- The Bible, the Book of Mormon, and Doctrine & Covenants Last Days scripture verses are cross referenced and organized for easy access and study. The Inspired version of the Bible has also been cross-referenced with the King James Bible. When differences exist between the two versions of the Bible, the King James Version is identified in parentheses. (e.g., John 5:11 KJV)
- Verses appearing in the Inspired Version only are marked "I.V. only."
- The Book of Mormon scriptures from the RLDS church have been cross-referenced for the LDS churches using the booklet, *The Book of Mormon Chapter and Verse RLDS-LDS Conversion Table* by Zarahemla Research Foundation, Independence, Missouri.

3- Provision:

The gathered information is provided in an easy-to-read manner for its intended audience: members of the former Reorganized Church of Jesus Christ of Latter Day Saints, the many Restoration Churches and any other interested parties.

The primary task of this book is to make this information available so the Saints[1], all concerned Christians, and anyone interested can become more aware of the crucial timing of the Last Days, and the necessity of preparing NOW. The time has come for individuals to make final decisions about their relationship with Jesus Christ.

Wake Up Call

This book is a unique source of information about the Last Days. It identifies Christ's warning signs in Matthew 24 and numerous other end times warnings scattered throughout the three standard books. It demonstrates how many of these signs are rapidly being fulfilled today. Matthew 24:42 says, "My elect who see all these things shall know that Christ is near, even at the door. But no one knows the hour or the day." When the signs are completely fulfilled, 'the Great Tribulation' will begin. In chapters 3 and 4 of this book, the warning signs are identified. In the chapters, which follow, numerous additional scriptures are provided to support each sign. The current fulfillment of many of these signs is also documented and the pages provide eye-opening reading for anyone interested in end time prophecies. Therefore, this is a wake-up call for all Christians who believe the scriptures are The Word of God.

Many authors have written about the Last Days, but interpretations of scripture are very different from one writer to the next. This book is written from the perspective of <u>the former</u> Reorganized Church of Jesus Christ of Latter Day Saints [2] and it uses scripture

---

[1] Saints is a name used in reference to membership of the RLDS church.

[2] The following books "Strong's Concordance of the Bible", "Cruden's Complete Concordance", "The Interpreter's Bible" (12 volumes), "The New King James Version of the Bible", "The New International Version of the Bible", "The Complete Jewish Bible", "Harper Collins Bible Dictionary", "Hard Sayings of the Bible", "The Bible Reader's Companion", "Illustrated Bible Handbook", "The Bible Timeline", and

from *The Inspired Version of the Bible, the Book of Mormon, and the Doctrine and Covenants.*

This book simply asks, **WHAT DO THE SCRIPTURES SAY WILL TAKE PLACE** in the Last Days.

To answer the question, I have attempted to place relevant verses of last day's scripture in chronological order so the pieces of the end times puzzle fall into place and answer readers' questions in a manner that is easy to follow. A strong effort has been made to keep each scripture within its proper context so it does not say something that is incorrect.

This document and each statement within are based on the content of:

- the Inspired Version of the Bible
- the Book of Mormon
- the Doctrine & Covenants

This document and each statement are supported by scripture within those three books. Nothing I have written is purposely taken out of context. As the person who compiled this book, I am solely responsible for any mistakes found on these pages.

Understanding Scripture Prophecy

Some prophetic verses of scripture have several levels of meaning and may refer to things that took place in the past as well as things that are to come. Passages referring to Christ's first and Second Coming often fall into this category. When using these verses, the attempt was made, through prayer, study, and research to gain a consistent understanding of scripture as a whole.

The prophets did not always understand their own visions or dreams. They tried to express their experiences in terms understood in their time, but these descriptions are often unclear to modern readers. Daniel's vision of the four beasts (Daniel 7) is an example.

However, today it is possible for us to understand some of the ancient visions because of the remarkable way they relate to current events.

It is also important to know that latter day signs may be misinterpreted. They may be purposely manipulated and shared incorrectly. We must be certain the signs we follow are accurate[3]. The three books of scripture containing Christ's warning signs are the 'only trustworthy source' of information about Christ's Second Coming. All books written by man, including this one, are subject to human error. No one but God knows the real order in which these events will occur.

"The Wall Chart of World History from Earliest Times to the Present" were all used as aids in writing this book.

[3] Christ's return has been watched for, by the individual Christian and Christian groups, dating from his Crucifixion and Ascension. Specific dates have been advertised to no avail. As of this writing, he has yet to return because ALL of the signs he said we must watch for have not yet occurred. Read more on this internet site: http://en.wikipedia.org/wiki/Rapture

Readers are encouraged to compare all the information in this book to their own scriptures and to pray for knowledge of God's truths.

My prayer is:

This book will find its way to people who need God's guidance, particularly during the Great Tribulation.

Readers will discover the truth of the prophetic scripture describing the Last Days as they study this book.

Readers will recognize the impact these scriptures have on the time in which we are now living.

Readers will spiritually prepare for the challenges the scriptures say are coming in these last days.

Readers will be blessed with more faith and power than ever before, in keeping with the will of our Lord and Savior Jesus Christ.

Readers will have the desire and courage to hold on to the rod of iron until the very end.

Suggestions for Individual or Group Use

This book can be used for individual or group study. It attempts to bring together important prophecies concerning the Last Days and provides numerous scriptures from the three standard books (the Bible, the Book of Mormon, and the Doctrine & Covenants) to help the understanding of each of the prophecies.

This manuscript should not be read like a novel, a history, or a textbook. It is a collection of unembellished facts concerning the Last Days supported by scripture from the Bible, the Book of Mormon, and the Doctrine and Covenants. Each topic is introduced by the question, "What do the scriptures say about __?" Numerous scriptures are provided to answer the questions.

A suggested approach: Gain an overall picture of the contents by reading chapters 1, 2, 3, and 4, which identify and examine each of Christ's warning signs.

Chapter 2 contains all essential information to prepare for Christ's Second Coming. A person could quit reading at this point and have all s/he needed to know to become part of Christ's kingdom. However, chapter 2 does not duplicate the valuable information in subsequent chapters. The balance of the chapters give a more complete picture of the Last Days and attempt to provide readers with an even better understanding of what the scriptures say will take place.

After reading 1, 2, 3, and 4, readers may choose to read the rest of the chapters in numerical order or read chapters that deal with subject matter on particular topics. However the chapters are approached, it is my hope all of them will be studied because of their importance, pertaining to God's plan, for this End Times-period.

As we approach the end times chapters 5, 6, and 7 concerning the restoration of Christ's Church and its relationship to the restoration become more relevant.

Chapters 8 and 9 are about God's ancient covenants with the Jews and their role in the Last Days.

Chapter 10 discusses the Antichrist.

Chapter 11 deals with the battle of Armageddon and the second Coming of Jesus Christ.

Chapter 12 discusses the defeat of Satan and looks at the millennium and the 1000-year reign of the Lord.

Chapter 13 deals with the Final Judgment.

Chapter 14 looks at scripture descriptions of Heaven and its rewards.

Chapter 15 provides scripture promises from God.

For group study, take turns reading and discussing portions of this book aloud. Refer to your own Bible, Book of Mormon, and Doctrine & Covenants to verify the accuracy of paraphrased scripture in this book.

Question how the paraphrased scriptures in this book compare to your personal understanding of God's word. Are there other scriptures, which more clearly define the topics?

This book was written after intensive study, but the author is neither a theologian nor an expert on scripture. Are there scriptures that present a different point of view than the author's? If a scripture does not relate appropriately to the topic, where does the problem lie?

Discuss any disagreement with the conclusions in this book and justify them by comparison to other scriptures. Don't worry about right or wrong statements. Consensus is not necessary.

It would be very helpful if readers will notify the author with additional scripture, thoughts, and suggestions.

Jeanne Roberts
djeanneroberts@gmail.com

Disclaimer

It has taken a long time to compile, write and correct this book. Yet, each time we review it, additional errors reveal themselves.

We are aware mistakes in punctuation, grammar, and capitalization still exist in this manuscript. Given the time in which we live and the present world conditions, we feel it is imperative to publish the book as it now stands.

Please overlook errors in punctuation, grammar, and capitalization but bring mistakes in scripture references and interpretation to our attention.

Scriptures in this book are not always written exactly as they appear in the Bible, Book of Mormon or Doctrine and Covenants. Many scriptures are paraphrased to make their content more understandable.

Whether therefore you eat, or drink, or whatever you do, do all to the glory of God.

I Corinthians 10:31

Introduction
Is the world really coming to an end?

After Christ's miraculous ascension into Heaven, Christians waited impatiently for His return. Throughout the next twenty centuries, believers expected Him within their lifetime. Expectations were based on incidents that appeared to fulfill portions of prophecy. They were always disappointed. Two thousand years passed and Christ did not come. Today, His future return is seldom discussed in Christian houses of worship, including the Community of Christ and many Restoration churches. Few people are waiting or watching. They prefer to ignore or ridicule discussions of the Last Days. Many Christians no longer believe His return will be literally fulfilled. Others argue it has already taken place, and some think His second coming is in the distant future. For most, the topic is no longer relevant, and they don't want to bother with speculation.

So, why should anyone get excited about this subject now?

1. It is important that we know what to expect.
2. It is important that we know what God expects of us.

According to scripture, Christ's return will be preceded by the Great Tribulation. During the tribulation, peace will be taken from the whole earth. The "man of perdition" (Antichrist) will be revealed and he will attempt to rule the world. He will promise peace but bring great destruction. Christians and Jews will be especially persecuted and no one will be safe from the wrath of this man. Jesus Christ warned His apostles about this time and He indicated that at the end of the tribulation, a great war will threaten to destroy the entire world. This war is described in Isaiah, Ezekiel, Daniel, Matthew 24, and the book of Revelation. (Specific scriptures are provided in this books chapter on the tribulation).

TODAY, many people discount the Last Days and the return of Jesus Christ but,

- **WHAT IF the scriptures are correct?**
- **WHAT IF Christ's signs in scripture are being fulfilled today?**
- **WHAT IF we are facing the End Times now?**

In spite of the popular *Left Behind* series by Tim LaHaye and Jerry Jenkins, most Christians know very little about the signs of the times. The majority of Christians believe this event remains in the distant future if it should ever take place at all. They fail to realize that the fulfillment of the signs means the Great Tribulation is almost upon us.

They remain unprepared for the Last Days. They are not "watching and waiting" (Matthew 24:49). They do not fully understand the scriptures and are unaware they forewarn what is to come.

Only believers, who are familiar with the prophecies, will recognize and understand the importance of the signs as they appear. They will be making prayerful preparations for Christ's return and will have His spirit to be with them during troubled times. Those who believe in the divinity of the Word are witnessing the fulfillment of some of Christ's signs now.

The Rapture

Many Christians believe in the 'Rapture' and that it will carry them out of the world before the Great Tribulation. This great 'escape' will solve all problems IF the pre-tribulation rapture theory is correct.

But, there are 3 different Rapture theories seriously considered by people in different churches.

- The Pre-Tribulation Rapture Theory suggests that God will remove all believers from earth before the tribulation begins. It indicates the faithful saints, living and dead, will be caught up in the Heavens to meet Christ before the Great Tribulation.
- The Mid-Tribulation Rapture Theory suggests believers will be caught up to meet Christ during the Tribulation.
- The Post Tribulation Rapture Theory implies believers will be removed from earth before the battle of Armageddon.

This IS NOT what the scriptures say and none of these theories was ever a part of the RLDS Church beliefs. Scripture tells us Christ will return to end the War of Armageddon (Thessalonians 4:16, 17) and at that time believers will be caught up to meet Him. Therefore, the rapture theories are in error and those who expect to be removed from earth will find themselves in the midst of calamity, unprepared for seven years under the domination of the Antichrist. Some may lose their faith, unable to withstand his persecution. However, Jesus promises to be with us forever.

Is another book about the End Times relevant?

Yes, when it emphasizes the warning signs that are seldom mentioned in other books about the Last Days.

The primary emphasis of most other literature is:

- the coming and reign of the Antichrist
- the Great Tribulation
- the war of Armageddon
- the return of the Lord

Although these topics are of great importance, emphasizing the Signs of the End Times may persuade Christians to prepare now.

Matthew 24:51
Therefore, be ready, for in such an hour when you think not, the Son of man will come.

Jesus is very concerned that His followers know He is coming, soon. He told us to be watching and waiting. The warning signs in scripture are provided for this purpose. The following verses from the Old and the New Testaments and the Doctrine & Covenants describe Christ's Second Coming.

Daniel 7:13, 14
I [Daniel] saw… one like the Son of man coming with the clouds of Heaven… and there was given Him dominion, and glory, and a kingdom that all people, nations, and languages should serve Him.

Matthew 16:2-4
When it is evening you say, "It will be fair weather for the sky is red" and in the morning, "It will be foul weather today for the sky is red and threatening." Hypocrites! You know how to discern the face of the sky but you cannot discern the sign of the times [See Mark 8:12, Luke 11:30-31, 12:54-56].

Doctrine & Covenants 43:5a-g, [February 1831, Kirtland, Ohio]
Hearken ye, for behold, the great day of the Lord is at hand. The day soon comes that the Lord shall utter His voice out of Heaven, the Heavens shall shake and the earth shall tremble and the trumpet of God shall sound both long and loud and say to the sleeping nation; "You saints arise and live: You sinners stay and sleep until I call again." Therefore, saints, prepare yourselves so that you are not found among the wicked. Lift up your voices and don't hold back. Call upon the nations to repent, both old and young, bond and free, saying, "Prepare yourselves for the great day of the Lord." For if I, who am a man, lift up my voice and call upon you to repent and you hate me, what will you say when the day comes when the thunders utter their voices from the ends of the earth, speaking to the ears of all that live, saying; "Repent and prepare for the great day of the Lord." What will you do when the lightning streaks forth from the east to the west and utters its voice to all that live and makes the ears of all that hear tingle, saying these words: "Repent now for the great day of the Lord is come" [See D & C 43:6-8].

Unexpected insights lie hidden in familiar portions of scripture. God reveals a little here and a little there according to the readiness of His children. It is possible to know Christ's return will take place soon. The signs He told us to watch for are appearing now.

The Fig tree is beginning to blossom.

Important Facts

<u>Many Bible scholars believe God has a six-thousand-year time line</u> for the world, from Adam to its final days[4]. Four thousand years separate the book of Genesis from the writings of the New Testament. An additional two thousand years bring us to the end of the twentieth century.

When the apostles asked Jesus about the Last Days, He described specific signs that would occur when these times were near. He called these signs "warning signals" or "birth pains," saying they would precede a period of tribulation unlike anything the world has ever known[5]. He also promised He would return to save believers, end the Great War, and establish His kingdom on earth. If we are in the Last Days, God's warning signs must be occurring now. In preparation, Christ told us to watch for the signals, grow in faith, pray diligently, and study His Word. The pages in chapter 3 and 4 identify, for your study, these "birth pains."

<u>All **scriptural** prophecies concerning the birth and work of Christ were fulfilled</u>. This should give us confidence to say scriptural prophecy concerning the last-days will also take place. This includes predictions of Christ's Second Coming. Jesus himself confirmed that He would one day come again, but He also said no one except His father knows the day or the hour of His coming, not even the angels in Heaven. <u>When ALL of the signs of His coming are fulfilled</u>, we will know Christ will soon appear (Matthew 24: 42-44). We can either believe His words or dismiss them as lies. There is no other alternative.

Today, words of the prophets are often misunderstood, misquoted, or taken out of context. Before accepting the opinion of any speaker or author, including this writer, the reader is advised to read all scripture references within the context of the entire chapter and to check unclear verses with other scriptures describing the same event or subject. It is helpful to compare different versions of scripture in order to improve the understanding of passages. A good concordance and a compendium of the scriptures are invaluable reference tools. Prayer also opens our understanding of God's Word.

The Bible, the Book of Mormon, and the Doctrine & Covenants are the only sources for reliable information about Christ's Second Coming. Everything else, including narrative in this book, is speculation based on imperfect human understanding of the scriptures. Therefore, this book emphasizes scripture, not the words of the author.

Essential Scripture Concerning the Last Days

Most of us are familiar with Christ's parable about the five wise and five foolish virgins (Matthew 25:1-12). The wise virgins were prepared for the coming of the bridegroom. The foolish were not and the door was shut against them. We have also read His words

---

[4] This author believes it is unnecessary to debate the age of the earth. The timeline we are concerned about is the period of six thousand years in which God specifically interacted with human beings.

[5] Although some people pinpoint historic events that might have fulfilled one or two WARNING SIGNS/BIRTHPAINS, ALL of the signals must be fulfilled during the same span of time. Historically, this has never taken place. It appears to be happening now.

about the rich man who gave certain talents to his servants and then took a long trip. We know the story in which Christ separates the sheep from the goats, and a fourth in which He says, "I was hungry and you gave me meat." However, unless all of Chapter 25 in the book of Matthew is read at one sitting, readers may not realize that these stories are part of a single sermon in which Christ is teaching His disciples about the Last Days. Each story illustrates a different point, but they must be read together in order to understand the four-point message of Christ's sermon:

(Summary)
Matthew 25:1-12
(1) The Wise and Foolish Virgins
Those who are wise will prepare for His Second Coming by having a ready reserve of spiritual oil that comes from a close relationship with Jesus Christ. Spiritual oil is produced through prayer, fasting, study of the scriptures, serving others, and living according to His guidelines. This must be done individually. It cannot be shared.

(Summary)
Matthew 25:13-31
(2) The Parable of the Talents
God expects His people to grow spiritually, mentally, and even materially, using gifts and talents He has given them to bless others, and develop new ones for the furtherance of His kingdom. Those who do are a blessing to Him. The others have no place in His kingdom.

(Summary)
Matthew 25:36-46
(3) I was hungry and you gave me meat.
He expects us to share what we have, caring for the poor, the hungry, the imprisoned, the ill, and the spiritually underfed, meeting the needs of people whenever we have the ability to do so.

(Summary)
Matthew 25:31-34 I.V; [Matthew 25:46 KJV]
(4) Come ye blessed of my Father, inherit the kingdom prepared for you.
Christ wants us to know that when He returns, He will separate His followers (the sheep) from those who have gone in other directions (the goats). His followers will be rewarded, but the rest will be condemned. (Matthew 25:32-35, 47) It is His will that all be saved, but He will not take our agency[6] from us. We must make the choice to live for Him or to follow a godless path[7].

A Solemn Warning to All People of God

Doctrine & Covenants 45:2a, b, c, d
Hearken, O you people of my church and you elders, listen together and hear my voice while it is yet day. And, don't harden your hearts for verily I say to you that I am Alpha and Omega, the beginning and the end, the light and the life of the world; a light that shines in darkness and the darkness doesn't comprehend it.

---

[6] Agency is, the individual's ability to make his own moral choices.
[7] This sermon material is also found in Mark, Luke, and John.

I came to my own and my own did not receive me but to as many as received me I gave power to do many miracles and to become the sons of God. To them that believed on my name I gave power to obtain eternal life. [John 1:11]

And so, I sent my everlasting covenant into the world to be a light to the world and a standard for my people and for the Gentiles to seek it, to be a messenger before my face to prepare the way for me. Therefore, come ye unto it.

Jesus Christ, Son of God, Light of the World, the Everlasting Covenant, is returning to earth. He will come as a thief in the night, unexpected by most of humanity. Only His followers will be watching for Him. At His return, He will fulfill all God's covenants with His people. [Also see: I Thessalonians 5:2-6; II Peter 3:10; Revelation 3:3, 16:15; D & C 103:2.]

Hebrews 8:10
"This is the New Covenant that I will make with the House of Israel after those days," says the Lord. "I will put my laws into their minds and write them in their hearts. I will be their God and they shall be my people."

Before Christ returns, there will be worldwide disturbances beginning with a period called the Great Tribulation, caused by the Antichrist. It will end with the war of Armageddon in which the Lord will intervene before our planet, as we know it, is destroyed. (Matthew 24: 21, 22; Revelation 19:11-16)

Revelations 19:11-16
And I saw Heaven opened, and behold a white horse; and He that sat upon him is called Faithful and True, and in righteousness He doth judge and make war; His eyes as a flame of fire; and He had on His head many crowns; and a name written, that no man knew, but himself. And He is clothed with a vesture dipped in blood; and His name is called The Word of God. And, the armies, which were in Heaven, followed Him upon white horses, clothed in fine linen, white and clean. And out of His mouth proceeds the Word of God, and with it He will smite the nations; and He will rule them with the word of His mouth; and He treads the winepress in the fierceness and wrath of Almighty God. And He has on a vesture, and on His thigh a name written, King of Kings and Lord of Lords.

King of Kings
and Lord of Lords.

Revelation 19:16

WHAT DO THE SCRIPTURES SAY ABOUT THE LAST DAYS?

Jesus said, "Now learn a parable of the fig tree: When its branches are still tender, and it begins to put forth leaves, you know that summer is near. So likewise, my elect who see all these things shall know that Christ is near even at the door. But no one but my father knows the day or the hour not even the angels of God in Heaven."

Matthew 24:41-43
Mark 13:45-47,
Luke 21:29-33,
D & C 45:5d

Each leaf on the Fig tree image represents 1 of 26 signs that must be fulfilled before Christ's second coming. As signs are fulfilled, we know Christ's return grows nearer.

All of the tree illustrations in this book have meaning. They are pictorial hints or indications of the MANY WAYS the "fig tree" is blooming, as the signs of the Last Days are fulfilled.

PART 1

Chapter 1

What do the scriptures say about Christ's second coming or the return of Jesus Christ in earth's last days?

Note: Some scripture is paraphrased in this chapter to clarify meaning.

―――――――

A Letter from God to the People of His Church

Doctrine & Covenants Section 1 [November 1, 1831]

1. Attention, people of my church, says the voice of Him who dwells on high and whose eyes are upon all. Yes, I say, pay attention you people from afar and you that are upon the islands of the sea. Listen together for the voice of the Lord is to all men and there is none who will escape and there is no eye that shall not see, neither ear that shall not hear, neither heart that shall not be penetrated and the rebellious shall be pierced with terrible sorrow. Their iniquities shall be spoken upon the housetops and their secret acts shall be revealed. The voice of warning shall be to all people by the mouths of my disciples whom I have chosen in these Last Days. They shall go forth and no one will be able to prevent them for I the Lord have commanded them.

2. Behold, this is my authority and the authority of my servants and my preface to the Book of My Commandments which I have given to be published for you, the inhabitants of the earth; therefore, fear and tremble, for what I the Lord have decreed in these commandments shall be fulfilled. And I say to you, they who go forth bearing this information to the inhabitants of the earth are given the power to seal, both on earth and in Heaven, the unbelieving and rebellious. Yes, they have the power to seal them up until the day when my wrath shall be poured out upon the wicked without measure; until the day when the Lord comes to give every man according to his work and according to the way he treats his fellowman.

3. Therefore, the voice of the Lord goes out to the ends of the earth so that all who pay attention will hear: Prepare yourself, prepare yourself for that which is to come, for the Lord is close at hand and the anger of the Lord is kindled. His sword is ready and it will fall upon the inhabitants of the earth. The arm of the Lord shall be revealed. The day will soon come that those who will not hear the voice of the Lord or the voice of His servants and will not pay attention to the words of the prophets and apostles will be cut off from among the people for they have turned their backs on my ordinances and have broken my everlasting covenant. They do not seek the Lord to establish His righteousness but every man walks in his own way, following the image of his own god whose image is the way of the world and whose substance is that of an idol which has become old and will perish when Babylon the great falls.

4. Therefore, I the Lord, knowing the calamity which is coming upon the inhabitants of the earth, called upon my servant Joseph Smith Jr. and spoke to him from Heaven and gave him commandments, and also gave commandments to others so they will proclaim these things to the world. All this is done so the things written by the prophets might be fulfilled; that the weak things of the world shall come forth and break down the mighty and strong ones; that man should not counsel his fellowman, neither trust in the arm of flesh. But, every man will speak in the name of God the Lord and the Savior of the world; that faith also might increase in the earth so my everlasting covenant will be established; that the fullness of my gospel might be proclaimed by the weak and the simple to the very ends of the world and before kings and rulers.

5. Behold, I am God and I have spoken it. These commandments are of me and are given to my servants in their weakness, in their own language, so they understand. Inasmuch as they erred it will be made known and inasmuch as they sought wisdom they will be instructed and inasmuch as they sinned they will be chastened so they might repent and inasmuch as they were humble they will be made strong and blessed from on high and receive knowledge from time to time.

6. And again, I say to you inhabitants of the earth, I the Lord am willing to make these things known to everyone for I am no respecter of persons. It is my will that all men know the day is speedily coming, the hour is not yet but is right at hand when peace shall be taken from the earth and the Devil shall have power over his own dominion. But the Lord shall also have power over His saints and shall reign in their midst and shall come down in judgment upon Idumea [8] or the world.

7. Search these commandments, for they are true and faithful and the prophecies and promises, which are in them, shall be fulfilled.

8. What I, the Lord, have spoken, I have spoken and I do not excuse myself. Though the Heavens and the earth pass away, my word shall not pass away but it shall all be fulfilled, whether by my own voice or by the voice of my servants, it is the same; for the Lord is God and the Spirit bears record and the record is true and the truth will remain forever and ever. Amen!

Can any warning from the Lord be more clear? He told us what He expects of His people, especially in these last days. Anyone who is not committed to Him and ignores His warning will not have His spirit with them in the coming years of turbulence.

Today Jesus must weep over the United States saying, "America! America! You who ignore your prophets and belittle them who are sent to you; how often I wanted to gather your children together even as a hen gathers her chicks under her wings but you would not. Behold, you are empty! I tell you now; you shall soon see me and know I am He of whom the prophets wrote, 'Blessed is He who comes in the name of the Lord, in the clouds of Heaven with all the holy angels.'" Then you will understand that He is coming

---

[8] Idumea - Ancient Edom (See Ezekiel 36:5.)

again on the earth for He was glorified and crowned on the right hand of God (Matthew 23:36-41).

Jesus Christ is coming back; His testimony confirms this. He identified signs of His coming in many places in scripture, even though the timing of His return remains unclear. Although He has not yet appeared, Christians still watch and wait. This watch is not futile. The Holy Spirit continues to work with those who are receptive. Believers pass this information from generation to generation, and hundreds of thousands of people accept the Lord. In our generation, the signs of Christ's Second Coming are being fulfilled. We still face the coming of the Antichrist and the Great Tribulation before Christ's return. But our shield and defender promised never to leave us. His appearance will end all destruction and warfare, ushering in one thousand years of peace. Christ's return will be a monumental surprise to most of the world for He will come as a thief in the night, just before humanity self-destructs. His coming will not be as the Lamb of God but as the roaring Lion of Judah. As He returns, the whole world will see signs and wonders in the Heavens and beneath the earth unlike anything ever known. The scriptures provide vivid description of that day.

What do the scriptures say about the Day of the Lord?

Isaiah 13:9, 10
Behold, the day of the Lord comes with wrath and fierce anger, to lay the land desolate. He shall destroy all sinners. The stars of Heaven and the constellations thereof shall not give their light. The sun shall be darkened in His going forth and the moon shall not cause her light to shine.

Isaiah 63:1-4
Who is this that comes from Edom with garments dyed from Bozrah? Who is this that is glorious in His apparel and travels in the greatness of His strength? It is I [the Christ] who speak in righteousness and am mighty to save. Why are my garments red like the man who treads in the wine vat? I have trod the winepress alone and no one was with me. I will tread them in my anger and trample them in my fury and their blood shall be sprinkled upon my garments and I will stain all my raiment; for the day of vengeance is in my heart and the year of my redeemed has come.

Joel 2:1, 30-32
Blow the trumpet in Zion and sound an alarm in my holy mountain; let all the inhabitants of the land tremble for the day of the Lord cometh and it is right at hand. And I will show wonders in the Heavens and in the earth, blood and fire and pillars of smoke. The sun shall be turned into darkness and the moon into blood before the great and terrible day of the Lord comes. And it shall come to pass that whosoever shall call on the name of the Lord shall be delivered for there shall be deliverance in Mount Zion and in Jerusalem and in the remnant whom the Lord shall call.

Matthew 24:34, 37-39 [Matthew 24:29, 30 KJV]
And immediately after the tribulation of those days, the sun shall be darkened and the moon shall not give her light and the stars shall fall from Heaven... the powers of Heaven shall be shaken and the sign of the Son of Man shall appear in the Heavens. Then all the tribes of the earth shall mourn. They

shall see the Son of Man coming in the clouds of Heaven with power and great glory. Whoever treasures up my words shall not be deceived.

I Thessalonians 5:1-6
Brothers, you have no need for me to write to you concerning the times and the seasons, for you know perfectly the day of the Lord will come as a thief in the night. For when people cry, "Peace and safety," then sudden destruction will come upon them as travail upon a woman with child and they shall not escape. But you, brothers, are not in darkness so the day will not overtake you as a thief. You are all children of light and children of the day. We are not of the night, nor of darkness. Therefore, let us not sleep as others do but let us watch and be sober.

II Peter 3:10
But the day of the Lord will come as a thief in the night, in which the Heavens shall shake and the earth shall tremble and the mountains shall melt and pass away with a great noise and the elements shall be filled with fervent heat. The earth also shall be filled and the corruptible works, which are therein, shall be burned up. If all these things will be destroyed, what kind of persons should you be in holy conduct and godliness, looking to and preparing for the day of the coming of the Lord when the corruptible things of the Heavens, being on fire, shall be dissolved and the mountains shall melt with fervent heat? Nevertheless, if we endure, we shall be kept according to His promise. And we look for a new Heaven and a new earth where the righteous will dwell. [See I Thessalonians 5:1-6:2.]

Jude 1:14
And Enoch also, the seventh from Adam prophesied, "Behold, the Lord comes with ten thousand of His saints to execute judgment and to convince the ungodly of their ungodly deeds and speeches which sinners have spoken against Him."

Revelation 16:15
Behold, I come as a thief. Blessed is he that watches and keeps His garments, [Robes of Righteousness, Isaiah 61:10] lest he walk naked and they see his shame.

III Nephi 11:4-9 [24:1-6 LDS]
Jesus told them, "The Father said to Malachi, 'Behold, I will send my messenger [John the Baptist] and he shall prepare the way before Me. And the Lord, whom you seek, shall suddenly come to His temple, the messenger of the covenant [Jesus Christ] in whom you delight. Behold, He shall come' says the Lord of hosts. 'But who may abide the day of His coming? And who shall stand when He appears? For He is like a refiner's fire and fuller's soap and He shall refine and purify the sons of Levi [the priests] and purge them as gold and silver so they may make an offering in righteousness to the Lord. Then, as in the days of old, the offering of Judah and Jerusalem shall be pleasant to the Lord.'"

For believers in Jesus Christ, His return is the most phenomenal event that will ever take place. Christ offers hope for a future in His presence.

There is no greater promise.

Jesus said, "Now learn a parable of the fig tree: When its branches are still tender, and it begins to put forth leaves, you know that summer is near. So likewise, my elect who see all these things shall know that Christ is near even at the door. But no one but my father knows the day or the hour not even the angels of God in Heaven."

Matthew 24:41-43
Mark 13:45-47
Luke 21:29-33,

The Fig Tree

Chapter 2

What do the scriptures say about Zion?

Note: Some scripture is paraphrased in this chapter to clarify meaning.

Hope for Christ's People: Zion, the Rest of God's Story

This chapter contains the most important message I can share. If you read no farther than the next few pages, you will discover the information needed to guide you through the challenging days ahead. The more you read, the more you will, of course, learn. The balance of the chapters identify the 26 signs of the Last Days and their fulfillment. They also describe the Great Tribulation and Christ's return to earth. Finally, they describe the Millennium, The Final Judgment, Heaven and the Glories of Heaven. Christians who read this manuscript have an opportunity to learn more about each of these events.

If you pay attention to world news, you are aware the world is 'out of kilter.'

- Scientists and environmentalists worry about global warming, air pollutants, oil spills, wildlife survival, acid rain, dying lakes, recycling, and the list goes on.
- Much of Hollywood joined the environmental bandwagon encouraging the public to "go green," but they usually fail to mention their own excesses.
- Super-storms of all kinds plague nations.
- Drought, floods, and poisonous contaminants threaten drinking water, crops, and livestock.
- We are further threatened by contaminated imports: toys, toothpaste, canned and dried foods for pets and humans, fresh meats, and vegetables.
- Families are torn apart by companies moving family members great distances apart from one another. Communication between local neighbors is almost a thing of the past.
- Sex abuse scandals strike homes, churches, businesses, and government.
- Individuals destroy their lives and the lives of others by abusing addictive/deadly substances.
- New and deadly diseases are emerging, affecting large populations.
- Healthcare costs are out of control, the new legislation is worse than the original problem, and many working people are still uninsured.
- Gas prices continue to skyrocket and road rage threatens motorists on the highways.
- The real estate market is dying. Unemployment levels continue to climb; people are losing jobs, homes, savings, and security. The nation's economy may never recover.
- Corporate and government mismanagement of funds is devastating businesses and faith in the economy across nations.
- Neither juvenile nor adult crime is under control.
- The nation's prisons are so overcrowded that dangerous felons are being released.

- Terrorism is a threat in every country in the world.
- The Middle East is a tinderbox that may soon escalate into major warfare.
- Alliances between nations are broken.
- Governments cannot be trusted to fix the problems.

This is just the beginning. When a man the Bible names the Antichrist is unveiled, the impact will send shock waves around the world. We will know this man when he reveals himself as a peacemaker, and he will sign a covenant with the state of Israel promising peace in the Middle East (Daniel 9:27). This "peacemaker" could appear at any time; Israel has already compromised much of her land (the Gaza Strip, Golan Heights and the West Bank)! When Israel signs the peace covenant offered, she will be signing her covenant with death (Isaiah 28:15).

Even so, this is an incredible time in which to live! You and I are taking part in historic events heralding the Last Days of earth. Some people reading this may live to see the Return of Jesus Christ! However, before He comes, a time called the Great Tribulation will occur. The whole world will be manipulated by the Antichrist in this period. He will persecute, torture, and kill Christians, Jews, and others who are his enemies. Everyone on earth will be forced to wear his mark (666) in order to buy or sell. The chaos caused by this man will come close to destroying the world (Armageddon, Revelation 16:14-21).

In Matthew Chapter 24, Jesus warns about this time-period. He also provides a list of signs that signal the beginning of the Tribulation (see Chapters 3 and 4). God will allow this worldwide disaster as His one last effort to call people to repentance and acceptance of Christ as their Savior. If the saints observe the message in the next few pages, detailed information about the Last Days becomes less necessary.

There is exciting hope in the promises of Jesus Christ.

- Jesus Christ is alive and He is in total control of this planet as well as the entire universe.
- He has planned safe haven for His people. Its name is Zion.
- Zion is Christ's kingdom on earth. It will not be complete until needed in the Great Tribulation, but the blessings of Zion are available now for those who obey God's directions.

From the restoration of Christ's church (April 6, 1830), members were directed by God to prepare for Zion. Many did not understand how to do this. They concentrated on physical preparations, but the more important spiritual ones were nearly overlooked. The spiritual conditions of Zion could be in operation now, but the saints, throughout generations, failed to grasp what must be done in order to be part of Christ's kingdom.

Christ's Kingdom of Zion has four specific components.

1. Zion is a spiritual condition.
It includes God's endowment of power on His obedient. Therefore, our preparation for Zion must be spiritual. It begins with a change of heart and a truly repentant spirit. This change is implemented as we adhere to the first four principles of the Gospel: faith, repentance, baptism, and laying on of hands to receive the Holy Spirit. These are outward signs of an inner transformation that must take place in order to achieve the

spiritual quality Zion requires. When these prerequisites are met, the Christian's goal is to become like the Savior. Jesus is not a remote mentor or guide. His love for us is real, and He seeks a lasting bond with each of us. This occurs through prayer, fasting, study, and meditation (listening to the voice of God). As this friendship grows, so does our spiritual condition. Men and women who develop this intimacy with the Lord make Zion possible. Their individual lives are zionic, their homes become zionic, and they strive to bring zionic conditions to the world around them, their neighborhoods, their places of work, and their places of worship. Developing zionic conditions requires sacrifice on the part of God's people.

Doctrine & Covenants 102:2c, d
Zion cannot be built up unless it is by the principles of the law of the celestial kingdom. Otherwise, I cannot receive her unto myself. And my people must be chastened until they learn obedience, if necessary by the things, which they suffer.

Doctrine & Covenants 140:5c, d
The work of preparation and the perfection of my Saints go forward slowly and zionic conditions are no further away nor any closer than the spiritual condition of my people justifies; but my word shall not fail, neither will my promises for the foundation of the Lord stands sure.

When the Saints' lives are zionic, they may claim the following promise:

John 14:13, 14
Whatsoever you shall ask in my name I will do so that the Father may be glorified in the Son.

2. Zion is a specific location.
The Doctrine & Covenants says Zion will begin at the Center Place, or the community called Independence in Jackson County, Missouri (D & C 57:1a, d). Early Saints gave up their homes and moved to the state to build a city for God. They were eager to participate, but the Civil War and human sin kept them from completing their task. Today many people no longer believe a specific location exists for Zion, but God promises Zion will be! The concept defies human reason, but the mind of God is far beyond human reason or logic. His promises are sure and His word is trustworthy (D & C 45:12a-d and 13a-b; 98:9f, g).

3. Zion is a place of safety for the Saints during the Great Tribulation.

Doctrine & Covenants 45:13, 14
And it shall come to pass... that every man who will not take his sword against his neighbor must flee to Zion for safety. And there shall be gathered into Zion people from every nation under Heaven and they shall be the only people not at war with one another. And it shall be said among the wicked[9],

---

[9] Scripture (Genesis 7:67-69; Isaiah 35:1-10; D & C 140:5c; D & C 63:13 a-g; D & C 36:12 c-g) says the wicked will not come into Zion. The wicked in this case may be anyone who does not obey and have a broken heart and a contrite spirit. It could be you or me.

"Let us not go up to battle against Zion for the inhabitants of Zion are terrible and therefore we cannot stand."

And it shall come to pass that the righteous shall be gathered out from among all nations and shall come to Zion singing, with songs of everlasting joy.

Difficult times are ahead. After the Great Tribulation, the Antichrist, assisted by Satan, will declare war against the Holy One of Israel (Christ). They will challenge Him with blasphemous curses, all the world's armies, and every loathsome weapon known to man. Armageddon will be the most destructive war the world has ever experienced. The Antichrist wants to destroy the Lord and rule earth. Satan intends to demolish God's power, ravage humankind, and annihilate the planet.

As chaos continues, astonishing signs will materialize on the earth and in the sky. Those who watch will be paralyzed with fear. Terrible pestilences will kill thousands. Earthquakes will strike with frequency and without warning in extraordinary places. The sun will be blackened and the moon will give no light. Even the stars will appear to tumble to earth. The bravest of mighty men will hide in caves and pray that the rocks will fall and cover them. But at that time, we shall also see the Heavens open and the Son of Man coming in the clouds of Heaven with power and glory. The mighty armies of God, fully arrayed in His Armor, stand ready for orders, and all the redeemed, both living and dead, will be caught up in the air to meet Him. (Matthew 24:5-44; Thessalonians 4:16, 17; Revelation 6:15, 16; 19:11-16)

This is the First Resurrection. [Revelation 20:5]

Christ will defeat His enemies with the Sword of the Spirit, His Word, for the Word of the Lord is the most powerful weapon in the universe. The Antichrist and his armies will be cast into the lake of fire and Satan will be bound for a thousand years. Nothing can stand between the Word of the Lord and the will of God. The book of Luke provides the following information.

> **Luke 21:25, 26**
> *In the generation in which the times of the Gentiles are fulfilled, there shall be signs in the sun, and in the moon, and in the stars. There will be great distress upon the nations of the earth…. The earth shall also be troubled and the waters of the great deep; men's hearts will fail them for fear and for looking at those things which are coming on the earth and the powers of Heaven shall be shaken.*

Throughout this time, the Lord promises protection for His people. Many will flee to Zion for safety. Those who live Zionic lives, and are led by the Spirit to stay in the midst of the tribulation, will have His spirit with them wherever they serve.

4. The city of Zion is an ancient spiritual and physical reality.
Zion, described in the book of Genesis (Inspired Version only), is a city filled with people who achieved perfection in the days of Enoch. Because of the righteousness of the people, God removed Zion from earth, reserving it until the latter days or the end of the world. In God's own time, before or during the tribulation, it will return. What this means

is unclear. Will an entire city descend on Jackson County, or will Saints from the biblical city return to witness the first resurrection? Certainly, the resurrected Saints and those still alive on earth will inhabit the millennium with Enoch and his people. We can only speculate. However, scripture provides tantalizing clues (Genesis 7:78; 14:34 IV.).

Genesis 7:70-73 [I.V. only]
I will cause righteousness and truth to sweep the earth as a flood, to gather out my own elect from the four quarters of the earth into a place which I shall prepare; a holy city that my people may gird up their loins [be preparing] looking for the time of my coming. For there shall be my tabernacle and it shall be called Zion, a New Jerusalem.

And, the Lord said to Enoch, "At that time you and all your city will meet them there and we will receive them into our bosom. They shall see us and we will fall upon their necks and they will fall upon our necks and we will kiss each other. And my home shall be there and it shall be Zion which shall come forth out of all the creations which I have made and for the space of a thousand years the earth shall rest." Then Enoch saw the coming of the Son of Man in the Last Days, to dwell on the earth in righteousness for the space of a thousand years.

Psalm 37:11
The meek shall inherit the earth and delight themselves in total peace.

Isaiah 65:21
And they shall build houses and inhabit them. They shall plant vineyards and eat the fruit of them.

I Corinthians 15:52-53
In a moment, in the twinkling of an eye, at the sound of the last trump, the dead shall be raised incorruptible and we also shall be changed…. This mortal body must put on immortality.

Doctrine & Covenants 63:13c-e, g
Blessed are the dead that die in the Lord from henceforth, when the Lord comes and old things shall pass away and all things become new. They shall rise from the dead, shall not die again, and shall receive an inheritance before the Lord in the holy city. He that lives when the Lord shall come and has kept the faith is blessed; nevertheless, it is appointed to him to die at the age of man. Children shall grow up until they become old, old men shall die but they shall not sleep in the dust. They shall be changed in the twinkling of an eye.

The people who live in Zion will be incredibly blessed:

- First, they will be in a place of safety where the Lord's spirit will watch over them during the troubled years.
- Second, when Christ returns, He will live with them in Zion.
- Third, Zion will exist throughout the thousand-year millennium. (See more about Zion in a later chapter.)

What do the scriptures say about the endowment?

As part of zionic spiritual growth, God will endow obedient saints with His own spiritual power. This may happen to an individual or to a group of the faithful. Individuals who submit themselves to God, allowing Him to direct their lives, begin to sense and respond to His will. As a result, zionic conditions develop and people are empowered to accomplish mighty things for Him. The following scriptures describe some of the things that may happen:

Isaiah 44:3
I will pour water upon him that is thirsty, and floods upon the dry grounds: I will pour my Spirit upon your seed, and my blessings upon your offspring.

Joel 2:28 and Acts 2:17, 18
I will pour out my Spirit on all flesh and your sons and your daughters shall prophesy; your old men shall dream dreams, your young men shall see visions and upon the servants and upon the handmaids in those days I will pour out my Spirit.

Zechariah 10:12
And I will strengthen them in the Lord; and they shall walk up and down in my name

John 7:37-39 [see KJV for differences in verse 39]
In the last day of the great feast, Jesus stood and cried, saying, "If any man thirst let him come to me, and drink. He that believes in me, as the Scripture has said, out of His belly shall flow rivers of living water." But He was speaking of the Spirit, which they who believe in Him should receive, for the Holy Ghost was promised to them who believe, after Jesus was glorified.

Acts 2:2-4
Suddenly there came a sound from Heaven as of a rushing mighty wind, and it filled all the house where they were sitting. And cloven tongues like fire appeared to them, and rested upon each of them. And they were all filled with the Holy Ghost, and began to speak with other tongues, as the Spirit gave them utterance.

Acts 19:6
And when Paul had laid his hands upon them, the Holy Ghost came on them; and they spoke with tongues, and prophesied.

Mosiah 11:104
And the Lord did pour out His Spirit upon them, and they were blessed, and prospered in the land.

Doctrine & Covenants 43:4c, d
You are to be taught from on high. Therefore sanctify yourselves [become holy] and you shall be endowed with power that you may give even as I have spoken.

©RSBlain Photography and Graphics

"If any man thirst
let him come to me,
and drink."

Matthew 24:41-43

Jesus said, "Now learn a parable of the fig tree: When its branches are still tender, and it begins to put forth leaves, you know that summer is near. So likewise, my elect who see all these things shall know that Christ is near even at the door. But no one but my father knows the day or the hour not even the angels of God in Heaven."

Mark 13:45-47
Luke 21:29-33,
D & C 45:5d

When the branches are still tender...

Chapter 3

What are Christ's Last Days warning signs?

Note: Some scripture is paraphrased in this chapter to clarify meaning.

Two types of Last Day Signs appear in the scriptures:

1. the signs that must be fulfilled before and during the tribulation
2. the signs to be fulfilled before Christ's reappearance

Now (2011), only three signs appear to be unfulfilled. One sign must be complete before the tribulation and two additional signs must be fulfilled before the Second Coming of Jesus Christ.

The Warning Signs That Precede the Great Tribulation and Christ's Return in the Last Days

Present Fulfillment Key: There are twenty-six scriptural prophecies identified in this book. They must be fulfilled before the Great Tribulation begins. The current prophecy status is indicated by (F), (OF), or (NYF).

(F) Prophecy that is already Fulfilled	(OF) Ongoing Fulfillment of Scripture	(NYF) Prophecy NOT YET FULFILLED

Identification List of the 26 Signs

SIGN 1 (OF)

> **Matthew 24:5-6 [Matthew 24:4, 5 KJV]**
> *Do not let yourselves be deceived by men who come in my name saying, "I [Jesus Christ] am Christ" but deceive many [by teaching false doctrine]. [Mark 13:10; Luke 21:8. Do not confuse sign #1 with signs #4 and 5.]*

SIGN 2 (OF)

> **Matthew 24:7 [Matt 24:9 KJV]**
> *They shall deliver you [Christ's followers] to be afflicted and shall kill you and you shall be hated by all nations for my name's sake. [Mark 13:11; Luke 21:12-17]*

SIGN 3 (OF)

> **Matthew 24:8 [Matthew 24:10 KJV]**
> *"Many shall be offended and betray one another and hate one another." The Book of Luke adds, "You shall be betrayed by parents and brothers and kinsfolk and friends and they will cause some of you to be put to death. And*

you shall be hated by all the world for my [Christ's] name's sake but not a hair of your head will perish." [Luke 21:15-17]

SIGN 4 (OF)

<u>Matthew 24:9, 23 [Matthew 24:11, 24 KJV]</u>
Many false prophets shall arise and deceive many people. And there shall arise false christs and false prophets who will show great signs and wonders and in as much as possible they will deceive the very elect who are part of God's covenant. [Mark 13:12b]

SIGN 5 (OF)

<u>Matthew 24:22, 23, 26 [Matthew 24:23, 24, 26 KJV]</u>
After the tribulation of those days, if anyone tells you Christ is here or Christ is there, do not believe him. In those days, false prophets and false christs shall arise who will show great signs and wonders, deceiving the very elect, according to the covenant, if possible. [Mark 13:23, 25, 28]

SIGN 6 (OF)

<u>Matthew 24:10, 11 [Matthew 24:12, 13 KJV]</u>
Sin will be everywhere and many people will no longer care about God or each other but he that remains steadfast, and is not overcome, shall be saved. [Mark 13:13, 35; I Timothy 3:1-7; D & C 45:4b, c]

SIGN 7 (OF)

<u>Matthew 24:25, 29, 30 [Matthew 24:6, 7 KJV]</u>
You will hear of wars and rumors of wars…. Nation shall rise against nation and kingdom against kingdom. [Mark 13:27, 32; Luke 21:9, 10a]

SIGN 8 (OF)

<u>Matthew 24:30 [Matthew 24:7 KJV]</u>
…There shall be famine and pestilences and earthquakes in diverse places. [Mark 13:34; Luke 21:10b]

SIGN 9 (OF)

<u>Matthew 24:32 [Matthew 24:14 KJV]</u>
The gospel of the kingdom will be preached in all the world as a witness to all nations. Then the end shall come and the destruction of the wicked. [Mark 13:36]

SIGN 10 (OF)

<u>I Thessalonians 5:3</u>
People will cry "Peace, Peace" but there will be no peace. [Ezekiel 7:25, D & C 1:6]

SIGN 11 (OF)

> **Daniel 12:4**
> *People will run to and fro and knowledge will be increased but God will confound the wisdom of the wise. [I Corinthians 1:19-25; I Corinthians 8:1-3; D & C 76:2; 108:11]*

SIGN 12 (OF)

> **II Peter 3:3-18**
> *People will reject the scriptures concerning the Last Days. [D & C 1:3c, d]*

SIGN 13 (OF)

> **I Timothy 4:1-9**
> *In the Last Days, there will be widespread acceptance of moral decay in society, corruption in religious thought and spiritual decay within the church. [II Timothy 3:1-7; D & C 1:3a-e; D & C 45:4b; 152:4]*

SIGN 14 (OF)

> **Galatians 1:8, 9**
> *There will be false teachers. [I Timothy 1:3-13; I Peter 2:6-8]*

SIGN 15 (F)

> **Genesis 50:30-33 [I.V. only]**
> *In the Last Days, God will raise up another seer from the descendants of Joseph [from Egypt] and he will bring forth God's word at that time.*

SIGN 16 (F)

> **Isaiah 29:11-26 [I.V. only]**
> *A book will come forth containing the words of those who slumbered in the dust. [See: Isaiah 29:11; Ezekiel 37:15-20; II Nephi 11:125-142]*

SIGN 17 (F)

> **Doctrine & Covenants 5:3, 32:2a**
> *Christ's church will be restored to its original form.*

SIGN 18 (F)

> **Genesis 6:7 [I.V. only]**
> *God's priesthood will be restored. [D & C 83:2c-g, 3, 4]*

SIGN 19 (NYF)

> **Doctrine & Covenants 63:9a-d**
> *Zion [Independence, Missouri] is to become a gathering place of safety for the Saints during the Tribulation. [D & C 45:13b, 14]*

SIGN 20 (NYF)

Doctrine & Covenants 57:1d
A Temple will be built in Independence, Missouri. [See: D & C 57:1d; 58:13]

SIGN 21 (OF)

Ezekiel 11:16-20
The Children of Israel return to their promised homeland. [See: Genesis 15:9-11; Exodus 23:30-32; Deuteronomy 30:1, 5-9; Jeremiah 23:7, 8; Ezekiel 11:16-20; I Nephi 7:23, 24, 36; RLDS, same as I Nephi 22:12 LDS.]

SIGN 22 (OF)

Jeremiah 3:17, 18
The tribes of Judah and the House of Israel will be reunited. [See: Ezekiel 37:22; Micah 5:3-4; I Nephi 4:31-33; RLDS-same as I Nephi 15:20 LDS.]

SIGN 23 (F)

Jeremiah 3:17, 18
The Jews will control all Israel, including Jerusalem and the Temple Mount. [Ezekiel 11:16-20; Joel 3:16-20; Zechariah 2:4]

SIGN 24 (NYF)

Malachi 3:1-4
The Temple must be rebuilt on the Temple Mount. [II Thessalonians 2:4, the Antichrist desecrates the temple.]

SIGN 25 (NYF)

Nephi 12:71, 72
The Book of Mormon will be accepted by the Jews. [See: II Nephi 11:27-34; II Nephi 12:71, 72; D & C 16:5a; 17:2d; 18:3c; 19:3c; 45:9a-d; 104:12, 13a, b; 105:2b; 108:3a.]

SIGN 26 (NYF)

Isaiah 28:28
The Antichrist will be identified. [See: Revelation 13:1-18, Revelation 14:9.]

At present, signs 24 and 25 must be fulfilled before the Second Coming of Jesus Christ. Sign 26 must be completed before the tribulation begins. All other signs must be and will have been fulfilled before He comes.

18

The Promise Repeated

Moroni 10:4-8

When you shall receive these things, I would exhort you to ask of God, the eternal Father, in the name of Christ, if these things are not true. And if you ask with a sincere heart, with real intent, having faith in Christ, He will manifest the truth to you by the power of the Holy Ghost. And by the power of the Holy Ghost, you may know the truth of all things.

Whatever thing is good is also just and true. Therefore, nothing that is good denies the Christ but acknowledges He is. And you may know He is, by the power of the Holy Ghost.

Therefore, I would exhort you, do not deny the power of God for He works by power according to the faith of men, the same today, and tomorrow and forever. Amen.

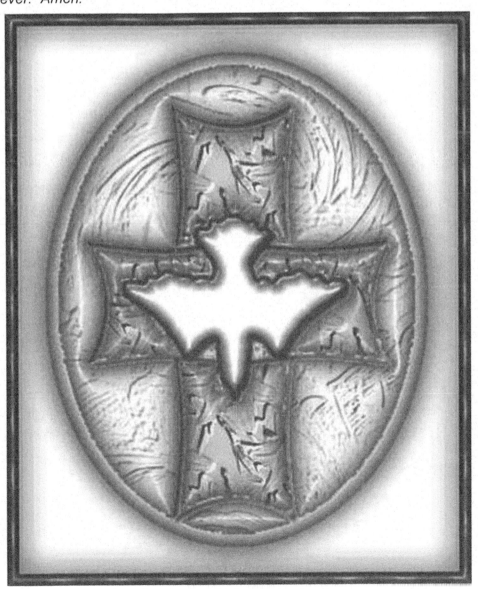

Jesus said, "Now learn a parable of the fig tree: When its branches are still tender, and it begins to put forth leaves, you know that summer is near. So likewise, my elect who see all these things shall know that Christ is near even at the door. But no one but my father knows the day or the hour not even the angels of God in Heaven."

Matthew 24:41-43
Mark 13:45-47
Luke 21:29-33,

The purpose of warning signs

Chapter 4

What do the scriptures say about Christ's warning signs?

Note: Some scripture is paraphrased in this chapter to clarify meaning.

The Importance of Signs

Signs are everywhere. There are traffic and destination signs, signs that identify products and their contents, and signs warning of dangerous areas for walking or driving. Our well-being depends on paying attention to signs.

The Purposes of Christ's Warning Signs

- **The first purpose is to provide convincing evidence that Jesus Christ is about to return**. The Bible warns that, before He comes, there will be a time of turbulence called the Great Tribulation (Matthew 24:21, 29). Many students of the scriptures have determined this will last about seven years[10], ending with the worst of man's world wars.

Christ will intervene to end this war, but He will come not as a lamb but as the Lion of Judah and King of the Universe. The signs that precede the tribulation are listed in Matthew 24 and in other scriptures identified in this manuscript. The world's current events indicate these signs are being fulfilled, right now.

Watching for Christ's return is nothing new. Since His ascension into Heaven, Christians have waited for His return, and His return has been predicted in almost every century. Believers looked for anything that appeared to fulfill one or more of these prophecies, but all of the forecasts were wrong.

Question:
Why were the forecasts incorrect?

Answer:
Many prophecies, referring to Christ's Second Coming, **were not yet fulfilled.**

Jesus told us **ALL of the signs in scripture must occur before His return.** People often take this with a grain of salt. Even believers become apathetic. Some 'Christians' no longer believe in the authenticity or authority of scripture. Others see the Last Days as something in the distant future that simply do not apply to them. That attitude may

---

[10] Though many students of the Scriptures have determined through their studies that the Great Tribulation will span about seven years, none of this author's reference positively identifies the length of the Great Tribulation.

have worked for them until the mid-twentieth century. But then, one after another, the signs began to appear. The "fig tree is producing leaves (Matthew 24:41)." **Today, all but three signs have been fulfilled.** This knowledge indicates the nearness of the Great Tribulation, but most of the world is unaware this is taking place.

The Signs Remaining to be Fulfilled

- The Antichrist, the Beast in Revelation, must reveal himself.
- A place of safety must be provisioned for His Saints. Preparation must be made in Independence, Missouri, for an influx of people fleeing the Great Tribulation. (D & C 45:13)
- The Jewish temple must be rebuilt, in the old city of Jerusalem[11]. This could take place during the first half of the tribulation.

The Antichrist, a powerful, charismatic, public figure, has not yet made himself known. Identifying this person is the key to knowing when the tribulation period will begin. He will announce himself by convincing the world he can bring peace to the Middle East and will succeed in doing this when everyone else has failed. But, the new world he creates will bring persecution and death to many thousands of people. Christians and Jews will be prime targets for his wrath. (See Chapter 9.)

- **The second purpose** of Christ's warning signs is **to encourage followers to prepare**. Spiritual preparation is by far the most important thing any of us can do to be ready for Christ's return and the many difficult challenges ahead.

Do we have a good relationship with the Lord? Have we repented of sin and been baptized in His name? We must study His Word and spend time talking to Him. The Father wants us to be aware of the times in which we live. He wants us to take necessary action before our options are much more limited. He implores us to repent of sin and live righteously. We must strengthen our faith in order to endure the times, which are coming. He invites us to draw closer to Him through prayer, fasting, meditation, and through the study and sharing of His Word with those who have not met Him. He will be with us, providing encouragement, strengthening our faith, filling us with peace, and removing our fears.

Physical and economic arrangements may or may not be of help, but we are expected to use the guidance and intelligence God gives us.

> **II Timothy 1:7**
> *God has not given us the spirit of fear; but of power and love and of a sound mind.*

> **I John 4:18**
> *There is no fear in love; perfect love casts out fear because fear has torment. He that is afraid is not made perfect in love.*

---

[11] The building of the temple is identified in scriptures indicating both the Antichrist and Jesus Christ will enter this building. The Antichrist will defile the temple in the last half of the tribulation, and Christ upon his return will re-enter it. Therefore, it is conceivable, the third temple, which must be in place before these events, could be built during the first three-and-a-half years of the tribulation. (See Chapter 8)

Physical preparation for disasters is addressed at the end of this book. However, there is no guarantee it will be useful during the tribulation. Much depends on where we find ourselves when trouble begins. Our real hope and help during any difficulty is Jesus Christ. We must learn to rely on and draw close to the Savior before chaos begins. (More information on spiritual preparation is included in Chapter 15.)

Christ's people must take these warnings and promises seriously. We no longer have the luxury of waiting for the distant future. Those who fail to take action will face serious consequences.

War, disease, and adversity will also take peace from the earth. Only those who remain close to Jesus Christ have the promise of His help through this adversity.

- **The third purpose** is to provide evidence that may convince skeptics that Christ is really returning.

Each fulfilled sign supports the truthfulness of scripture. Those who are observant will know Christ is near, even at the door (Matthew 24:42). As these signs are fulfilled, the scriptures concerning them are validated. Some who are skeptical may see the light and accept Him as Savior and Lord. Chapter 10 is devoted to His return.

Christ's warning signs are for our protection during the Tribulation.

Matthew 24:1, 2, 4
As Jesus left the temple His disciples came to Him saying, "Master, tell us about the buildings of the temple you said will be destroyed." And Jesus replied, "...I tell you not one stone will be left upon another. They shall all be thrown down." ...Then they asked, "Tell us when these things concerning the destruction of the temple shall take place, and what will happen to the Jews? What is the sign of your coming and the end of the world?" [See Mark 13:1-4 and Luke 21:5-7.]

Christ did not answer the questions about the temple or the Jews directly but as He predicted, Romans destroyed the buildings in AD 70, and the Jews were dispersed throughout the world. He replied to the third question by providing a list of signs. Those who watch for them will know when He is about to return.

At that time the sign of the Son of Man will appear in the sky, and all the nations of the earth will mourn. They will see the Son of Man coming on the clouds of the sky, with power and great glory

Matthew 24:30

SIGN 1
Deception by False Ministers

> ### Matthew 24:5, 6 [Matthew 24:4, 5 KJV]
> *Do not let yourselves be deceived by people who come in my name saying I am Christ; and shall deceive many. [See Mark 13:10 and Luke 21:8. This refers to anyone using Christ's name to teach false doctrine. See signs 4 & 5 for false christs.]*

> ### Doctrine & Covenants 63:15d
> *Let all men beware how they take my name in their lips for many who use the name of the Lord...in vain are under condemnation for they have no authority. Therefore, let the church repent of their sins and I the Lord will acknowledge them. Otherwise, they shall be cut off.*

(Present Fulfillment)
- Deceptions in the name of Christ
- Ministers selling the Gospel of Jesus Christ for financial gain
- Clergy teaching portions of scriptures, ignoring the heart of Christ's message
- Preachers twisting the message of the Gospel into something it is not
- Sex abuse of children by trusted ministers
- Various cults teaching in the name but not in the spirit of Jesus Christ
- Past and present use of Christianity in defense of Nazism and persecution of Jews, etc

Many people teach in the name of Jesus Christ declaring Him to be the Son of God. Grievously, their message and personal behavior are not compatible with God's Word. The scriptures provide the standard by which we must judge the accuracy of things men and women teach. Therefore, it is our responsibility to study the Word for ourselves, to pray, and seek God's direction to avoid being misled. The same guidelines are appropriate for all of us when we are unsure about right and wrong.

The Lord provided the following counsel to Joseph Smith as he translated the Book of Mormon. These words are recorded in the Doctrine and Covenants.

> ### Doctrine & Covenants 9:3b-d
> *You must study it out in your mind. Then you must ask me if it is right. And if it is right, I will cause your bosom to burn within you; therefore, you shall feel that it is right. If it is not right, you shall have no such feelings but you shall have a stupor of thought that shall cause you to forget the thing, which is wrong.*

SIGN 2
Affliction

Matthew 24:7
They shall deliver you [Christ's followers] up to be afflicted and shall kill you and you shall be hated by all nations for my name's sake. [See Mark 13:11 and Luke 21:12-19.]

(Present Fulfillment)

Oppression of believers has grown steadily for more than a century. In many parts of the world, Christians are executed for their belief in Jesus Christ. Persecution was particularly strong in former communist nations, and although the political situation has changed, harassment, violence, imprisonment, and death still threaten Christians in China, India, Africa, Haiti, Iran, Iraq, Saudi Arabia, Vietnam, Myanmar, North Korea, Laos, Sudan, and in other Islamic nations. The newsletter Christian Currents from Jacksonville, Oregon, reports that Christians were martyred in about forty countries between 2001 and the end of 2007.

Anti-Christian sentiment is also growing in the United States, and as proponents gain power in government, the courts, and the media, it will become more difficult and eventually dangerous to profess a belief in Jesus Christ. Already, some in the news media call the Bible "hate literature." This mindset is infecting many Americans who strongly oppose any influence of Christianity in public places.

Christians who believe in three books of scripture, the Inspired Version of the Bible, the Book of Mormon, and the Doctrine and Covenants, are a threat to many people. Latter Day Saints were driven from their homes and killed in the 1830s when Joseph Smith founded the church. Today, some Christian denominations still describe the RLDS church as a dangerous cult. The Community of Christ rarely experiences this harassment because its name change is not widely associated with the Book of Mormon. Use of the Book of Mormon is diminishing within the Community of Christ.

People who remain faithful to the original doctrine of the RLDS church. believing Jesus Christ restored His church in 1830 and that He provided three unique books of scripture can still expect misunderstanding and abuse from some in the Christian community.

SIGN 3
Betrayal

Matthew 24:8 [Matthew 24:10 KJV]
Many shall be offended and betray one another and hate one another.

Luke 21:11-13 [Luke 21:12, 13 KJV]
But before all this, they will lay their hands on you and persecute you, delivering you up to the synagogues and prisons and you will be questioned by kings and governors for my name's sake. Don't worry about answers beforehand; for I will give you a mouth and wisdom which none of your adversaries will be able to withstand or contradict.

Luke 21:15 [Luke 21:16 KJV]
You shall be betrayed by parents and brothers and kinsfolk and friends and they will cause some of you to be put to death. And you shall be hated by all the world for my name's sake but not a hair of your head will perish. [Mark 13:12a]

(Present Fulfillment)

The Constitution of the United States guarantees many freedoms to citizens. However, we are quickly moving in a direction causing loss of freedoms, especially for Christians and Jews. This is a deliberate betrayal of this country's founding principles. Much of this is evident in current newspapers, magazines, and TV programs, for example:

- The American Civil Liberties Union declaration of war on marriage reported in September 2005 by the Alliance Defense Fund (marriage between a man and woman versus gay marriage) and attempting to force the Boy Scouts of America to accept gay leadership.
- Efforts to remove Judeo/Christian monuments, and literature, from government buildings and schools
- Efforts to ban prayer from schools, pro games, courts, congress, and public places
- Politically correct speech protecting freedoms of all but Christians and Jews
- Harassment of Christians through the courts
- A rise in vandalism against churches and synagogues
- Anti-Semitism and hate crimes in America and other parts of the world

Violence against Christians and Jews is common in many countries and cultures. People are beaten, jailed, tortured, and killed as neighbor turns against neighbor. In Russia, during the Communist regime, authorities encouraged parents and children to report each other for Christian activities. Today, in China, Christians are arrested with the possibility of disappearing. As anti-Semitism reemerges, Jews are renewed targets for tyranny and killing. Similar persecution takes place in India, Africa, Asia, South America, Arab countries and other parts of the world.

Eventually, under the worldwide government of the Antichrist, it will be illegal everywhere to be a Christian or a Jew or to own a book of scripture. Hatred for believers in Christ will increase and their testimony for the Lord is an easy excuse to kill them. Everyone will be compelled to join the one world religion to worship the Antichrist. (Rev. 13:8)

26

SIGN 4
Deception by False Prophets

Matthew 24:9, 23 [Matthew 24:11, 24 KJV]

False prophets shall arise and deceive many. And there shall arise false christs and false prophets who shall show great signs and wonders and, in as much as is possible, they will deceive the very elect who are part of God's covenant. [Mark 13:12b]

III Nephi 6:27-32 [6:14, 15 LDS]

Beware of false prophets who come to you in sheep's clothing. Inwardly they are ravening wolves. You shall know them by their fruits. Do men gather grapes of thorns, or figs of thistles? Even so, every good tree brings forth good fruit; but a corrupt tree brings forth evil fruit. A good tree cannot bring forth evil fruit; neither can a corrupt tree bring forth good fruit. Every tree that does not bear good fruit is hewn down and cast into the fire. Therefore, by their fruits you shall know them.

(Definition)
PROPHECY: True prophecy provides a message from God through divine inspiration to His people. It may or may not predict or foretell future events.

(Definition)
DIVINE INSPIRATION is the belief that God provided, the transcribers of the Three Standard Books, the words which were written. Again, the correctness of any scripture depends on whether it is translated correctly, in subsequent versions. True prophets speak under divine inspiration.

F. Henry Edwards[12] said, "Prophets are not the originators but the messengers. A prophet of God interprets, declares, preaches, expounds, or speaks for the Lord. He is an authoritative spokesman for God who delivers [God's] divine messages or interprets [God's] divine will. In order to have prophecy we must have one who sends the message [God], one who conveys the message [the prophet] and one who is meant to receive the message [the sheep of His pasture]."

It is a great and distinct honor to be a prophet of the living God. That is why there were so many false prophets (Old and New Testament) in Israel and scripture tells us there will be false prophets appearing in the Last Days as well.

A FALSE PROPHET purposely provides false information in an attempt to lead people away from the one true God. The question is, why would anyone want to be a false prophet to lead people away from God? A false prophet's motivation could be a desire for power or acceptance, money, leverage, better personal relationships, politics, revenge or evil purposes, and combinations of any on the list.

---

[12] F. Henry Edwards was a prolific author for the R.L.D.S. Church. He served in various important capacities, including counselor to church presidents Israel A. Smith and President W. Wallace Smith.

SIGN 5
False Christs

> ### Matthew 24:22, 23 [Matthew 24:23, 24 KJV]
> *After the tribulation of those days, if anyone tells you Christ is here or Christ is there, do not believe him. For in those days false christs and false prophets shall arise, and they will show great signs and wonders, deceiving the very elect according to the covenant, if possible. [See also Mark 13:23, 25, 28 and Matthew 24:22, 23 both part of the section on the tribulation.]*

(Present Fulfillment)

More than one person has claimed they were Jesus Christ. Toward the end of the twentieth century, several claims emerged in the United States. The most prominent included David Koresh, leader of the Branch Davidians, who died with many of his followers at Waco, Texas. A second was Jim Jones, pastor of the People's Temple, who led many of his followers to a suicidal death by poisoning. And Heaven's Gate, the flying saucer people who left behind serene, dead bodies as their souls "traveled to Heaven via a spaceship." Less well known, eastern mystic Guru Maharaj-Ji, considered Supreme Master of his time (just like Krishna, Rama, and Christ). As we draw closer to Christs return, more imposters will appear.

We might wonder how anyone can take these claims seriously. Yet, false christs do attract followers, and though most of these movements are limited in numbers, some grow in size. Their messages may sound scriptural, but they are not consistent with God's Word. They all deceive and therefore harm their adherents. Some followers lose their earthly lives. Some will also lose their spiritual lives unless they find the real Jesus Christ, the only Savior. Therefore, Christians must be well versed in scripture to keep themselves, their families, and friends from deception.

During the Great Tribulation, **the Antichrist will claim to be Christ**, and much of the world will believe him. He will conduct worldwide persecution of Christ's real disciples. Jesus warned His followers about this. (Daniel 8:24; Daniel 7:5, 19-21; Rev. 13:1, 7)

> ### Matthew 24:26, 27, 37
> *Jesus said, "I have told you before…if they shall say to you, 'He is in the desert'; don't go to look for me. 'He is in the secret chambers'; do not believe it. For, <u>as the light of the morning comes out of the east and shines to the west, covering the whole earth, so shall the coming of the Son of Man be</u>… After the tribulation of those days, when the powers of Heaven are shaken, the sign of the Son of Man shall appear in the Heaven, and all tribes of earth will mourn and they shall see the Son of Man coming in the clouds of Heaven, with power and great glory."*

"As the light of the morning comes out of the east and shines to the west, covering the whole earth, so shall the coming of the Son of Man be." Matthew 24:27

This promise cannot be duplicated by false christs.

SIGN 6
Sin Is Rampant.

Matthew 24:10, 11, 31 [Matthew 24:12, 13 KJV]
Sin will be everywhere and many people will no longer care about God or each other. But he that remains steadfast, and is not overcome, shall be saved. [Mark 13:13, 35;
I Timothy 3:1-7; D & C 45:4b, c]

Doctrine & Covenants 45:4b-e
The love of men shall grow cold and iniquity shall abound and when the time of the Gentiles has come, a light shall break forth among them that sit in darkness and it shall be the fullness of my gospel. But, they do not receive it for they do not perceive the light and they turn their hearts from me because of the precepts of men. In that generation the times of the Gentiles shall be fulfilled and there shall be men standing in that generation that shall not die until they see an overflowing scourge because a desolating sickness shall come over the land. However, my disciples shall stand in holy places, and shall not be moved. But among the wicked, men shall lift up their voices and curse God, and die… and there shall also be earthquakes in many different places and other desolations. Yet, men will harden their hearts against me. And they will take up their swords against one another, and they will kill each other…. But, my disciples shall stand in holy places, and shall not be moved.

Revelation 3:17-22 [An Admonition]
Because you say, 'I am rich and increased with goods and have need of nothing' and that I do not know that you are wretched, and miserable, and poor, and blind, and naked, I counsel you. "Buy gold tried in fire from Me so you may be rich, and have white raiment, that you may be clothed, and the shame of your nakedness is not public. Anoint your eyes with salve so you may see. As many as I love, I rebuke and chasten. Be zealous and repent. Behold, I stand at the door and knock. If anyone hears My voice and opens the door, I will come in to him and will eat with him and he with Me. I will invite all those who overcome, even as I also overcame, to sit with Me on My throne as I am sitting with My Father on His throne. If you have an ear, listen to what the Spirit says to the churches."

(Definition) SIN: Any transgression of divine law or any requirement of right, duty or propriety; made known through the revealed Word of God; any lack of holiness, any defect of moral purity and truth, in the heart or life, by commission or omission. This includes criminality, delinquency, depravity, evil, immorality, iniquity, ungodliness, unrighteousness, viciousness, wickedness, or wrongdoing. Historically, the seven deadly sins are defined as anger, gluttony, pride, sloth, envy, covetousness, and lechery.

Mark 7:14-21 Jesus Condemns Sin
When Jesus entered the house, His disciples asked Him about His remark, "Food that enters into a man does not defile him but the things that come out of him [thoughts, words, or behavior] are the things which defile him for they come out of his heart. If any man has ears to hear, let him hear…. Don't you

understand? Nothing digested by a man can defile him because it does not enter into his heart but into his belly and becomes waste when the food is purged. Evil, which comes out of men, defiles men. Wicked thoughts, adulteries, fornications, murders, thefts, covetousness, wickedness, deceit, lasciviousness, an evil eye, blasphemy, pride and foolishness come from within their hearts; all these evil things come from within and defile men."
[See Mark 7:6-16; Luke 9:11-20.]

Galatians 5:19-21
The works of the flesh are obvious. They are these: adultery, fornication, uncleanness, lasciviousness, idolatry, witchcraft, hatred, variances [13], emulations [14], wrath, strife, and seditions [15]. They are heresies [16], envying, murders, drunkenness, reveling [17], and all things that are similar.

I Timothy 4:1-9
The Spirit warns in the latter times some shall depart from the faith giving heed to seducing spirits and doctrines of devils; speaking lies in hypocrisy, having their conscience seared as with a hot iron. They forbid people to marry and command people to abstain from meats, which God has created to be received with thanksgiving of them who believe and know the truth.

II Timothy 3:1-7
In the Last Days perilous times shall come. Men shall be lovers of themselves, covetous, boasters, proud, blasphemers, disobedient to parents, unthankful, unholy, without natural affection, truce breakers, false accusers, incontinent, fierce, despisers of those that are good, traitors, heady, high-minded, lovers of pleasure more than lovers of God; having a form of godliness but denying the power thereof. Turn away from them…. They are ever learning, yet never able to come to the knowledge of the truth.

Doctrine & Covenants 59:2c
You shall not steal or commit adultery, kill or do anything similar.

Doctrine & Covenants 152:4
The Spirit further says, "I, God have not forsaken you nor have I changed in regard to the great and important work of the Restoration which I have called you to do. Neither have I turned from you my people. This is true in spite of the fact some of you have turned away from me, and my purposes. Some have been led to inactivity and even lulled to sleep by the spirit of carelessness and indifference. Some have been overcome by the grosser sins of the world, the spirit of revelry, wanton living, use of drugs, drinking and fornication and have fallen away. And still others have turned away for personal aggrandizement, rejecting my leadership because of trivial offenses. All who have done any of these things are counseled to repent with a contrite

---

[13] Variance is defined as discrepancy, discord, dissension.

[14] Emulations are defined as striving to equal or surpass another or competition, selfish rivalry.

[15] Sedition is defined as language or conduct directed against the public order.

[16] Heresies are defined as any course, conduct, or instruction that tends to produce dissension and schism in the church.

[17] Reveling is defined as carousing, boisterous festivity.

heart and heaviness of spirit while there is yet time. You are further admonished to covenant with me anew so you may again be clean men and women and find peace. My promises are sure; my yoke is easy and my burden is light for those who love me and walk in the light of my Spirit."

(Present Fulfillment)
Blatant disregard for the laws of God is evident to most people today, and the sins specified in this section are committed daily, throughout the world.

If we walk in the light, as He is in the light, we have fellowship with one another. And, the blood of Jesus, His Son, cleanses us from all sin. If we say we have no sin, we deceive ourselves and, the truth is not in us. If we confess our sins, He is faithful and just to forgive us our sins and to cleanse us from all unrighteousness.

I John 1:7-9

SIGN 7
Wars and Rumors of Wars

Matthew 24:25, 29, 30 [Matthew 24:6 KJV]
Jesus continues, "You will hear of wars and rumors of wars. I speak to you for the sake of my elect. Nation shall rise against nation and kingdom against kingdom. [Mark 13:27, 31, 32; Luke 21:9-10]

Revelation 6:3, 4
And when He had opened the second seal, I heard the second beast say, Come and see. And there went out another horse that was red; and power was given to him that sat thereon to take peace from the earth, and that they should kill one another; and there was given unto him a great sword.

(Summary)
Revelation 6:3, 4
The rider on the red horse represents war. This is the rider who "takes peace from the earth" and "wields a great sword[18]." Thousands will die when this seal is broken.

Mormon 4:28 [Mormon 8:29 LDS]
[The records of the Book of Mormon] shall come in a day when they shall hear of fires and tempests and vapors of smoke in foreign lands and they shall also hear of wars and rumors of wars and earthquakes in different places.

Doctrine & Covenants 45:4a [also Matthew Chapters 24 and 25]
In that day you shall hear of wars and rumors of wars and the whole earth shall be in commotion and men's hearts shall fail them and they shall say that Christ delays His coming until the end of the earth.

Doctrine & Covenants 45:11c
You hear of wars in foreign lands but I say to you they are very close, even at your doors and not many years in the future you shall hear of wars in your own lands.

Doctrine & Covenants 63:2a-c
I the Lord utter my voice and it shall be obeyed. Wherefore, I say, "Let the wicked take heed and let the rebellious fear and tremble and let the unbelieving hold their lips for the day of wrath shall come upon them as a whirlwind and all flesh shall know that I am God. And he that seeks signs shall see signs but not unto salvation."

(Present Fulfillment)
Wars have taken place throughout the centuries. Although they were deadly, the destructive power of weapons was limited. People even sat on hillsides to watch some battles. However, those hostilities cannot begin to compare with current warfare with its technological advances. In less than a hundred years, we have progressed from

---

[18] The book of Revelation (Revelation 6:1-2) describes a sealed scroll held in the hand of God the Father. The seven seals on the book can be opened only by the Lamb of God, Jesus Christ. He alone is worthy to break the seals to expose the contents. Each seal represents a decree from God affecting men on earth. The seals in the book of Revelation are often parallel with signs in Matthew 24.

relatively primitive conflicts to a time when it is possible to destroy the whole earth. Modern weapons are able to reach every location on this planet. We no longer watch battles from hillsides. There will be no place to hide when nuclear weapons are discharged. The twentieth century and now the twenty-first have experienced constant fighting in one part of the world or another. The Internet currently documents 148 wars between 1900 and 2000. This does not include the current crisis in Iraq, Iran, Egypt, Afghanistan and other Arab countries. Since World War I, there has been very little peace[19].

Matthew 10:30 [Matthew 10:34 KJV]
Jesus said, "Don't think that I come to bring peace to the world, I come to bring a sword."

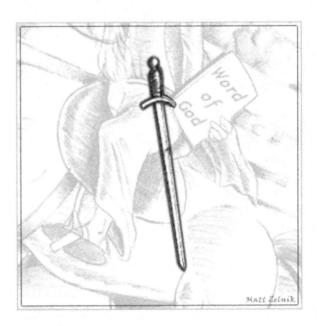

John 14:16, 26, 27
Jesus also said, "I will pray to the Father to send the Comforter or the Holy Ghost to you in my name and He shall teach you all things and bring to your remembrance all the things I have taught you. My peace I leave with you. My peace I give to you, not as the world gives but as I give it to you. Don't let your heart be troubled and don't let it be afraid."

War will persist in many places of the world (possibly in the United States) from now throughout the tribulation. The cost in lives, devastation, and dollars will exceed our worst imagination. With the economic crisis and continued warfare, the collapse of nations is possible. This could lead to anarchy, hunger, and terror as people try to provide for very basic human needs. We can only pray for Jesus to come quickly.

---

[19] See internet http://en.wikipedia.org/wiki/list_of_wars_and_disasters_by_death_toll

SIGN 8
Famines, Pestilences, and Earthquakes

> <u>**Matthew 24:30 [Matthew 24:7 KJV]**</u>
> *…There will be famine and pestilences and earthquakes in different places.*

> <u>**Revelation 6:5, 6 [The Third Seal on the Scroll Is Broken.]**</u>
> *And when the Lamb of God opened the third seal, I [John] heard the third beast say, "Come and see." And I beheld a black horse[20], and he that sat on him had a pair of balances in his hand. And I heard a voice…say, "a measure of wheat for a penny and three measures of barley for a penny and don't hurt the oil and the wine."*

The rider on the black horse represents famine, which starves the poor by inflating prices far above their normal level. The penny represents a day's wages, perhaps enough to buy a quart of wheat to feed one person or three quarts of less nutritious barley, which might be a day's ration for a small family. However, wine will be plentiful. Because of the food shortage, people may be tempted to drink instead of eat. The effects of too much alcohol on individuals and families is devastating.

> <u>**Revelation 6:7, 8 [The Fourth Seal on the Scroll Is Broken.]**</u>
> *And, when the Lamb had opened the fourth seal, I [John] heard the voice…say, "Come and see." And I looked and beheld a pale horse and the one who sat on him was Death and Hell followed him. And power was given to them over one-fourth of the earth, to kill with hunger and with death and with the beasts of the earth.*

© RSBlan Photography and Graphics

---

[20] Revelation 6:5, 6 describes a famine that will have a huge death toll. The black horse represents famine.

Doctrine & Covenants 45:4f [See also Matthew 24:30.]
There shall be earthquakes in diverse places and much desolation; yet men will harden their hearts against me and they will take up swords against one another and kill each other.

(Present Fulfillment)
Natural disasters do occur throughout time. However, they are noticeably increasing. A weekly syndicated column called *Earthweek, a Diary of the Planet* by Steve Newman (*Tribune Media News*) appears in papers throughout the country. Through this source it is possible to track natural events from around the world that otherwise might go unnoticed. It records evidence of major outbreaks of disease, earthquakes, hurricanes, tsunamis, typhoons, volcanic eruptions, and wildfires, displacement of animals from their natural habitat, change in global weather patterns, enormous mudslides, and other natural catastrophes. (For more, search Natural Disasters on Wikipedia.org.). Nearly as soon as individuals and world aid organizations assist in one area, another area is in dire need.

On August 29, 2005 Hurricane Katrina, a category 3 storm, hit the states of Louisiana and Mississippi. It was one of the greatest natural disasters ever to touch the United States of America. The rescue of residents was poorly managed, and at least 1,836 people lost their lives. The destruction of property, homes and business covered an area the size of Great Britain. Recovery from this calamity will take years, affecting the whole United States economically, psychologically, politically, and spiritually. Those who were directly affected and those who died are tragic examples of the fragility of humankind in a very unpredictable world.

After Hurricane Katrina, the groundwater in New Orleans filled with poisons. Although many of the city water lines were unbroken, water in the pipes was contaminated. Restoring safe water to affected communities was a major problem. The conditions were ripe for an outbreak of fatal diseases. Mass evacuation avoided disaster, but it also created numerous other problems.

On September 23, 2005, Hurricane Rita (another category 3 storm) ravaged the Texas and Louisiana coasts. Satellite imaging revealed that Katrina and Rita produced one of the nation's largest forestry disasters in recorded history. The storms killed or severely damaged some 320 million trees in Mississippi and Louisiana. Researchers say this will significantly add to greenhouse gas buildup, putting as much carbon from dying vegetation into the air as the rest of American forests take out in a year of photosynthesis.

In 2007, a huge wave created a wall of water and mud a half mile wide in Mexico. The water and mud buried homes in San Juan Grijalva, and an entire village in Chiapas, Mexico. Tropical Cyclone Sidr crippled Bangladesh, and hurricane-force winds with high seas sank three vessels laden with chemicals, spilling oil from a tanker in one of Russia's worst environmental disasters.

In September 2008, Hurricane Ike targeted Texas and Louisiana coastlines with devastating results. Some of the cities may never be completely rebuilt. The winds from the hurricane moved northward, reaching as far as Ohio. In many parts of the Buckeye state, winds in excess of 80 mph continued for hours, causing power outages that lasted for days. Fallen trees, numerous accidents, and deaths ranged from Cincinnati northward toward Cleveland, Ohio.

After the U.S. hurricanes, a 2008 earthquake in Pakistan took more than 50,000 lives, but human error and greed are often involved in a significant number of other disasters. Poaching and deforestation threaten the extinction of some primates in South Africa. Rampaging monkeys in New Delhi terrorize neighborhoods encroaching upon their natural habitat.

Our food supply is also at risk. High gas prices encouraged farmers to turn corn into ethanol, reducing the amount of this vegetable available for food. In September 2006, an E-coli outbreak in various parts of the United States was traced to fresh and bagged spinach in markets. Later, lettuce was similarly affected. Aug 17, 2010 an Iowa egg producer recalled 380 million eggs after their being linked to an outbreak of salmonella poisoning. Recalls of butchered meats, canned foods, and fresh vegetables are becoming common. Pet food imports from China killed numerous animals. Many toys imported from that country were recalled because they contained lead.

Early in 2010, a massive earthquake devastated portions of Haiti leaving many residents buried under collapsed buildings, and survivors fighting for food brought in by relief organizations. Many children were orphaned and residents in the affected part of the country had little shelter. World relief organizations responded immediately, but the situation was overwhelming. Bodies were shoveled into mass graves to prevent disease.

On Feb. 28, 2010, a magnitude 8.8 earth tremor hit Chili causing a tsunami with 10-foot waves headed for other parts of the world. The death toll and the relief efforts paralleled those in Haiti, and survival for many of the residents was in grave doubt. By the time massive flooding hit Nashville, Tennessee, (2010), national relief efforts for disasters were sadly depleted. Much of the city had to fend for itself.

Spring of 2010, the explosion of a BP oil well in the Gulf of Mexico, created an oil spill that dumped millions of gallons of oil into the gulf's waters. The oil washed inland to the eastern coast of the United States destroying beaches, dunes, wildlife sanctuaries, and jobs in fishing and tourist industries. This national disaster will take eons of time to dissipate. The wildlife destroyed is a catastrophe in itself. China had a similar catastrophe only weeks later.

In March of 2011 a devastating earthquake and tsunami that hit Japan was described as creating more damage than WWII.

National news articles documented increases in plant diseases and poisons polluting the water, ground, and air in 2006. This intensifies the growing number of famines. *Earthweek* recorded invasions of locusts and grasshoppers stripping fields in third world countries nearly overnight. Famine is a reality in poor countries, war zones and in parts of the world where the desert is rapidly advancing.

An unprecedented number of new and unusual human diseases are rapidly spreading throughout the world, creating health and economic crises. For the last twenty years, formerly unknown, deadly diseases have confounded the medical world. In 2004 and

2005, *Earthweek* documented some of the newly discovered maladies. These include the Usutu virus, Ebola virus, Marburg virus, Cryptosporidium, toxic shock syndrome, and flesh-eating bacteria. On April 11, 2005, it was reported in national newspapers that the Marburg hemorrhagic fever that killed 123 people in the Congo in 1998 was spreading to war-torn Angola. Two hundred people were affected. Of these, 173 died.

Other communicable diseases, mad cow disease, Legionnaire's disease, SARS (severe acute respiratory syndrome), and river blindness (in Africa) appeared in the last thirty years. A super-bug called MRSA (a Methicillin resistant staphylococcus aureus) attacked people, in western countries, who were hospitalized or in nursing homes. The same illness was reported among American high school athletes, children in day-care centers, prisoners in various institutions, and people who should not have been vulnerable to this ailment.

Other news sources describe pestilences of many kinds that are occurring in various countries. The most obvious one is the AIDS epidemic, which has become a worldwide problem. Billions of dollars spent on researching this disease resulted in some progress but no cure. Many people live longer with the illness, and the number of babies born with HIV has been reduced. However, this illness remains a preventable catastrophe that will claim many more lives before it is conquered. Much of South Africa has already been decimated by AIDS.

A worldwide pandemic of Asian bird flu was averted in February. However, the H5N1 strain of bird flu mutated to a form that remains a serious threat to humans and may yet cause many deaths.

In 2009, the whole world was threatened by the killer H1N1 pig virus and people throughout many parts of the world were vaccinated.

Diseases thought to be extinct or under control are resurfacing and are nearly immune to modern medicine. Anthrax, cholera, dengue, yellow fever, diphtheria, and tuberculosis are again claiming lives. Even polio has reemerged.

Statistically, it takes an average of ten years for a person to die from AIDS. The Ebola virus kills in ten hours. Individually these calamities would not be prophetic fulfillment, but the numbers are increasing dramatically. The growing worldwide population also complicates matters. Whenever disaster occurs, the loss of life is staggering. All of this indicates that significant changes in nature are taking place. Scriptures indicate these challenges will grow in number.

It is time to pay attention.

SIGN 9
The gospel is preached throughout the world.

Matthew 24:32 [Matthew 24:14 KJV]
The gospel of the kingdom will be preached in all the world as a witness to all nations. Then the end, the destruction of the wicked, shall come. [See also Mark 13:36.]

Doctrine & Covenants 2:6a
My work shall go forth, for as knowledge of a Savior has come to the world through the testimony of the Jews, so shall the knowledge of a Savior come to my people and the Nephites and the Jacobites and the Josephites and the Zoramites through the testimony of their fathers. This testimony shall come to the knowledge of the Lamanites and the Lemuelites and the Ishmaelites who dwindled in unbelief because of the iniquity of their fathers whom the Lord chose to destroy because of their iniquities and abomination. For this purpose, the plates [Book of Mormon] are preserved which contain these records so the promises the Lord made to His people might be fulfilled and the Lamanites might come to the knowledge of their fathers. Know the promises of the Lord, believe the gospel, rely upon the merits of Jesus Christ and be glorified through faith in His Name so through their repentance they might be saved. Amen.

Doctrine & Covenants 18:3b, c
...The Book of Mormon, which is My word to the Gentiles, contains the truth and the Word of God... which soon may go to the Jews of whom the Lamanites are a remnant so they may believe the gospel and not look for another Messiah.

(Present Fulfillment)

With the advent of radio, TV, satellite communications, and the Internet, ministers and missionaries are preaching the gospel where it has never before been heard. Individual Christian men and women are devoting their lives to reaching people for Christ in remote places of the world. SAT 7, Christian satellite television for the people of the Middle East and North Africa, is bringing many Muslims to Christ. Restoration churches, RLDS and the LDS church, continue their work in bringing the words of the Book of Mormon to the Jewish people, American Indians and others around the globe. Although its message still has many places to go, it is traveling faster than ever before. People of every nation now have an opportunity to receive Christ's gospel. We can support this effort through gifts to Christian organizations and missionary efforts of our choice.

SIGN 10
People will cry "Peace, peace!" but there will be no peace.

Ezekiel 7:25
Destruction will come and they shall seek peace but there shall be none. [This scripture has implications for both the Babylonian captivity and the time, which precedes the Second Coming.]

I Thessalonians 5:2, 3
You know perfectly the day of the Lord will come as a thief in the night. When they say peace and safety, sudden destruction will come upon them as birth pains upon a woman with child. And they shall not escape. [See: Jeremiah 6:14; 8:9, 11, 15; 8:15; Isaiah 48:22, 57:21; Daniel 8:25; Luke 12:60-65; Micah 3:5-7; Ezekiel 7:25; 13:10, 16.]

Mormon 4:39 [8:31 LDS]
In that day, there shall be murders, robbing, lying, deceiving, whoredoms and all manner of abominations. There will be many who will say, "Go ahead and do what you want for the Lord will not punish you at the last day."

Doctrine & Covenants 1:6b
The day is speedily coming, the hour is not yet but is close at hand when peace shall be taken from the earth and the Devil shall have power over his own dominion. But, the Lord also shall have power over His saints and shall reign in their midst and shall come down in judgment upon the world.

(Present Fulfillment)

Today the world is filled with anger, violence, terrorism, war, rage within homes, and unprecedented destruction in the air and on the highways. People everywhere, including within the Community of Christ, are crying for peace. Since the beginning of the twentieth century, the world has struggled with major wars and threats of major wars. Sophisticated weapons and bombs are in the hands of governments and terrorists. Ambassadors attempt to reason with dictators about the dangers of building nuclear weapons, and biological warfare is an unseen killer used in Iraq and elsewhere. Fear surrounds the globe and men cry, "Peace, Peace," but there is no peace.

The scriptures indicate there will be no world peace until Christ returns, but the apostle John records this comforting promise from Jesus Christ.

John 14:27
Jesus promises, "Peace I leave with you. My peace I give to you but not as the world gives peace. Do not let your heart be troubled or afraid."

Jesus can deliver the inner peace each believer needs in a world completely in turmoil. Faith and trust in Him are the essentials for obtaining this peace.

SIGN 11

"People will run to and fro and knowledge will be increased but the wisdom of the wise will be confounded." Daniel 12:4

Proverbs 3:7
Be not wise in your own eyes. Fear the Lord and depart from evil.

I Corinthians 1:19-31
It is written: I will destroy the wisdom of those who think they are wise and will bring to nothing the understanding of those who appear to be prudent[21]. Where are the wise? Where is the scribe? Where is the disputer [22] of this world? Has not God made the wisdom of this world into foolishness? The world by its wisdom does not know God but it pleases God by the foolishness of preaching to save them that believe. The Jews require a sign and the Greeks seek after wisdom; but we preach Christ crucified! This is a stumbling block to the Jews and foolishness to the Greeks but to the Jews and Greeks who believe, Christ is the power of God and the wisdom of God. The foolishness of God is wiser than men and the weakness of God is stronger than men.

Brothers, not many wise or mighty or noble men receive your calling, for God has chosen the weak things of the world to confound things which are mighty and the base things of the world and things which are despised, to bring down things that are mighty so that no man will glory in his own presence. But, you are of Christ Jesus. He is God's wisdom, righteousness, sanctification and redemption to us. According to the written word, he that gives glory should glory in the Lord.

I Corinthians 8:1-3
Knowledge makes people proud but charity edifies them. If any man thinks he know something, he does not know anything he ought to know. But if a man loves God, that man is known to Him.

DOCTRINE & COVENANTS 76:2c
The wisdom of the wise shall perish and the understanding of the prudent shall come to naught. By my Spirit I will enlighten them and by my power I will make known to them the secrets of my will; yes, even those things which eye has not seen nor has the ear heard nor have these things yet entered into the heart of man. [See Psalms 138:6; II Chronicles 7:14.]

(Present Fulfillment)

What a vivid description of our modern world! In a little over a hundred years, we have progressed from the horse-and-buggy to putting men on the moon. We can travel around the world in hours instead of months; we navigate the deepest oceans and send unmanned craft deep into space. We cure many diseases, and scientists explore how to make life as well as extend it. Human pride is an important factor in SIGN 11. Many men equate knowledge, education, and "book learning" with wisdom. The more they

---

[21] Prudent synonyms are diplomatic, discerning, levelheaded, rational, discreet, shrewd, and sensible.
[22] Synonyms for disputer are doubter, challenger, and one who questions the truth.

40

learn, the more they impress themselves. This is especially true in churches where the scriptures are no longer regarded as truth and current perceptions (the way men want things to be) are substituted for the Word of God. Christ says, "The wisdom of the wise shall perish." We will all be humbled before the Lord.

"People will run to and fro and knowledge will be increased but the wisdom of the wise will be confounded."

Daniel 12:4

SIGN 12
People will reject the scriptures concerning the Last Days.

There will be widespread acceptance of moral decay in society, corruption in religious thought, and spiritual decay within the church.

II Peter 3:3-5, 8-12
In the Last Days, there will be scoffers who pursue their own lusts and deny the Lord Jesus. They will say, "Where is the promise of his coming?" or "what makes you think He will come now?" …They are willingly ignorant.

I don't want you to be ignorant about the coming of the Lord. Remember, one day is like a thousand years with God and a thousand years is like one day. The Lord is not late in keeping His promise and coming, the way some think of lateness. Instead, He is longsuffering toward us. He is reluctant that anyone should perish and is providing time for everyone to repent.

But the day of the Lord will come as a thief in the night; the Heavens will shake and the earth will tremble and the mountains will melt and disappear with a great noise and the earth will be filled with fervent heat and all of the corruption which is in it will be burned up. Therefore, if all these things will be destroyed, what kind of people should you be in holy conduct and godliness, while you watch and prepare for the day of the coming of the Lord?

I Nephi 7:50 [Nephi 22:23 LDS]
The time shall come speedily when all churches, those built for gain or power over the flesh, and those which are built to be popular in the eyes of the world, and those which seek lusts of the flesh and the things of the world and do all manner of iniquity, and all those which belong to the kingdom of the devil, will fear, tremble and quake. They will be brought down into the dust and consumed as stubble.

Mormon 4:51, 52 [Mormon 8:38 LDS]
Oh, you polluted people, you hypocrites, you teachers who sell yourselves for that which will rot! Why have you polluted the holy church of God? Why are you ashamed to take upon you the name of Christ?

(Present Fulfillment)
Today, the authority of scripture is questioned in many churches, including the Community of Christ. Passages that teach the virgin birth, the resurrection, and Christ's Second Coming are called metaphor and folktales. They are attributed to nineteenth century theology, both unenlightened and unscientific beliefs of the early church.

Because of this, it is now difficult to find RLDS reference books such as the *Compendium to the Scriptures* or the *Compendium of Faith and Doctrine* based on the Inspired Version, Book of Mormon, and Doctrine and Covenants. However, both books are major assets for members who want to explore basic beliefs of the Restored Church. Students of these scriptures realize the purpose of a compendium is to provide, in one place, scripture references to all the basic teachings of the Restoration. These books emphasize that Christ is returning soon and will build His kingdom on earth.

Isaiah 5:20, 21, 23, 24
Woe to them that call evil good and good evil; that put darkness for light and light for darkness; that put bitter for sweet and sweet for bitter! Woe to those who are wise in their own eyes and prudent in their own sight, which justify the wicked for reward and take the righteousness of the righteous from him. Therefore as the fire devours the stubble and the flame consumes the chaff, so their root shall be rotten and their blossom shall go up as dust because they have cast away the law of the Lord of hosts and despised the word of the Holy One of Israel.

©RSBlain Photography and Graphics

SIGN 13
Moral decay and corruption are widespread.

I Timothy 4:1-9
In the Last Days, there will be widespread acceptance of moral decay in society, corruption in religious thought, and spiritual decay within the church.

(Definition)
MORALITY pertains to character and behavior from the point of view of right and wrong; obligation to duty, moral conduct, chastity, virtue, conforming to that which is right, good, righteous, virtuous, dutiful, ethical, excellent, faithful, good, honest, honorable, incorruptible, just, righteous, true, and upright. This covers the entire scope of human conduct.

Moral Decay in Society: Today many people reject concepts of right and wrong. If something feels good, do it! More and more business leaders are involved in illicit transactions. Corruption is found in the highest levels of government and churches. School textbooks advocate political correctness rather than truth. Spirituality, religion, politics, history, current events, and other subjects of importance are significantly influenced and modified by politically correct viewpoints. History is written by the "winners" rather than based on fact. Homes and marriages are often insecure havens where anger and violence threaten the well-being of all family members. Divorce is easier than working out marital differences. Concepts of morality, as defined above, have been trampled in much of the modern world.

Corruption in Religious Thought: The September 2005 *NewsMax* magazine reported on Hollywood's "New Gods" which influence celebrities and young people seeking alternative forms of spirituality. Although numerous sources address this topic, *NewsMax* magazine captured the subject quite well.

"With the old religions losing their hold on many people, stars and their fans are seeking a new, modern, more hip faith. Many are turning to New Age philosophies which became popular in Western culture in the 1970s."[23]

The spring 2005 issue of *NewsMax* said that the term New Age refers to a collection of esoteric teachings including spiritualism, channeling, astrology, Gnosticism, theosophy, Transcendental Meditation, and Wicca, an exclusive form of witchcraft. It also includes religions such as Buddhism, Hinduism, and Taoism. Interest in New Age increased in the late 1980s when actress Shirley MacLaine's autobiographical book *Out on a Limb* became a bestseller.

Scientology is one of these new religions, according to Scientology[24] magazine. It is the subject of the movie *War of the Worlds* and Scientology was founded as a church in 1954 in Los Angeles. It is a philosophical religion conceived by science-fiction writer L. Ron Hubbard, the author of *Dianetics: the Modern Science of Mental Health*, published in 1950.

---

[23] "Hollywood and Their New Age Faith," *NewsMax* magazine, Sept. 5, 2007
[24] Famous adherents of Scientology include noted personalities Tom Cruise, Katie Holmes, John Travolta, Kirstie Alley, Lisa Marie Presley, Juliette Lewis, Jenna Elfman and film producer Douglas Urbansky.

Kabbalah [25], part of ancient Jewish traditions, is based on mystical aspects and interpretations of the Old Testament. The word is derived from the Hebrew term for "reception," and it claims to have secret knowledge that has been kept hidden from nonbelievers. Kabbalah relates to esoteric wisdom and contemplative practices facilitating communion and, sometimes, even the union of the individual and their god. It refers to receiving the inner, hidden, or esoteric meaning of divine revelation. Former insurance salesman Philip Berg launched the modern Kabbalah movement. He took the ancient teachings of Kabbalah and converted them into a New Age mystical philosophy promising improved sex, immortality, and a changed world. About fifty thousand students attend weekly programs at fifty branches worldwide.

Buddhism is also attracting Hollywood insiders, thereby influencing many young people. Richard Gere, Steven Seagal, and Philip Glass are some of its noted adherents. In the 1960s, the Beatles looked to the Maharishi Mahesh Yogi and Transcendental Meditation. Because of the Beatles' involvement, this philosophy has advocates all over the world.

These are by no means all of the new religions perpetuated and promoted by Hollywood. However, many come and go before gaining public attention. David Zucker, producer, director, and writer, said, "Mainstream Hollywood rejects the notion of good and evil. Religions which do not emphasize moral absolutes are attractive to folks in Tinsel town."

NewsMax magazine published a profound quote from public relations expert Michael Levine who advises many famous clients, including, Barbra Streisand, Ozzy Osbourne, Demi Moore, and Michael J. Fox. "One thing missing from their worldview," according to Levine, is the conventional notion of evil. "Nobody is evil," he explains. "If you ask them whether Charles Manson was evil, they would say, 'Well, I wouldn't do what he's done, but it's not for me to judge.'"

Certainly, Hollywood is not the only source of religious corruption. Radio and TV programming, school textbooks, liberal-minded teachers, magazines, and computer information increasingly contain objectionable materials that influence the minds of gullible people. All of this demonstrates sign 13 is being fulfilled.

Spiritual Decay in the Church: Christian churches are under attack from within. Corrupted thought among some religious leaders is causing widespread spiritual and moral decline. Many liberal leaders are challenging age-old Christian doctrine, changing the gospel and teaching a watered-down version of scriptural truths. People who are hungry for the Word of God may have difficulty finding a church teaching the basic principles of the gospel.

Many people join a church for social reasons rather than a relationship with Jesus Christ. Their concern for God's Word is limited. They no longer believe the scriptures are relevant and are willing to accept modified changes in church doctrine to justify degraded behavior. Their dwindling faith in the Son of God and in His Word serves themselves rather than their creator. Church attendance has little influence on the rest

---

[25] Noted personalities who are a part of the Kabbalah movement are Madonna, Guy Ritchie, Britney Spears, Demi Moore, Rob Lowe, Elizabeth Taylor, Paris Hilton, Naomi Campbell, Rosie O'Donnell, Winona Ryder, Sharon Osbourne, Barbra Streisand, and Monica Lewinski.

of their lives and immorality of all kinds is overlooked or tolerated. Recent scandals of sexual abuse within various churches reveal only a portion of the decay within.

Corruption among church leaders and parishioners is an appalling but common offense. Theft in office, misuse of trust, and blatant abuses of scripture, incest and other forms of sex abuse are the most insidious forms of corrosion taking place. New Age thought is also creeping into the church. Concepts of good and evil have changed. The scriptures are being modified for use by special-interest groups who want them to reflect their points of view and activities that God calls abominations are expected to be accepted. Preachers shy away from controversial topics, and a whole generation has never heard the verses of scripture that should guide their choices in life. Young people may never hear Christ's essential message. Many live as unmarried couples and children are born out of wedlock. Homosexual relationships are viewed as a choice, not as a perversion.

We are failing our children and ourselves if we allow Christ's restored gospel to be lost once again. It is completely unacceptable for any church purporting to be a House of the Living God to twist Christian doctrine into an unrecognizable form. Jesus Christ must be introduced to others as the only Savior. He is Savior, judge, and best friend to those who follow Him. We know Him through prayer and study of the Bible, the Book of Mormon, and the Doctrine and Covenants.

Mormon 4:41-43, 49-51 [Mormon 8:32, 36, 38 LDS]
It [God's records] shall come in a day when churches are built up which shall say, "Come unto me and for your money you shall be forgiven of your sins." O you wicked and perverse and stiff-necked people! Why have you built churches to gain riches and prestige for yourselves? Why have you transfigured the Holy Word of God to bring damnation upon your own souls?

Your churches, yes, every one of them, have become polluted because of the pride of your hearts. Behold, you love money, and your substance, and your fine apparel and the adorning of your churches more than you love the poor, and the needy, the sick, and the afflicted…. Why have you polluted the holy church of God?

Mormon 4:66-68 [Mormon 9:7, 8, 9 LDS]
*And again **I speak to you who deny the revelations of God** and say they are gone; there are no revelations, nor prophecies, nor gifts, nor healing, nor speaking with tongues nor the interpretation of tongues. Behold I say to you, **he that denies these things does not know the gospel of Christ. He has not read the Scriptures or, if so, he does not understand them.** Do we not read that God is the same yesterday, today and forever and in Him there is neither variableness, nor shadow of changing?*

The scriptures stress the importance of sexual morality.

Our scriptures, the Old and New Testament, the Book of Mormon, and the Doctrine and Covenants, speak with God's authority about chastity (no sex outside of marriage), the sanctity of marriage, and sexual morality. The subject appears in these books more than two hundred times. Reading them contextually, they convey a clear message admonishing the people of God to remain pure and free from sexual perversions. God

46

considers sexual immorality so serious that Alma says it the most abominable of all sins, except for murder or denying the Holy Ghost. (Alma 19:5, 7, 13, 16; Alma 39:3, 10 LDS)

First and foremost in God's plan for humanity is the sanctity of marriage. Human sexual behavior is intended by God to be expressed solely within the confines of heterosexual, monogamous marriage. Since God is love, sexual activity can be considered as a true act of love only when confined within the parameters clearly established in His Word. Scriptural guidance on human sexual behavior is positive and life giving. It is an expression of God's perfect love and desire to protect those He has created. Any deviation from its intended purposes is rebellion against His wisdom and goodness. It sets the man or woman at enmity with Him until the person repents and comes into agreement with God's design. The idea that man has the right to choose his own methods of sexual expression is opposed in scripture.

Words in scripture, which identify unacceptable sexual behavior.

(Definitions)
ADULTERY
Sexual relations between two people when one or the other is married to a third person. It is also defined as any sexual act or thought in violation of the scriptures.

FORNICATION
Debauchery, copulation, sexual intercourse between unmarried persons; impurity, adultery, harlotry, incest.

SODOMY
Carnal copulation between same-sex partners or with beasts. The word derives from the Genesis account of Sodom and Gomorrah. It is referred to in the scriptures in Genesis 13:11, 19:6-16, 18-25 (I.V.) or Genesis 13:13, 19:4-17 (KJV).

LASCIVIOUSNESS
Characterized by lust, lewd, lecherous, licentious, wanton behavior. Lacking moral discipline. Having no regard for accepted rules or standards.

INCEST
Sexual intercourse between people who are too nearly related for legal marriage.

Scripture identifies sexual behavior, which is unacceptable to God.

> ### Leviticus 18:22
> *You shall not lie with mankind as with womankind. It is an abomination.*

> ### Leviticus 20:13
> *If a man lies with a man as he lies with a woman, both of them have committed an abomination: they shall surely be put to death and their blood shall be upon them.*

Romans 1:18, 21, 24-30

The wrath of God is revealed from Heaven against all ungodliness and unrighteousness of men who do not love the truth but remain in unrighteousness. Because, when they knew God, they did not glorify Him as God, neither were they thankful but became vain in their imaginations and their foolish hearts were darkened. Professing themselves to be wise, they became fools. Therefore, God gave them up to uncleanness through the lusts of their own hearts to dishonor their own bodies between themselves. They changed the truth of God into a lie and worshipped and served the creature more than the Creator who is blessed forever. Amen.

For this cause, God gave them up to vile afflictions for even their women changed their natural use to that which is against nature. Likewise, the men, leaving the natural use of the woman, burned in their lust one toward another; men with men working that which is unseemly and receiving in themselves that recompense of their error which was deserved. And even as they did not like to remember their knowledge of God, God gave them over to a reprobate [shameless] mind, to do those things which are not legitimate; being filled with unrighteousness, fornication, wickedness, covetousness, maliciousness, full of envy, murder, debate, deceit, malignity, whisperers, backbiters, haters of God, despiteful, proud, boasters, inventors of evil things, disobedient to parents, without understanding, covenant-breakers, without natural affection, implacable, unmerciful; and those who know the judgment of God and know that they who commit such things are worthy of death, are inexcusable, for they not only do the same but have pleasure in them that do them.

I Corinthians 6:9, 10

Do not be deceived. Neither fornicators, or idolaters, or adulterers, or those who are effeminate, or those who abuse themselves with mankind, or thieves, or those who are covetous, or drunkards, or revilers, or extortionist shall inherit the kingdom of God.

I Corinthians 6:18

Flee fornication. Every sin that a man commits is against the body of Christ, and he who commits fornication sins against his own body.

I Corinthians 6:18 KJV [significantly different]

Flee fornication. Every sin a man does is outside the body but he that commits fornication sins against his own body.

Ephesians 5:3

As saints, don't let fornication or any uncleanness or covetousness be found among you….

Doctrine & Covenants 42:7d, e

You shall love your wife with all your heart and shall cling to her and no one else. He that looks upon a woman with lust denies the faith and shall not have the Spirit; if he does not repent, he shall be cast out. You shall not commit adultery and he who commits adultery and does not repent shall be cast out. You shall forgive an adulterer who repents with all his heart and forsakes it and does not do it again; if he does it again, he shall not be forgiven and shall be cast out.

All of these scriptures warn against sexual immorality because these behaviors are destructive, in one way or another, to individuals who practice them. I am particularly concerned about the devastating effects of homosexuality. Before I am accused of perpetrating "hate messages" against homosexuals, let me say that I have already lost several close family members and friends to the scourge of AIDS. I care deeply about each one of these people, and continue to mourn their loss. It is not the people I hate. It is the illness and its cause.

At every opportunity, I discuss these scriptures with relatives and friends who continue to live gay or alternative lifestyles. We discuss the illnesses afflicting people involved in all open sexual relationships. Many still blindly reply, "Yes, but it won't happen to me." The statistics are against them. The numbers show that the longer these relationships are practiced, the greater the risk of contracting one or more sexually related illnesses. In 2004, the U.N. World Health Organization reported 40 million known HIV-positive cases in the world. There were 5 million new cases that year and 3 million deaths. Tragically, AIDS, herpes, gonorrhea, and many other infections affect those who reject God's sexual guidelines. Talented people, who otherwise have much to offer, are dying prematurely. None of this would happen if self-discipline and abstinence were practiced. Most disturbing, because the behavior leading to this incurable illness is a choice, it is also a form of consensual suicide and murder.

Can you imagine you hear the voice of the Lord saying to you in that day, Come to me you blessed, for behold, your works have been the works of righteousness upon the face of the earth? ...Can you look up to God at that day with a pure heart and clean hands?"

Alma 3:36 [5:19 LDS]

ADDITIONAL SCRIPTURES
Adultery Cruden's Complete Concordance, KJV

Exodus 10:14	Leviticus 20:10	Deuteronomy 5:18
Proverbs 6:32, 30:20	Jeremiah 3:8, 9; 5:7; 7:9; 13:27; 23:14; 29:23	Ezekiel 16:32; 23:37, 43
Hosea 2:2; 4:2, 13, 14	Matthew 5:27, 28; 28:32; 15:19; 19:18	Mark 7:21; 8:38; 10:11, 19
Luke 16:18; 18:20	John 8:3, 4	Romans 2:22; 13:9
Galatians 5:19	James 2:11; 2	Peter 2:14
Revelation 2:22		

Concordance Supplement the Inspired Version of the Holy Scriptures

Matthew 5:29, 30, 36; 12:34; 15:18; 16:4; 19:9	Mark 7:20; 8:41; 10:9, 10, 17	Luke 16:21-23

The Book of Mormon

Mosiah 1:19, 44 (1:13, 2:13 LDS)	Mosiah 7:121 (11:15 LDS)	Alma 11:29 (16:18 LDS)
Alma 14:6 (23:3 LDS)	Alma 16:11 (30:10 LDS)	Helaman 2:45 (4:11 LDS)
Helaman 3:4 (7:5 LDS)	III Nephi 5:76-80 (12:27-32 LDS)	

Doctrine and Covenants

D & C 42:7, 20, 22	D & C 59:2	D & C 63:4, 5
D & C 66:5	D & C 76:7	

ADDITIONAL SCRIPTURES
Lasciviousness, Cruden's Complete Concordance KJV

Mark 7:22; 2	Corinthians 12:21	Galatians 5:19
Ephesians 4:19; 1	Peter 4:3	Jude 1:4

Concordance Supplement for the Inspired Version of the Holy Scriptures

Mark 7:20; 1	Peter 4:3	

Concordance to the Book of Mormon

Jacob 2:66 (3:12 LDS)	Alma 11:29 (Alma 16:18 LDS)	Alma 21:11 (Alma 45:12 LDS)
Alma 21:122 (47:36 LDS)	IV Nephi 1:18 (IV Nephi 1:16 LDS)	

ADDITIONAL SCRIPTURES
Sodomy, Cruden's Complete Concordance, KJV

Deuteronomy 23:17; 1	Kings 14:24; 15:12; 22:46	II Kings 23:7

Concordance Supplement Inspired Version of the Holy Scriptures
Sodom and Gomorrah

Genesis 19:6, 12, 30, 31, 34	Isaiah 3:9	

Book of Mormon

II Nephi 8:47	II Nephi 13:19 LDS	II Nephi 10:19
II Nephi 23:19 LDS	Alma 19:5, 7	

ADDITIONAL SCRIPTURES
Fornication Cruden's Complete Concordance, KJV

Deuteronomy 22:5	Leviticus 18:22, 23	Matthew 5:32; 15:19; 19:91
Mark 7:22; 19:9	John 8:41	Acts 15:20, 29; 21:25
Romans 1:29; 1	Corinthians 5:1, 9-11; 6:9, 13, 18; 7:2; 2	Corinthians 12:11, 21
Galatians 5:19	Ephesians 5:3	Colossians 3:5; 1
Thessalonians 4:3	Hebrews 12:16	Hebrews 13:4
Jude1: 4-8	Revelation 2:21; 9:21; 14:8; 17:2, 4; 18:3; 19:2	

Concordance Supplement for the Inspired Version

Matthew 5:36; 15:18; 19:9	Mark 7:20	Acts 21:25
I Corinthians 6:18; 7:2; 10:8	Revelation 2:21	

Book of Mormon

Jacob 2:66 (3:12 LDS)	Helaman 3:64 (8:26 LDS)	III Nephi 5:80 (12:32 LDS)

President W. Wallace Smith was the last prophet/president to receive guidance for the church on morality. On March 29, 1976, at the Reorganized Church of Jesus Christ of Latter Day Saints World Conference in Independence, Missouri, he presented the following words in his prophetic document, recorded as Section 152, 4a-d in the Doctrine and Covenants.

Doctrine & Covenants 152:4a-d

The Spirit states further: "I, God, have not forsaken you nor have I changed in regard to the great and important work of the Restoration which I have called you to do. Neither have I turned from you my people. This is true in spite of the fact some of you have turned away from me and my purposes. Some [of you] have been led to inactivity, yes, even lulled to sleep by the spirit of carelessness and indifference. Some have been overcome by the grosser sins of the world, the spirit of revelry, wanton living, and use of drugs, drinking, and fornication and have fallen away. And still others have turned away for personal aggrandizement, rejecting my leadership because of trivial offenses.

All who have done any of these things are counseled to repent with a contrite heart and heaviness of spirit while there is yet time. You are further admonished to covenant with me anew that you may again be clean men and women and find peace. My promises are sure; my yoke is easy and my burden is light for those who love me and walk in the light of my Spirit."

Morality: The guidance provided by Brother Wallace Smith is desperately needed today. Gross sin, as defined by scripture, is worldwide. In general, from about 1960, morality plummeted to a very low level. Sexual immorality followed. This problem infiltrates our own world church. Many members profess a belief in God but do not carry scriptural admonition into daily life. Attendance is dropping and the doors of many congregations are permanently closed. We no longer teach our church history, the basic beliefs of our church, or the things that make Latter Day Saints unique. The new curriculum of the '60s and '70s eliminated most of this information, and what is now taught is diluted, centering primarily on peace and justice.

Another concern: In some places, New Age philosophy is incrementally entering the church. Among our own people, there is a growing belief in New Age meditation and other deceptive forms of spiritualism. Many Christians are attracted to false prophetic gifts, such as spiritualism, clairvoyants, horoscopes, séances, crystal balls, Ouija boards, and Tarot card readings. These were once considered superstition or games for amusement, but through these mystical practices, more and more people, including teenagers, are being drawn into witchcraft, a worship of plural gods and goddesses, and various forms of Satanism. The occult is no longer underground. There is a large market for all of this information. Books and artifacts can be found in gift shops, most bookstores, department stores, specialty catalogs, and inside respectable homes in most communities. Skilled charlatans convert young people attracted by demonic sources of power and successfully undermine the faith of many unsuspecting youth. My own small community in Ohio has an active coven of witches.

Deuteronomy 18:10-12
There shall not be found among you any one that makes his son or his daughter pass through fire or that uses divination or an observer of times or an enchanter or a witch or a charmer or a consulter with familiar spirits or a wizard or a necromancer. All who do these things are an abomination to the Lord and because of these abominations, the Lord thy God will drive them out from you.

II Corinthians 11:13, 15
There are false apostles, and deceitful workers who transform themselves into the apostles of Christ. This is no marvel; for Satan himself is transformed into an angel of light. Therefore, it is not surprising if his ministers are also transformed as ministers of righteousness, whose end shall be according to their works.

I Timothy 4:1, 2
Now the spirit speaks expressly, that in the latter times some shall depart from the faith, giving heed to seducing spirits and doctrines of devils: Speaking lies in hypocrisy; having their conscience seared as with a hot iron; forbidding to marry, and commanding men to abstain from eating meat, which God has created to be received with thanksgiving by them who believe and know the truth. For every creature of God is good, and nothing is to be refused, if it is received with thanksgiving, for it is sanctified by the Word of God and prayer.

This is no marvel for
Satan himself is transformed into an angel of light.

II Corinthians 11:14

Although there are numerous religions practiced throughout the world,

Jesus said,

"I am the way, the truth and the life.
No man comes to the father except by me."

John 14:6

Therefore, any religion that does not include Christ is a form of fraudulent spiritualism that takes its adherents away from the only real God. Fraudulent spiritualism is the foundation for the Antichrist's coming new world religion. Its source is Satan.

ADDITIONAL SCRIPTURES

Leviticus 19:1-8	Leviticus 20:1-6	Deuteronomy 18:9-14; 32:16,17
Isaiah 8:19-22; 19:3	I Timothy 4:10	II Corinthians 11:14
Revelation 12:12	II Nephi 9:57	Helaman 5:23, 24, 41, 45-49
Mormon 1:19, 20		

How is it many church leaders no longer believe in a literal Satan? Even science agrees "opposites exist in ALL things"! Simply illustrated, there is black and white, male and female, good and evil, moral and immoral, <u>Heaven and Hell, God and Satan</u>. It is important to recognize and remember this dichotomy[26].

© ArtToday Photographs and Graphics

---

[26] Dichotomy—a division into two mutually exclusive, opposed, or contradictory groups.

God is!
God said unto Moses, "I am that I am." (Exodus 3:14)
"I am Alpha and Omega."

Revelation 1:8

GOD IS and SATAN EXISTS also.

Satan is the source of all evil and all occult powers. (See: Genesis 3:4, 5:2, Corinthians 11:14; Revelation 12:9, 20:2.)

Occult activities exist in many forms and they are practiced by a variety of people. Until recently, these activities were considered superstitions not verified by science. Although still not scientifically understood, there is now considerable evidence that evil power exists within the occult, and it is capable of deadly harm to those who are influenced by it.

Witchcraft is a very old world religion closely associated with other forms of the occult. Many witches practice a nature or earth-centered form of spirituality, and rituals differ widely. Some worship a goddess. Covens are growing, and within the last few years, organized witches even demanded religious recognition from the U.S. government[27].

Many bookstores carry a variety of titles attempting to create interest in witchcraft and the occult. This writer is not an expert on these subjects. However, the scriptures are clear: involvement in witchcraft or any form of the occult is forbidden! Therefore, I believe all of these practices put individuals at serious risk mentally, physically, and spiritually.

God continues to warn about involvement in all forms of evil. His position in scripture is very clear. He will not tolerate sin. Occult activity, idolatry, immoral sexual activity, and behaviors that harm the human body (smoking, drunkenness, drug abuse, gambling, overeating, and lies) are not part of His plan for humanity. His Word emphatically speaks against all false prophetic gifts, immorality, and other sin. He continues to encourage His people to keep themselves clean in mind, body, and spirit, preparing to live in His presence.

We are already reaping the consequences of our failure to teach moral absolutes. How many of our members, including some within our leadership and priesthood of the church, have AIDS? How many have died? How many are addicted to pornography or are involved in extramarital affairs? How many homes have been broken and lives forever altered? This is not what God wants for His church.

---

[27] This information was contained in an article published in the Kansas City Star, Scott Bauer, May 27, 2008

SIGN 14
There will be false teachers.

Matthew 23:5
Do not be called Teacher, for only Christ is your master and you are all brothers and sisters…. Do not be called master for only one is your master, Christ who was sent by your Heavenly Father so you might have life. He that is greatest among you shall be your servant. Whoever exalts himself shall be humbled and he who humbles himself shall be exalted by the Lord.

Galatians 1:8
[Paul said] "Though we or an angel from Heaven preach any other gospel to you than that which we have preached, let him be accursed."

I Timothy 1:3-11
…Charge the leaders so they teach no other doctrine or pay attention to fables and endless genealogies, which create questions rather than edifying the faith in a Godly manner. Now, the end of the commandment is charity out of a pure heart and of a good conscience with real faith. Some have swerved and have turned aside to vain jangling. They want to be teachers of the law but they do not understand what they are saying or what they affirm. We know that the law is good if a man uses it lawfully for the law is not made for righteous men but for the lawless and disobedient…. Any other thing is contrary to sound doctrine, according to the glorious gospel of the blessed God, which He committed to my trust.

I Peter 2:6-8
Behold, I lay in Zion a chief cornerstone, elect, and precious. He that believes in Him shall not be confounded. He is precious to you who believe, but to the disobedient who stumble at His word, He is a stone of stumbling and a rock of offense. For the stone, which the builders threw away, has become the Head of the Corner [of the church].

II Nephi 12:3, 5-21 [2 N 28:3-17 LDS]
It shall come to pass in that day, the churches which are built up but not for the Lord will say to one another, "Behold, I am the Lord's" and the other shall say, "I am the Lord's." And they shall contend with each other and their priests shall argue with one another and they will teach with their own learning and deny the Holy Ghost, which should inspire their words. And they deny the power of God, the Holy One of Israel. They will say to the people, "Listen to us. There is no God today for the Lord, the Redeemer has done His work, and now He has given His power to men. Don't look for miracles by the hand of the Lord. His work is finished and He is no longer a God of miracles. Eat, drink and be merry for tomorrow we shall die but it will be well with us."

Others will say, "Eat, drink and be merry but fear God. He will justify small sins. It's all right to lie a little, take advantage of others or dig a pit for your neighbor. There is no harm in this. Go ahead and do these things, for tomorrow we die and even if we are guilty, God will beat us with a few stripes but we shall still be saved in His kingdom."

Yes, there will be many who teach in this manner, false and vain and foolish doctrines and shall be puffed up in their hearts and seek to hide this counsel from the Lord. Their works shall be in darkness and the blood of the saints will cry from the ground against them. They have gone out of the way and have become corrupted. Because of pride and false teachers and false doctrine, their churches have become corrupted. Their churches are lifted up because of pride and they are puffed up.

These leaders/teachers rob the poor to pay for their fine sanctuaries and fine clothing. They persecute the meek and the poor in heart because of their pride. Because of pride, they have stiff necks and hold their heads high. They commit abominations and whoredoms, and all except a few humble followers of Christ have gone astray.

Nevertheless, they err because they are taught by the precepts of men. Oh the wise and the learned and the rich who are puffed up in the pride of their hearts and all those who preach false doctrines or commit whoredoms and pervert the right way of the Lord; Woe, woe, woe be to them! The Lord God Almighty says, "They shall be thrust down to Hell." Woe to them that turn aside the just for a thing of no value and revile against that which is good, saying that it is of no worth, for the day shall come that the Lord God will speedily visit the inhabitants of the earth and in that day that they are fully ripe in iniquity, they shall perish. But if the inhabitants of the earth repent of their wickedness and abominations, they shall not be destroyed, promises the Lord.

Mormon 4:43 [Mormon 8:33 LDS]
Why have you transfigured the Holy Word of God, that you might bring damnation upon your souls?

ADDITIONAL SCRIPTURES
False Teachers/Bad Shepherds

Isaiah 56:10, 11, Blind watchmen, poor shepherds	Jeremiah 23:1-4, Pastors that scatter the flock
Jeremiah 25:35-37, Judgment on shepherds	Ezekiel 34: See whole chapter, Reproof of shepherds
Zechariah 10:2, 3 Missing shepherds	Galatians 1:8, 9, Teach truth
I Timothy 1:3-12, Poor teachers of law	II Nephi 12:12-20 (8:10-16 LDS), Teachers of foolish doctrines

ADDITIONAL SCRIPTURES
How the Wisdom of the Wise Shall Perish

Job 5:13, 14 to end	Jeremiah 8:8, 10	Jeremiah 9:23-26
Proverbs 3:5-35	Proverbs 23:4	I Corinthians 1:19-31
I Corinthians 3:18-23	Isaiah 29:26	Isaiah 42:21, 22

(Present Fulfillment)

Many religious leaders profess to have God's truth, yet they lead their followers astray in a variety of directions[28]. These men are masters at making the scriptures appear to say things that are not written there. All of these people qualify as false teachers because of the things they teach or taught. Though they frequently quote scripture, God's Word is twisted to their advantage and is therefore no longer in harmony with the Three Standard Books. Some teachers become wealthy from the gullibility of followers. Christ's disciples must pray and search the scriptures to confirm the truth of things men teach.

Matthew 24:5, 6
Jesus said to His listeners, "Take heed that no man deceive you for many shall come in my name saying, 'I am Christ' and they shall deceive many."

Matthew 24:22, 23
After the tribulation of those days, which shall come upon Jerusalem, if any man shall say to you, 'Christ is here, or Christ is there, do not believe him. In those days, there shall also arise false christs and false prophets who shall show great signs and wonders and, if possible, they shall deceive the very elect who are the elect according to the Covenant.

Deuteronomy 18:19
[God says] "Whoever fails to pay attention to my words which he speaks in my name will be held accountable."

©RSBlain Photography and Graphics

---

[28] Self-proclaimed saviors, David Koresh, leader of the Branch Davidians; Jim Jones, pastor of the People's Temple; Marshal White, leader of the Heaven's Gate UFO organization; and Guru Maharaj Ji, who claims to be God's prophet have been discussed. Others periodically emerge claiming to be Christ himself. Avoid them and warn others against them.

Jesus said, "Now learn a parable of the fig tree: When its branches are still tender, and it begins to put forth leaves, you know that summer is near. So likewise, my elect who see all these things shall know that Christ is near even at the door. But no one but my father knows the day or the hour not even the angels of God in Heaven.

Matthew 24:41-43
Mark 13:45-47
Luke 21:29-33,
D & C 45:5d)

Each numbered Fig leaf represents one of the twenty-six signs that must be fulfilled.

SIGN 1 Deception	SIGN 2 Affliction
SIGN 3 Betrayal	SIGN 4 False Prophets
SIGN 5 False Christs	SIGN 6 Sin is Rampant
SIGN 7 Wars and Rumors of Wars	SIGN 8 Famine, Pestilence, Earthquakes
SIGN 9 The Gospel Is Preached Throughout the World	SIGN 10 People Cry Peace, Peace
SIGN 11 People Run To and Fro and Knowledge Is Increased	SIGN 12 People Reject the Scriptures Concerning the Last Days
SIGN 13 Moral Decay and Corruption	SIGN 14 False Teachers
SIGN 15 God Will Raise Another Prophet	SIGN 16 A Book Comes Out of the Dust
SIGN 17 Christ's Church Will Be Restored in the Last Days.	SIGN 18 God's Priesthood Will Be Restored in the Last Days
SIGN 19 Zion Is a Gathering Place of Safety During the Tribulation	SIGN 20 The Temple Will Be Built in Missouri
SIGN 21 The Children of Israel Return to Their Promised Land	SIGN 22 The Tribes of Judah and the House of Israel Will Be Reunited
SIGN 23 The Jews Control Israel Including the Temple Mount	SIGN 24 The Temple is Rebuilt in Israel
SIGN 25 The Gospel is Taken to the Jews	SIGN 26 The Antichrist Will Be Revealed

"Behold, I lay in Zion a chief cornerstone, elect and precious."

I Peter 2:6

Jesus said, "Now learn a parable of the fig tree: When its branches are still tender, and it begins to put forth leaves, you know that summer is near. So likewise, my elect who see all these things shall know that Christ is near even at the door. But no one but my father knows the day or the hour not even the angels of God in Heaven."

Matthew 24:41-43
Mark 13:45-47
Luke 21:29-33,
D & C 45:5d

...and it begins to put forth leaves...

60

Chapter 5

A History of the Restoration of Christ's Church, Part 1

Note: Some scripture is paraphrased in this chapter to clarify meaning.

What do the scriptures say about the restoration of Christ's church in the Last Days?

SIGN 15
In the Last Days God will bring forth a prophet descended from Joseph in Egypt.

Genesis 50:30 [I.V. only]
[God made a promise to Joseph, son of Israel, as Joseph lay dying.] The Lord said, "I will raise up a prophet [seer] out of your offspring and give him power to bring forth My Word to your descendants. Not only will he bring forth my word but he will convince them of my word which shall have already gone forth among them in the Last Days."

(Present Fulfillment)
Another Joseph Is called by God: During America's Christian revival (1820 to 1840), a fourteen-year-old, Joseph Smith, wanted to join a local church. He was confused by conflicting doctrines. God would not teach one group to worship in a particular way and teach another opposing principles. Joseph believed that if God had a church, it would not be split into factions. He was familiar with James 1:5: "If any man lacks wisdom, let him ask of God who gives to all men liberally and does not upbraid, and it shall be given him." Joseph took this scripture literally, and withdrew into a wooded grove to pray. There he saw a vision of two people enveloped in brilliant light. One pointed to the other and said, "This is my beloved Son. Hear ye Him." During this vision, Joseph learned errors existed in all denominations. The Lord made it known that none of them was His church and Joseph should not join any of them. He received God's promise that the fullness of the gospel would be revealed to him in the future.

When this experience was discovered, Joseph was subjected to ridicule and persecution, but he would not deny his encounter with God. On September 21, 1823, while praying, Joseph was again confronted by an unexpected light. An angel informed him that God's covenant with ancient Israel was about to be fulfilled and preparation for Christ's Second Coming must begin immediately. From this messenger, Joseph learned of his call to be a chosen instrument in God's hands, bringing about fulfillment of several signs that must take place before Christ's return[29].

Genesis 50:33 [I.V. only]
The Lord said to Joseph, "I will bless that seer; and those who seek to destroy him shall be confounded. I give you this promise for I will remember you from generation to generation. His name shall be called Joseph and it shall also be the name of his father and he SHALL BE LIKE YOU. The thing which the Lord brings forth by His hand shall bring my people salvation."

---

[29] RLDS Church History, Volume 1, Herald House, Independence, Missouri, MDCCCXCVI
The Story of the Church, Inez Smith Davis, Herald Publishing House, Independence, Missouri 1943

SIGN 16
A book will come out of the dust.

Isaiah 29:1, 2, 4 [I.V. only]
Isaiah prophesied, "Woe to Ariel[30], the city where David dwelt.... I will distress Ariel. ...And I the Lord will camp against her and lay siege.... She shall be brought down and shall speak out of the ground and her speech shall be low out of the dust and her voice shall be as one who has a familiar spirit, out of the ground and her speech shall whisper out of the dust."

Isaiah 29:14
...He shall deliver the words of the book, which are the words of those who have slumbered in the dust...

The Story of the Book from the Dust is exciting and profound.

Briefly, Lehi, a descendant of Ephram (son of Joseph in Egypt), was directed by God to leave Jerusalem before it was sacked by the Babylonians (about 600 B.C.). Lehi obeyed, taking with him, his family and some of the holy records of his people. The trip by foot and sea was treacherous, but God eventually led the little band to Central America. In time, they became two great nations, known as the Nephites and the Lamonites. Prophets in the New World kept a history of their people and God's interactions with them. These records included the words of Isaiah, which were part of the sacred records, Lehi brought to the new world. All of the words were embossed or pressed into thin sheets of metal. The sheets, called plates, appeared to be made of gold. The plates were passed down from generation to generation so that the people would know their history and God's intimate involvement with them. The plates tell the story of three tribes of people who descended from the Jews, the Jaredites, Nephites, and Lamonites. The records also testified of Christ's appearance to them after His resurrection. He came to bring the gospel to the Lost Tribes of Ephram (son of Joseph). The complete record became known as the Book of Mormon, a second witness to the divinity of Jesus Christ. In it, Christ's gospel is emphasized and some Bible passages are clarified. It also provides a history of the people who migrated here from Jerusalem, prior to the birth of Christ. It also records that many Nephites fell away from God over the centuries. Because of their disobedience, most were killed in brutal warfare. Moroni, the last of the Nephite writers, carefully hid the book in a hill called Cummorah at approximately AD 421. He knew God would bring it forth at a later date.

September 21, 1823[31], the young Joseph Smith had an unexpected vision. An angel told him about historical records written by ancient Hebrew prophets, who lived on this continent hundreds of years ago. He was guided by the angel to a nearby hill (Manchester, New York), where he found a large stone protruding from the ground. Following directions, he removed the earth around the boulder and he lifted the rock.

---

[30] Isaiah 29:1 identifies Ariel as the city where David dwelt. Some scholars believe this refers to Bethlehem, the place of his birth. Others indicate it is Jerusalem, his capitol. See Halley's Bible Handbook by Henry H. Halley, Regency Reference Library, Zondervan Publishing House, Grand Rapids , Mich. 1965

[31] The date used is from *The Story of the Church* by Inez Smith Davis, Harold Publishing House, Independence Missouri, 1943.

Inside the hole was a stone box containing the golden plates[32], (the book coming forth from the dust) hidden by Moroni. It was covered with curious writing.

Joseph also saw a strange instrument called the Urim[33] and Thummim. This object was attached to an ancient breastplate. The boy wanted to examine these artifacts more closely, but he was forbidden to touch them. Several years passed before he was permitted to remove this treasure from its hiding place.

Finally, on September 22, 1827, Joseph was allowed to retrieve the box and take it home. Many difficulties followed. As the story of the golden treasure spread throughout the neighborhood, Joseph had to protect the plates from theft. He knew the writing must be translated and published, but he was poor and uneducated. He was forced to be completely dependent on God for the work entrusted to him. The Lord prepared other men to assist in translation, and to help in the protection of the plates.

The Urim and Thummim, which was found with the plates, enabled Joseph to translate the unfamiliar language. Somewhat similar to eyeglasses, it was made of two transparent stones set in the rims of a bow fastened to a breastplate. By peering through the stones, the unfamiliar language could be read. The content was written by a variety of prophets whose testimony of God filled the pages. As Joseph translated, he learned that Jesus Christ visited an ancient civilization in Central America. He also learned the things Christ taught during His stay on this continent parallel the things He taught his disciples during His life in Israel. They are the same as the words recorded in the Bible. For those who believe in Christ, new insight was provided with this information.

In February 1828, a friend named Martin Harris visited Joseph. With permission, he took copies of the characters on the plates and Joseph's translation to a noted professor skilled in the interpretation of ancient languages. Professor Anthon, from the state of New York, confirmed the translation[34] was accurate. Characters not yet translated were verified as Egyptian, Chaldaic, Assyrian, and Arabic. Professor Anthon signed a certificate that authenticated the characters and their translation. However, when he learned how they were obtained, he destroyed the certificate, saying there was no such thing as the ministering of angels. He said if Joseph would bring him the plates, he would translate them. Harris informed the professor that a portion of the book was sealed, and it was forbidden to bring the plates to anyone. The professor replied[35], "I cannot read a sealed book (Isaiah 29:20, 21)." At another time, the same copies with characters were taken to a Dr. Mitchell[36] who agreed with Professor Anthon in respect to both the characters and the translation.

---

[32] Golden plates refers to thin metal sheets that may or may not have been real gold. A stylus or thin pointed stick was used to impress the characters into the soft metal.

[33] According to Cruden's Complete Concordance, the literal translation of Urim and Thummim is "lights and perfections." They were worn attached to the breastplate of the Jewish high priest when he inquired of God. See Deuteronomy 33:8.

[34] This information was obtained from RLDS Church History, volume 1, page 19. In 1828, no one thought to document more on Professor Anton's credentials. No additional information has been uncovered.

[35] Isaiah 19:17-28: "I cannot read a sealed book."

[36] The story of Dr. Mitchel is located in RLDS Church History, Volume 1, page 19. In 1828 no one thought to further document more information on Dr. Mitchel's credentials. No additional information is available.

On June 1, 1829, Joseph completed the translation, which was published as the Book of Mormon. The first printed edition was finished on March 26, 1830. The book was translated into many languages and distributed worldwide. People in many parts of the world have been converted to Christ through its message. The testimony of this book is that Jesus Christ is Lord, the same today and forever, and he will come again at the appointed time. Eventually, the Bible and the Book of Mormon will come together to correct false doctrines, overcome theological disagreement, establish peace among the children of Israel, and bring them to a knowledge of God's covenants with their ancestors.

What does the Bible say about the Book of Mormon?

Genesis 50:31 [I.V. only]

"The descendants of Joseph [in Egypt] shall write about their experiences with God and the descendants of Judah shall also keep a written record. These two documents shall eventually come together and confound false doctrines and contentions and establish peace among your descendants and bring them to the knowledge of their fathers in the latter days and also to the knowledge of my covenants," promises the Lord.

Ezekiel 37:16-22 I.V. [37:15-22 KJV]

Therefore, son of man, take one stick [scroll] and write on it for Judah and for the children of Israel, his companions; then take another stick and write upon it for Joseph and his son Ephraim and for all the House of Israel, his companions. And join them into one stick and they shall become one in your hand.

And when the children of your people ask, "What does this mean?" say to them, "The Lord God says, 'Behold, I will take the stick of Joseph which is in the hand of Ephraim and the tribes of Israel and will put them with the stick of Judah. This will MAKE THEM ONE STICK[37] and they shall be one in my hand.'" And, say to them, "This is what the Lord God says: 'Behold, I will take the children of Israel from among the heathen where they have gone and will gather them on every side and bring them into their own land. And I will make them one nation in the land upon the mountains of Israel and one king shall be king to them all and they shall no longer be divided into two nations or kingdoms.'"

Isaiah 29:11-15 [I.V. only]

And the Lord God shall bring forth to you the words of a book and they shall be the words of those who have slumbered. And the book shall be sealed and in the book shall be a revelation from God, from the beginning of the world to the ending thereof. Now because of the things, which are sealed, they shall not be delivered in the day of wickedness and abominations of the people. Therefore, the book shall be kept from them. But the book shall be

---

[37] The word *stick* in Ezekiel 37 refers to a scroll that the Hebrews used like a book or tablet to record information. The Stick of Judah is the Old Testament. The Stick of Joseph through the genealogical lineage of Ephraim is the Book of Mormon. Together with the Inspired Version of the New Testament and the Doctrine and Covenants, they become our present set of scriptures. Ezekiel 37:17 "They shall be one in my hand."

delivered to a man and he shall deliver the words of the book, which are the words of those who slumber in the dust, to another person. But he shall not deliver the words that are sealed. The book was sealed by the power of God and the revelation, which was sealed, shall be kept in the book until God's own due time. Then it will come forth, for it reveals all things from the foundation of the world until the end.

Isaiah 29:16 [I.V. only]
And the day will come that the words of the book which were sealed shall be read upon the housetops by the power of Christ and all things shall be revealed to all mankind who ever lived or ever will live, even to the end of the earth.

Isaiah 29:17-19 [I.V. only]
The book shall be hidden from the eyes of the world until that day when it is delivered to the man of whom I have spoken. No one shall see it except three witnesses and the man to whom the book is delivered. They shall behold it by the power of God and shall testify to the truth of the book and the things therein. Only a few others will view it according to the will of God and they will bear testimony of His Word to the children of men. The Lord God has said that the words of the faithful shall speak as though from the dead. Therefore, the Lord God will proceed to bring forth the words of the book and through as many witnesses as He chooses He will establish His Word. Woe to him who rejects the Word of God. [Also, see Habakkuk 2:2, 3, 14; Psalms 85:10-12; D & C 2:6; 18:3c.]

Isaiah 29:20, 21 [I.V. only, see KJV next.]
The Lord God shall say to him to whom the book was delivered, 'Take these words which are not sealed and deliver them to another, that he may show them to the learned, saying, 'Read this, I pray thee.' And the learned shall say, 'Bring me the book and I will read it.' But the learned man will say this for the glory of the world and for gain and not for the glory of God. The messenger shall say, 'I cannot bring the book for it is sealed.' Then the learned man shall say, 'I cannot read it.'

- **Note the difference in the two verses above.**

Isaiah 29:22, 23 [I.V. only]
Then the Lord God will deliver the book and the words in it to a man who is not learned and the man who is not learned will say, "I am not learned." Then the Lord God shall say to him, "The learned shall not read them for they have rejected them and I am able to do my own work. Therefore, you shall read the words, which I shall give to you. Do not touch the things which are sealed for I will bring them forth in my own due time and I will show the children of men that I am able to do my own work."

Isaiah 29:11 KJV
And the vision of all is become unto you as the words of a book that is sealed, which men deliver to one that is learned, saying, "Read this, I pray thee," and he replied, "I cannot; for it is sealed."

- **Note the difference in the two verses above.**

Isaiah 29:22 KJV
And the book is delivered to him that is not learned, saying, "Read this, I pray thee," and he replied, "I am not learned."

Isaiah 29:24, 25 [I.V. only]
Then the Lord said to Joseph Smith, "When you have read the words which I have commanded you and obtained the witnesses which I have promised you, then you shall seal up the book again. Hide it up unto me, that I may preserve the words which you have not read until I shall see fit in mine own wisdom to reveal all things unto the children of men. For behold, I am God; and I am a God of miracles; and I will show to the world that I am the same, yesterday, today, and forever. I do not work among the children of men except according to their faith."

Isaiah 29:26 [Isaiah 29:13, 14 KJV]
And again, the Lord shall say to him that reads the words that are delivered to him. "Forasmuch as this people draw near to me with their mouth and honor me with their lips but have removed their hearts far from me and their fear toward me is taught by the precepts of men, I will proceed to do a marvelous work among these people. Yes, [I will do] a marvelous work and a wonder. The wisdom of their wise and learned shall perish and the understanding of their prudent shall be hid."

Isaiah 29:29, 30 [Isaiah 29:17-19 KJV]
"But," says the Lord of hosts, "I will show to the children of men that in a very little while Lebanon shall be turned into a fruitful field and the fruitful field shall be esteemed as a forest. And IN THAT DAY the deaf shall hear the words of the book; and the eyes of the blind shall see out of obscurity and out of darkness. The meek shall increase and their joy shall be in the Lord. The poor among men shall rejoice in the Holy One of Israel."

Mormon 4:27-40, 44
Search the prophecies of Isaiah for I cannot write them. Yet, I say to you that those saints who have gone before me, who have possessed this land, shall cry yes, they will cry to the Lord even from the dust, and as the Lord lives, He will remember the covenant which He made with them.

The Lord knows their prayers on behalf of their brothers. And He knows their faith, for in his name, they could remove mountains, and in His name, they could cause the earth to shake, and by the power of His word, they caused prisons to tumble to the earth. Yes, even the fiery furnace could not harm them neither wild beasts, nor poison serpents because of the power of His word.

And their prayers were also in behalf of him [Joseph Smith] who the Lord would cause to bring these things forth [the words of the Book of Mormon], and no one can say, 'They shall not come'-for they surely shall, for the Lord has spoken it!

They [the words of the Book of Mormon] shall come out of the earth by the hand of the Lord, and no one can prevent it. And it shall come in a day when it shall be said that miracles no longer happen. And it shall come as though someone is speaking from the dead.

And it shall come in a day when the blood of saints shall cry to the Lord because of secret combinations and the works of darkness. Yes, it shall come in a day when the power of God shall be denied and churches become defiled and members are lifted up in the pride of their hearts, yes, even in a day when leaders of churches and teachers are full of pride, even envying them who belong to their church.

Yes, it shall come in a day when there shall be fires and tempests and vapors of smoke in foreign lands, and people shall also hear of wars and rumors of wars and earthquakes in divers places. It shall come in a day when there shall be great pollutions upon the face of the earth. There shall be murders and robbing and lying and deceiving and whoredoms and all manner of abominations. There shall be many who will say, 'Do this or do that and it won't matter for the Lord will uphold these things at the last day'. But woe unto them for they are in the gall of bitterness and in the bonds of iniquity.

Now look into the revelations of God, For behold, The time is coming when all these things must be fulfilled.

Mormon 4:44

Jesus said, "Now learn a parable of the fig tree: When its branches are still tender, and it begins to put forth leaves, you know that summer is near. So likewise, my elect who see all these things shall know that Christ is near even at the door. But no one but my father knows the day or the hour not even the angels of God in Heaven."

Matthew 24:41-43
Mark 13:45-47
Luke 21:29-33,
D & C 45:5d

...you know that summer is almost here.

Chapter 6

A History of the Restoration of Christ's Church, Part 2

Note: Some scripture is paraphrased in this chapter to clarify meaning.

What do the scriptures say about the restoration of Christ's church in the Last Days.

SIGN 17
Christ's church will be restored in the Last Days.

On April 6, 1830, God restored Christ's church on earth. Joseph Smith and a small group of men, designated by the Lord, assisted in this work. The story of those events is widely published. In this chapter, scripture passages are examined to determine what components must be part of the Church of Jesus Christ.

Matthew 9:18-21 [I.V. only]
Then the Pharisees said to Him, "Why won't you receive us with our baptism, seeing we keep the whole law?" But Jesus said to them, "You do not keep the law. If you kept the law, you would have received me, for I am He who gave the law. I don't receive you with your baptism because it doesn't gain you anything. When that which is new is come, the old is ready to be put away."

Matthew 9:22, 23 I.V. [Matthew 9:16, 17 KJV]
No man puts a piece of new cloth on an old garment for that which is put in [patched] actually takes from the garment and the tear is made worse. Neither do men put new wine into old bottles because the bottles will break and the wine will spill out. Instead, they put new wine into new bottles and both are preserved [saved].

Jesus told the Pharisees that He would not mend an old garment with new cloth or put new wine into an old goatskin bottle. In the same manner, He must incorporate the gospel of the kingdom into a completely new church or the church itself would be contaminated.

Christ's restored Church reveals Him as the Rock of Revelation.

Matthew 16:16-19 [Matthew 16:15-18 KJV]
Jesus asked the apostles, "Whom do you say that I am?" Simon Peter replied saying, "You are the Christ, the Son of the living God." And Jesus said to him, "Blessed are you, Simon Bar-Jona for flesh and blood has not revealed this to you but my Father who is in Heaven. And I say to you **Peter;** *upon this rock [of revelation], I will build my church and the gates of Hell shall not prevail against it.*

The Catholic Church and many other denominations interpret this paragraph to mean that Jesus will build His church upon Peter the rock. However, this is NOT substantiated by any other scripture. Throughout the Three Standard Books, the Rock is a reference to Jesus Christ. A church built on Peter or any other apostle would have a very shaky foundation. Correctly read, Jesus acknowledges Peter as a blessed man who received a revelation from God convincing him of Christ's divinity. Notice, in the Inspired Version above, that Peter's name is followed by a semicolon, indicating the end of that thought. Jesus completes His sentence with, "Flesh and blood has not revealed this to you" (revelation comes only through the Holy Spirit) "and upon this rock (of revelation) I will build my church."

Part of the confusion is that Peter's name (Petra) means "stone." However, though this may be no more than coincidence; like all the rest of us, Peter was a sinful human being prone to many mistakes, including the betrayal of Jesus. Although he became steadfast following Christ's crucifixion, he was hardly the rock on which Christ's church could be built.

Christ's church is built upon the rock of revelation; which is himself.

This is verified in all three books of scripture.

> ### II Samuel 22:32, 47
> *For who is God, save the Lord? And who is a rock, save our God? The Lord lives and blessed be my rock. Exalted be the God of the rock of my salvation.*
>
> ### Psalm 118:22
> *The stone, which the builders refused, has become the head stone of the corner.*
>
> ### II Nephi 3:66
> *Behold, my voice shall forever ascend up to you, my rock and my everlasting God. Amen.*
>
> ### Doctrine & Covenants 6:16
> *Do not be afraid, little flock. Do good and let earth and Hell combine against you. If you are built upon my Rock, they cannot prevail.*
>
> ### Doctrine & Covenants 32:3a
> *This is my gospel. You shall have faith in me or you cannot be saved. Upon this rock, I will build my church.*

Criteria that Distinguish Christ's Church

- **CHRIST'S CHURCH MUST BE CALLED BY CHRIST'S NAME.**

  > ### III Nephi 12:16-19 [27:3-7 LDS]
  > *[Christ was asked what the name of His church should be. Christ responded,] "Have you not read the Scriptures which say, you must take upon you the name of Christ, which is my name? For you shall be called by this name at the last day; and <u>whoever takes my name upon him, and</u>*

70

endures to the end, shall be saved at the last day. Therefore, whatever you shall do, do it in my name. Therefore, call the church in my name and call upon the Father in my name so He will bless the church for my sake. How can it be my church unless it is called by my name?"

- **CHRIST'S CHURCH MUST BE HIS BODY ON EARTH.**

(Summary)
I Corinthians 12:12, 13, 27
"As a body is one but has many parts and all those many parts are members of that one body, so also is [the body of] Christ. For by one Spirit we are all baptized into one body." [Paul's testimony is, "the body of Christ is Christ's church."]

Ephesians 4:4, 5
There is one body and one Spirit… one Lord, one faith, one baptism, one God and Father of all, who is above all and through all and in all. But to every one of us is given grace according to the measure of the gift of God.

Jesus says there is only one body, one Spirit, and one church that He brought among men. There is only one Lord, one faith, one baptism. Today more than 265 different Christian denominations claim to have Christ's truth, yet each of them teaches something different.

- **CHRIST'S CHURCH MUST TEACH HIS GOSPEL WITHOUT MAN'S ADDITIONS OR OMISSIONS.**

The gospel is the grace of God revealed to fallen man, through Jesus Christ, our mediator. The word *gospel* means "good tidings." It is used to describe the message of Christ as demonstrated by His life, doctrine, actions, death, resurrection, and ascension. The gospel is found in the Bible and the Book of Mormon, which are both the Word of God. The Inspired Version of the Bible contains many corrections and additions given to Joseph Smith through the power and revelation of the Holy Spirit. People have no authority to change the scriptures. However, God still speaks today and only He may correct scriptures that have translation errors or add to the Word He has already given.

Genesis 5:44 [I.V. only]
The gospel [of Christ] began to be preached from the beginning, declared by holy angels who were sent forth from the presence of God and by God's own voice and by the gift of the Holy Spirit. And all things were confirmed to Adam by a holy ordinance and the gospel was preached and a decree was sent forth that it [the gospel] would be in the world until the end.

Christ taught His gospel during the time He spent on earth. This is recorded in the books of Matthew, Mark, Luke, and John, and in the Book of Mormon (III Nephi Chapters 4-13 RLDS Chapters 8-29 LDS).

John 7:16, 17 [The Gospel came from the Father.]
Jesus said to them, "My doctrine is not mine but His who sent Me. If any man will do His will, he shall know whether the doctrine is of God or of me."

> ### John 13:34, 35
> *Jesus said, "A new commandment I give to you that you love one another as I have loved you. By this all men will know that you are my disciples because you have love for one another."*

- **CHRIST'S CHURCH MUST TEACH THE PRINCIPLES OF HIS GOSPEL**

Christ gave himself in life and in death to perfect the church, its organization, gospel message, and gifts of the Spirit. He said the Principles of the Gospel were the door into His church and that they were essential guides for those who follow Him.

The Principles of the Gospel

- **Faith**
- **Repentance**
- **Baptism by Water**
- **Laying On of Hands to receive the Holy Spirit (baptism by fire)**
- **Resurrection of the Dead**
- **Eternal Judgment**

FAITH
The First Principle of the Gospel

> #### Romans 10:16 [10:17 KJV]
> *Faith comes by hearing and hearing by the Word of God. [Faith is not inherent or instinctive. It comes by recognition of the truth through hearing and reading God's Word.]*

> #### Hebrews 11:1
> *Now faith is the assurance of things hoped for, the evidence of things not seen.*

> #### Hebrews 11:6
> *Without faith, it is impossible to please God. He who comes to God must believe that God is and that He rewards those who diligently seek Him.*

REPENTANCE
The Second Principle of the Gospel

Sin is rebellion against God and against the way of life that He planned for us. This rebellion is expressed as we move in the opposite direction from his divine purpose or as we move in his direction with less speed than we should. Repentance is feeling pain or sorrow for our sin, something done or left undone. It is changing unacceptable behavior and entering into a new way of life according to his direction. Whether or not we like it, we are all sinners. Repentance must be continuous. It is complete when we are totally obedient to all his commandments and go forward with Him to a more perfect way of living.

Genesis 5:1-3 [I.V. only]

And the Lord God called upon men everywhere by the Holy Ghost and commanded them that they should repent and as many as believe in the Son and repent of their sins shall be saved. And all those who do not believe or repent shall be damned.

Acts 2:38-39

Repent and be baptized, every one of you, in the name of Jesus Christ for the remission of sins and you shall receive the gift of the Holy Ghost. And this promise is to you and to your children and to all that are afar off, even as many as the Lord our God shall call.

(Summary)
Alma 9:40-41 [Alma 12:24 LDS]

Temporal death comes upon mankind; nevertheless, space was granted to man in which he might repent. Therefore, this life became a probationary state; a time to prepare to meet God; a time to prepare for that endless state which follows the resurrection of the dead and our Judgment by Christ.

Moroni 8:29 [8:26 LDS]

The first-fruit of repentance is baptism. Baptism comes by faith to fulfill the commandments. The fulfilling of commandments brings remission of sin and the remission of sins brings meekness and lowliness of heart. Then because of meekness and lowliness of heart, the visitation of the Holy Ghost comes. He is the comforter who is filled with hope and perfect love, whose love endures by diligence in prayer until the end comes when all the saints shall dwell with God.

Faith and repentance are the first steps to Christian life. Faith, the assurance of things hoped for, must be accompanied by repentance, which is a change of mind, behavior, and attitude from self-centeredness to inspired hope and trust. This change is demonstrated by a new lifestyle, habits, and conduct.

Deathbed repentance does not work.

Alma 16:227-235 [Alma 34:33 LDS]

...Now is the time and the day of your salvation. Therefore, if you will repent and do not harden your hearts, the great plan of redemption shall immediately be brought about for you.

Behold, this life is the time for men to prepare to meet God. Today is the day for men to perform their labors...Therefore; I beseech you that you do not procrastinate the day of your repentance until the end, for this day is given us to prepare for eternity. If we do not improve our time, while in this life, the time of darkness will come and no labor can be performed.

You cannot say, when you are in that awful crisis, "I will repent; I will return to my God." No, you cannot say this for that same spirit which possesses your body at the time you leave this life will have power to possess your body in the eternal world. If you have procrastinated the day of your repentance until death, you have become subjected to the spirit of the devil and he claims you. Therefore, the Spirit of the Lord has withdrawn from you and has no place in you and the devil has all power over you. This is the final state of the wicked. This I know because the Lord has said He does not dwell in unholy temples but in the hearts of the righteous.

Sin against the Holy Ghost is unpardonable.

Luke 12:12 [12:10 KJV]
Whoever speaks a word against the Son of Man and repents shall have forgiveness but he who blasphemes against the Holy Ghost cannot be forgiven.

Hebrews 6:4-6
God has made it impossible for those who were once enlightened, tasted of the Heavenly gift, received the Holy Ghost, tasted the good Word of God and the powers of the world to come, to repent, if they fall away, because they crucify the Son of God anew and put Him to open shame. [Also See: Matthew 12:26, 27; Mark 3:23, 24; Hebrews 10:26, 27; II Peter 2:20, 21; I John 5:16; II Nephi 13:18; II Nephi 31:14 LDS; Alma 19:8 RLDS; Alma 39:6 LDS; D & C 76:4.]

This admonition must not be taken lightly. The Holy Spirit directs the life of a spirit-filled person. When He directs us to action and we deliberately fail to do it, we may be precariously close to committing the sin against the Holy Spirit.

BAPTISM
The Third Principle of the Gospel

To baptize means to immerse, submerge, or wash by immersing. Baptism is commanded by God for the remission of sin and **is essential** to our salvation. Salvation is the incredible gift God offered mankind through the sacrifice and blood of His only Son. Without Him, we would have no hope. Salvation is given to us through the grace and mercy of God the Father whose Son chose to die in our place. Through baptism, we are sanctified or made holy. (Ephesians 5:26) Some churches believe salvation is a free gift. SALVATION IS NOT FREE! It cost the life of God's Son, Jesus Christ.

Salvation has four requirements.

- **Faith in and acceptance of Jesus Christ**
- **Repentance of sin**
- **Baptism in Christ's name**
- **Endurance to the end, be steadfast, hold firm, do not be overcome. (Matthew 10:22; Mark 13:13)**

Titus 3:3-7
[The New International Version Study Bible]
At one time, we were foolish, disobedient, deceived and enslaved by all kinds of passions and pleasures. We lived in malice and envy, being hated and hating one another. But when the kindness and love of God our Savior appeared, He saved us. We were not saved because of righteous things we had done but because of His mercy. He saved us through the washing of rebirth and renewal by the Holy Spirit, whom He poured out on us generously through Jesus Christ our Savior. Being justified by His grace, we become heirs having hope of eternal life.

Alma 5:24-25 [7:14-16 LDS]
You must repent and be born again for the Spirit says, "If you are not born again, you cannot inherit the kingdom of Heaven. Therefore, come and be baptized unto repentance so you may be washed from your sins and so you may have faith on the Lamb of God who takes away the sins of the world, who is mighty to save and to cleanse from all unrighteousness." [See Romans 6:3-5; II Corinthians 5:17.]

LAYING ON OF HANDS TO RECEIVE THE HOLY SPIRIT
The Fourth Principle of the Gospel

The Laying On of Hands has five primary purposes.

- **Conferring the Holy Spirit upon newly baptized Christians**
- **Conferring authority and ordain priesthood**
- **Blessing children**
- **Assisting healing**
- **Praying for specific, serious needs of individuals**

The Laying On of Hands confers the gift of the Holy Spirit following baptism.

Jesus indicates there are two baptisms, the first by water and the second by the power of the Holy Spirit (baptism by "fire"). After baptism by water, Elders of the church lay their hands on the heads of new church candidates and pray that God will confer the gift of the Holy Spirit upon them. This is called the baptism by fire. This ordinance may take place on the day of water baptism or another day after the newly baptized person has a chance to pray about the experience.

When the laying on of hands is performed, new church candidates receive the baptism by fire through the Holy Spirit. This is a holy moment. God's spirit now resides within new Christians. The experience is wonderful and may be emotional, but visible signs and miracles from God should not be anticipated. They sometimes take place. But more often, those who receive this blessing do not recognize that anything out of the ordinary has happened. Emotions and spiritual manifestations DO NOT determine the legitimacy of God's blessing. However, lives and purpose have been reborn. New spirit-filled Christians are counseled to pray diligently, seeking God's guidance to open their lives so the Spirit within can begin its work. God's purpose, in this new beginning, will be revealed in those who watch for the prompting of His Spirit, which now resides inside them. When individuals receive both baptisms, they are reborn or born again, into the kingdom of God. They become God's new children, adopted into the House of Israel, with all the privileges of His chosen people. At that time, they also become members of Christ's church.

John 3:3
Jesus said, "Except a man is born again, he cannot see the kingdom of Heaven."

John 3:5
Jesus said, "Except a man is born of water and the Spirit, he cannot enter into the kingdom of God."

Acts 8:14-17
When the apostles in Jerusalem heard that men and women in Samaria had received the Word of God, they sent Peter and John who, when they arrived, prayed for them that they might receive the Holy Spirit. This had not taken place even though they were baptized in the name of the Lord Jesus. Then Peter and John laid their hands on them and they received the Holy Ghost.

Alma 16:117 [Alma 31:36 LDS]
Alma clapped his hands upon them and they were filled with the Holy Ghost.

ADDITIONAL SCRIPTURES for Laying On of Hands to Receive the Holy Spirit

Acts 9:17	Galatians 3:5	Ephesians 4:30
I Timothy 4:14	Moroni 2:1, 2	D & C 17:8, 18; 32:3
D & C 34:2; 49:2g, h; 52:3; 53:2; 55:1; 68:4		

The Laying On of Hands is used to ordain priesthood members.

Individuals called of God to priesthood responsibility are ordained by the laying on of hands by the Elders of the church. At that time, the Elders also confer the authority and duties of their priesthood office upon them.

Alma 4:1 RLDS [Alma 6:1 LDS]
Alma ordained priests and elders by laying on his hands, according to the order of God.

III Nephi 8:70, 71 RLDS [III Nephi 18:36 LDS]
When Jesus finished speaking, He touched the disciples whom He had chosen with His hand, one by one, until He had touched them all...and the disciples bore record that He gave them power to give the Holy Ghost.

Doctrine & Covenants 42:4
It shall not be given to anyone to go forth and preach my gospel or to build up my church unless he is ordained by someone who has authority and has himself been properly ordained.

ADDITIONAL SCRIPTURES
Laying On of Hands for Priesthood Ordination

Leviticus 8:12	Mark 3:13	John 15:16
Acts 6:6	Acts 13:3	Acts 14:23
I Timothy 2:7; 4:14; 5:22	II Timothy 1:6; 2:7; 4:4	Jacob 1:8
Mosiah 9:51 RLDS same as	Mosiah 18:18 LDS	
Mosiah 11:97 RLDS same as	Mosiah 25:19 LDS	
Alma 10:103 RLDS same as	Alma 15:13 LDS	
Alma 14:8 RLDS same as	Alma 23:4 LDS	
Alma 21:26, 27 RLDS same as	Alma 45:22, 23 LDS	
III Nephi 8:70-73 RLDS same as	III Nephi 18:36-38 LDS	Moroni 2:1; 3:1-3

The Laying On of Hands is used to bless children.

Mark 10:12-14 [Mark 10:14-16 KJV]
...Suffer the little children to come unto me and forbid them not, for of such is the kingdom of God. Whosoever shall not receive the Kingdom of God as a little child shall not enter therein. And, He took them in His arms, put His hands upon them, and blessed them. [Matthew 19:14, 15; Luke 18:15-17; III Nephi 8:23 RLDS, III Nephi 17:21 LDS]

Doctrine & Covenants 17:19
Every member of the Church of Christ, having children, is to bring them before the congregation of the church where the Elders will lay their hands upon them in the name of Jesus Christ and bless them in His name.

The Laying On of Hands is used to pray for healing of the sick.

James 5:14, 15
Is anyone sick among you? Let him call for the Elders of the church and let them pray over him, anointing him with oil in the name of the Lord. And, the prayer of faith shall save the sick, the Lord shall raise him up, and if he has committed sins, they shall be forgiven him.

Doctrine & Covenants 42:12d
Two or more Elders of the church shall be called and shall pray for and lay their hands upon them in my name. [See Mark 6:7]

RESURRECTION OF THE DEAD
The Fifth Principle of the Gospel

When a man or woman dies, the spirit separates from the body. The spirits of righteous people go to paradise, and those of the wicked go to Hell. The spirits of little children who die always inherit eternal life.

Alma 19:33-35
There is a time appointed that all shall come forth from the dead. No one knows when this time will come. Only God knows the appointed time.

Alma 19:36, 37
Now there must be a space between the time of death, and the time of the resurrection. And I would inquire what became of the souls of men, from this time of death, to the time appointed for the resurrection?

Alma 19:42-47
Now concerning the state of the soul between death and resurrection, it has been made known to me by an angel, that the spirits of all men, good or evil, as soon as they are departed from this mortal body; are taken home to God who gave them life. And the spirits of those who are righteous are received into a state of happiness, which is called paradise; a state of rest; a state of peace, where they shall rest from all their troubles, cares and sorrow. Then the spirits of the wicked who are evil... shall be cast into outer darkness; there shall be weeping, and wailing and gnashing of teeth, because of their own iniquity. Now this is the state of the souls of the wicked, in darkness, and a state of awful, fearful, looking for the fiery indignation of the wrath of God upon them, and they remain in this state until the time of their resurrection.

Doctrine & Covenants 85:4a, b
Through the redemption which [Christ] made for you, is also brought to pass the resurrection from the dead. And the spirit and the body is the soul of man. And the resurrection from the dead is the redemption of the soul; and the redemption of the soul is through Him who quickens all things, in whose bosom it is decreed, that the poor and meek of the earth shall inherit it

Paradise is a temporary place of rest for the spirits of the righteous.

Alma 19:44 RLDS [Alma 40:12 LDS]
It shall come to pass that the spirits of those who are righteous are received into a state of happiness called paradise; a state of rest, a state of peace where they shall rest from all their troubles, care and sorrow.

Hell is a temporary prison house.

The scriptures do not describe Hell as a place of eternal burning. Instead, it is described as a prison for fallen angels and for all wicked or unrighteous spirits who did not accept Christ during their lives. These unrighteous spirits must wait in this prison until the Second Resurrection. Spirits who never heard of Jesus Christ are also in Hell. For them, Hell is a place of learning [I Peter 3:18, 19, 20]. These spirits have the opportunity to hear Christ's gospel message and accept or reject His salvation. [I Peter 3:18, 19, 20]

Psalm 9:17
The wicked shall be turned into Hell along with all the nations that forget God.

Isaiah 42:7
[Christ will] open blind eyes, to bring the prisoners out from the prison and those who sit in darkness out of the prison house.

Mosiah 8:58-60
There are those who have part in the first resurrection. Those who died before Christ came. They died in ignorance, not having salvation declared to them. The Lord restores those souls and they have part in the first resurrection, and have eternal life, redeemed by the Lord.

The First Resurrection (Resurrection of the Righteous)

The Doctrine & Covenants provides a vivid picture of Christ's Second Coming and the resurrection of the dead.

Doctrine & Covenants 85:27
There shall be silence in Heaven for the space of half an hour, and immediately after the curtain in Heaven shall be unfolded, as a scroll is unfolded after it has been rolled up, and the face of the Lord shall be unveiled. And the saints that are on the earth, who are alive, shall be quickened, and caught up to meet Him. And they who have slept in their graves shall come forth; for their graves shall be opened, and they also shall be caught up to meet Him in the midst of the pillar of Heaven. These are Christ's first fruits who will descend with Him first, and they who are on the earth, and in their graves, who are first caught up to meet Him; at the sounding of the trumpet of the angel of God.

At the second coming of Jesus Christ, all the righteous, both dead and alive will be caught up in the air to meet Him (Thessalonians 4:16, 17). This is the First Resurrection! The dead will receive perfect spiritual bodies and will live forever. Those who are still alive will live to an old age. Then, though they die, they will be changed in the twinkling of an eye, and receive perfect, eternal bodies. They will live in the presence of Christ for a thousand years until the eternal judgment. (D & C Section 76 beginning with 3D to 8C, and Sections 85:1-18)

The Doctrine & Covenants Section 85:28 A and B provides insight into the lives of those who were good people but who never heard the Gospel of Jesus Christ.

Doctrine & Covenants 85:28 A, B
And after this, another angel shall sound which is the second trump and then comes redemption of those who are Christ's at His coming who have received their part in that prison which is prepared for them that they might receive the Gospel and be judged according to men in the flesh.

Those in Hell who never had an opportunity to hear the Gospel message but who accepted Him in this prison will be freed and caught up with the righteous. They will join the righteous and live for 1000 years in the Millennium. This is substantiated by numerous Bible scriptures.

Isaiah 24:22
They shall be gathered together, as prisoners are gathered in the pit, and shall be shut up in the prison, and after many days, they shall be visited. [The visitor was Jesus Christ who descended into Hell at His death].

Isaiah 42:6, 7
I the Lord have called thee in righteousness, and will hold your hand, and will keep you, and give you for a covenant of the people, for a light of the Gentiles; to open the blind eyes, to bring out the prisoners from the prison, and them that sit in darkness out of the prison house. I am the Lord; that is my name; and my glory I will not give to another.

Isaiah 49:9
…That you may say to the prisoners, "Go forth"; to them that are in darkness, "show yourselves"…

Isaiah 61:1
He has sent me to bind up the broken-hearted, to proclaim liberty to the captives, and the opening of the prison to them that are bound.

I Peter 3:18, 19
For Christ also once suffered for sins, the just for the unjust, being put to death in the flesh, but quickened by the Spirit, that He might bring us to God. For this cause also, He went and preached unto the spirits in prison.

I Peter 4:6
Because of this, the gospel is preached to them who are dead, that they might be judged according to men in the flesh, but live in the spirit according to the will of God.

Doctrine & Covenants 110:22
Let the dead speak forth anthems of eternal praise to the King Immanuel, who has ordained before the world was that which would enable us to redeem them out of their prisons; for the prisoners shall go free.

After Christ's return to earth, He will end the war of Armageddon. Resurrected souls will take part in the thousand-year millennial kingdom of Zion living eternally in the presence of Jesus Christ. The rest will wait in the prison house for the second resurrection.

John 11:25, 26
I am the resurrection and the life; he that believes in me, even though he is dead, shall live. And whoever lives and believes in me shall never die.

Romans 6:3-5
Do you not know that those of us who were baptized into Jesus Christ were baptized into His death? We are buried with Him by baptism into death [being placed under the water] but as Christ was raised up from the dead [so we are raised up from the baptismal waters] by the glory of the Father and should walk in newness of life. And because we have been planted together in the likeness of His death, we shall also be in the likeness of His resurrection.

I Thessalonians 4:16, 17
For the Lord shall descend from Heaven with a shout, and the dead in Christ shall rise first. Then they [the righteous] who are alive shall be caught up...with them...to be with the Lord forever.

II Nephi 6:31 RLDS [II Nephi 9:13 LDS]
At the First Resurrection, the paradise of God must deliver up the spirits of the righteous [who have died].

Mosiah 8:51-56
How beautiful upon the mountains are the feet of Him who brings good tidings, and is the founder of peace! Yes, even the Lord who has redeemed His people, and granted them salvation; If it were not for the redemption, which He made for His people, planned from the foundation of the world, all mankind would perish.

But behold, the bands of death are broken. The Son reigns and has power over the dead. Therefore, He brings to pass the resurrection of the dead. This is a first resurrection.

Alma 19:58 [40:23-LDS]
The soul shall be restored to the body and the body to the soul and every limb and joint shall be restored to its body, even a hair of the head shall not be lost but all things shall be restored to their proper frame.

THE FINAL JUDGMENT
Sixth Principle of the Gospel

The Second Resurrection follows the thousand year reign. The souls of those who remained in Hell are brought forth to stand before God with all those who were part of the First Resurrection. Everyone who ever lived will appear before Christ (God) in perfect, resurrected bodies. They are there for the final judgment and His designation of their place in eternity.

Revelation 20:13, 14
And I saw the dead, small and great, stand before God; and the books were opened; and another book was opened, which is the book of life; and the dead were judged out of those things which were written in the books, according to their works.

And the sea gave up the dead, which were in it; and death and hell delivered up the dead which were in them; and they were judged every man according to their works.

This point confuses many Christians. We are saved by God's grace, BUT we are judged by our works. The things we choose to do during life determine our place or reward in the hereafter.

John 5:25, 28-31

The hour is coming, and now is, when the dead shall hear the voice of the Son of God. And they who hear shall live.... Marvel not at this; for the hour is coming, in which all who are in their graves shall hear His voice, and shall come forth; those who have done good, in the resurrection of the just; and they who have done evil, in the resurrection of the unjust. And all shall be judged by the Son of Man. For as I hear, I judge, and my judgment is just; for I can do nothing of myself; but the will of the Father who sent me.

Romans 14:10-12

...We shall all stand before the judgment seat of Christ. ...And every knee shall bow to Him. And every tongue will swear to God and we will give an account of ourselves [our works] to God. [See James 2:14-18, Revelation 20:11-13.]

II Corinthians 5:10

All people must appear before the judgment seat of Christ so everyone will be rewarded for the deeds [works] done while alive on earth, whether good or bad. [See James 2:14-18; Revelation 14:13; Revelation 20:11-13.]

Alma 8:98-104

The day is coming that all shall rise from the dead and stand before God and be judged according to their works. Now there is a death called temporal [earthly death] and the death of Christ shall loose the bands so all shall be raised from this temporal death. The spirit and the body shall be reunited in its perfect form. Both limb and joint shall be restored to its proper frame, even as we are now.

And we shall be brought to stand before God, knowing as we know now, having a bright recollection of all our guilt. Now this restoration shall come to all, both old and young, bond and free, male and female, wicked and the righteous. Not so much as a hair of their heads will be lost but all things shall be restored to perfection and shall be brought and arraigned before the bar of Christ the Son and God the Father and the Holy Spirit, which is one eternal God, to be judged according to their works, whether they are good or evil.

The Role of Repentance

Luke 5:31, 32

Jesus answering said to them, "They that are whole do not need a physician, but they that are sick. I did not come to call the righteous, but sinners to repentance."

Luke 13:3

Jesus said, "I tell you except you repent, you shall all perish."

Mark 3:22

Jesus answered: "All sins which men have committed, when they repent, shall be forgiven them, for I came to preach repentance unto man."

The justice of God is beyond our ability to fathom. Even the wicked, who were thrust into Hell, have opportunity for redemption. Christ makes repentance possible even in the prison, for it is still His intent to save as many souls as He can. Life in eternity will be tolerable for them, although far removed from the rewards received by the faithful.

Read more in:
- Chapter 12 for the Millennium
- Chapter 13 for the Second Resurrection and the Final Judgment
- Chapter 14 for the Kingdom of Heaven

SIGN 18
Christ's church includes His restored priesthood.

Genesis 6:7 [God's Promise Concerning the Priesthood, I.V. only]
Now this same priesthood, which was in the beginning, shall also be at the end of the world.

What happened to the historic priesthood?

While Moses was on the mountain conversing with God, the children of Israel built a golden calf to worship. As he descended from his experience, Moses was horrified to see the behavior of God's people. In anger, Moses broke the tablets of commandments God had given him.

Exodus 34:1 I.V. [Exodus 34:1 KJV includes the first three lines only.]
And the Lord said to Moses, "Make two more tables of stone like the first and I will write the words of the law on them also, in the same way they were written on the first set of tables which you broke. But they will not be the same as the first, for I will take away the priesthood from the midst of these people. Therefore, my holy order and the ordinances thereof shall not go before them and my presence shall not be in their midst because it would destroy them."

(Summary)
Doctrine & Covenants 83:2c, 3, 4
This section of the Doctrine & Covenants describes the priesthood as it was given to Adam and those who followed Him. This passage is consistent with similar scriptures in the book of Genesis. If mankind had not been rebellious, all God's priesthood would have continued forever as the holiest order of God. Priesthood members hold the key to the mysteries of the kingdom, including the key of the knowledge of God. However, because of disobedience, the higher priesthood did not remain with men. Christ restored it while on earth, but it was lost again because of human failure.

The Aaronic order continued to serve the people, but the Melchisedec priesthood, established by God at the time of Adam, was lost for about three thousand years. Even the memory of the purpose for God's higher priesthood eventually disappeared. Remaining offices were a poor facsimile of God's original design. During Christ's earthly ministry, He reorganized His church restoring both orders of priesthood among His followers. The Melchisedec order was forfeit again in the Dark Ages when men, coveting their own authority, lost touch with the Holy Spirit.

Doctrine & Covenants 83:4a-e
Now, Moses, who taught the Children of Israel in the wilderness, sought diligently to sanctify the people so they might behold the face of God. But, they hardened their hearts and could not endure God's presence…Therefore, God took Moses and the holy priesthood out of their midst but the lesser priesthood continued. The Aaronic priesthood holds the key of the ministering of angels, the preparatory gospel, which is the gospel of repentance and of baptism and the remission of sins and the law of carnal Commandments. The Lord allowed these to continue with the house of Aaron, among the children of Israel, until the birth of John whom God raised

up filled with the Holy Ghost from his mother's womb. John was baptized while he was yet in his childhood, ordained to the Aaronic priesthood by the angel of God when he was eight days old…to make straight the way of the Lord before the face of His people to prepare them for the coming of the Lord in whose hand is given all power.

Jesus Christ is our High Priest.

Hebrews 5:4-6
No man takes this honor [priesthood] for himself. He must be called of God as Aaron was. Even Christ did not glorify himself to be made a high priest but God said to Him, "You are my Son. Today I have begotten you…You are a priest forever after the order of Melchisedec.

Alma 9:63-73 [13:1-3 LDS]
"Remember the Lord God ordained priests after His holy order to teach these things to the people. Priests were ordained after the order of His Son so the people would learn to look to Jesus for redemption. Priesthood members were ordained in this manner: They were called and prepared from the foundation of the world, according to the foreknowledge of God, of their strong faith and good works, after an opportunity to choose good or evil. Therefore, they chose good, exercising great faith and are called with a holy calling provided by a preparatory redemption for them. They have been called to this holy calling because of their faith, while others rejected the Spirit of God because of the hardness of their hearts and blindness of their minds.…

…Therefore, these men were called by His holy calling and ordained into the high priesthood of the holy order of God, to teach His commandments to the children of men, that they might also enter into His rest.

This high priesthood was after the order of His Son, established from the foundation of the world. It is without beginning of days or end of years, being prepared from eternity to all eternity, according to His foreknowledge of all things.

Jesus is the rock on which the church and its priesthood are founded.

The whole structure of the church, including the priesthood, is established on the rock of divine revelation. The church derives its stability from the power of His spirit and the force of His divine personality. Both the Melchisedec and Aaronic priesthoods were restored by Christ before the Church of Jesus Christ of Latter Day Saints was organized in 1830. (See sign 17, Christ's Church Restored—The Rock of Revelation.)

"No man takes this honor for himself."

Hebrews 5:4

Priesthood Offices Identified in the New Testament and Doctrine and Covenants

Aaronic Priesthood
Deacons

Philippians 1:1	I Timothy 3:8-13	D & C 17:12; 83:22

Teachers

I Corinthians 12:28, 29	Hebrews 5:12; Ephesians 4:11	D & C 17:11

Priests

Luke 1:5, 5:14	Acts 6:7	D & C 17:10

Melchisedec Priesthood
Elders

James 5:14	Acts 14:23	I Peter 5:1
D & C 17:8, 9		

High Priests

Hebrews 5:1-6, 8:3	D & C 17:17; 104:5; 120:2; 125:10	

Bishops

Philippians 1:1	I Timothy 3:2-4	D & C 68:2; 104:32

Evangelists

Ephesians 4:11	D & C 125:3, 4	

Seventies

Luke 10:1, 18	D & C 104:13	

Apostles

Matthew 25:34	Luke 11:50	I Corinthians 12:11, 12
Ephesians 4:11	Romans 1:1	I Corinthians 12:28
D & C 6:5; 17:17; 104:5 (Apostles are High Priests before being ordained as Apostles.)		

Prophets

Luke 11:50-51	I Corinthians 12:28	Acts 15:6
I Corinthians 12:28, 29	Ephesians 4:11	Acts 13:1
D & C 99:6; 104:42 (pertains to the president of the church)		

Pastors are usually Elders.
However, in congregations where no Elder is present, a Priest may assume this position.

Authority of the Priesthood

Priesthood members must be called and given authority by God through His divine revelation.

John 15:16
Christ said, "You have not chosen me but I have chosen you and ordained you that you should go and bring forth fruit [be productive] that your fruit should remain."

Hebrews 5:4, 5, 10
No man takes this honor to himself but he that is called of God, as Aaron was. Christ did not glorify Himself... He was called of God as a high priest after the order of Melchisedec.

Moroni 2:1, 2 [2:1, 2 LDS]
Christ laid His hands upon His chosen twelve, calling them by name saying, "You shall call on the Father in my name, in mighty prayer and after you have done this, you shall have power to give the Holy Ghost to him on whom you lay your hands. You shall do this in my name for this is the work of my apostles." [See Corinthians 12:27-31; Moroni 3:1-3 or 3:1-4 LDS.]

Moroni 3:2, 3
After they had prayed unto the Father in the name of Christ, they laid their hands upon them and said, "In the name of Jesus Christ I ordain you to be a priest." Or if he be a teacher, "I ordain you to be a teacher—to preach repentance and remission of sins through Jesus Christ by the endurance of faith on His name to the end. Amen." And after this manner did they ordain priests and teachers, according to the gifts and callings of God unto men. And they ordained them by the power of the Holy Ghost, which was in them.

Mission Duties and the Purpose of Priesthood

(Summary)
I Peter 5:1-3
Elders are described as overseers, to be examples to the church.

Mosiah 4:4 [Mosiah 6:3 LDS]
[King Benjamin] appointed priests to teach the people that they might hear and know the commandments of God, reminding them of the oath which they made with God.

Mosiah 11:17-20 [Mosiah 23:17, 18 LDS]
None received authority to preach or to teach unless it was given to him from God. Therefore, Alma having received this authority, as high priest, was able to consecrate priests and teachers and none were consecrated except they were just men. Therefore, they watched over their people and nourished them with things pertaining to righteousness.

ADDITIONAL SCRIPTURES
Mission Duties, and Purpose of Priesthood

Genesis 14:17, 18, 26-29	Psalms 110:1, 4
Hebrews 5:5, 6; 7:1-3, 11, 15, 17	Alma 9:54 RLDS same as Alma 12:33 LDS
Alma 9:63-73 RLDS same as Alma 13:1-9 LDS	Alma 10:1-17 RLDS same as Alma 13:10-20 LDS
D & C 42:8; 72:1; 83:2-4; 84:3; 104:9	

- **CHRIST'S CHURCH MUST INCLUDE THE GIFTS OF THE SPIRIT.**

The Gifts of the Spirit

- **Wisdom, a Word of Knowledge**
- **Faith**
- **Gifts of Healing**
- **Working of Miracles**
- **Prophecy**
- **Discerning of Spirits**
- **Diverse Kinds of Tongues**
- **Interpretations of Tongues (Corinthians 12:8-10)**

Congregations that are not experiencing these gifts are missing the fullness of God's Spirit. By opening our minds to the will of God, and praying in unison until the gifts are given, the congregation will be recharged, excited about the Lord, and strengthened by a new commitment of members. The Spirit will also attract new members and build a growing church.

> **Luke 11:14**
> *If you who are evil know how to give good gifts to your children, how much more shall your Heavenly Father give good gifts, through the Holy Spirit, to those who ask Him? [See Mark 16:16-19; I Corinthians 12:7-11; Ephesians 4:7, 8; Moroni 10:3-12.]*

- **CHRIST'S CHURCH MUST BE FILLED WITH THE FRUITS OF THE SPIRIT.**

The Fruits of the Spirit are important Christian characteristics. These characteristics grow within individuals and congregations as the Holy Spirit is encouraged to work in the church.

> **Galatians 5:22, 23**
> *The Fruit of the Spirit is love, joy, peace, long-suffering, gentleness, goodness, faith, meekness, temperance; against such, there is no law.*

Ephesians 5:8-10 adds righteousness to the Fruit of the Spirit.

II Peter 1:5-7 adds virtue, knowledge, patience, godliness, brotherly kindness and charity to the Fruit of the Spirit.

D & C 4:2 adds humility and diligence to the Fruit of the Spirit.

ADDITIONAL SCRIPTURES
Fruits of the Spirit

John 13:35	Philippians 4:8	Romans 6:22
Colossians 1:20; 3:12-15	Jas. 3:17	Alma 5:39-42; 10:28, 16:239
Moroni 7:48-53	D & C 11:4	

- **CHRIST'S CHURCH MUST BE UNCHANGEABLE.**

   <u>**Malachi 3:6**</u>
   I am the Lord. I do not change.

   <u>**Hebrews 13:8**</u>
   Jesus Christ is the same yesterday, today and forever.

   <u>**James 1:17**</u>
   Every good and perfect gift is from above and comes from the Father of lights, who does not change like shifting shadows.

Therefore, the church, His Body on earth, must remain the same perfect organization that he originally built.

These scriptures are overlooked by many in the church. This should not take us by surprise. In the Last Days, even the very elect, who are part of the covenant, will be deceived (Matthew 24:23). Nevertheless, those who are wary and place their trust in Christ and His scripture will be watching and waiting, preparing to meet the Savior. They also have a responsibility to reach out and pray for those who are being deceived.

WARNING
Even Christ's church will be polluted.

   <u>**Mormon 4:44-56**</u>
   Behold! Look at the revelations of God; for the time is coming, at that day, when all these things must be fulfilled. The Lord has shown me great and inconceivable things concerning that, which shall shortly come forth among you at that day. I speak to you as if you were present, and yet you have not even been born. But Jesus Christ has shown you to me, and I know what you are doing.

   I know that you walk in the pride of your hearts; and there are only a few who do not lift themselves up in the pride of their heart. Most wear very fine apparel, causing envy and strife and malice and persecutions and all manner of iniquity. And your churches, yes every one, have become polluted because of the pride of your hearts.

   You love money, and your substances, and your fine apparel, and the adorning of your churches more than you love the poor, and the needy, and the sick, and the afflicted.

Oh, you pollutions! You hypocrites! You teachers who sell yourselves for that which will rot! Why have you polluted the holy church of God? Why are you ashamed to take upon you the name of Christ? Why do you not think that the value of endless happiness is greater than that misery which never dies because of the praise of the world?

Why do you adorn yourselves with that which has no life, and yet allow the hungry, and the needy, and the naked, and the sick, and the afflicted, to pass by you without being noticed? Yes, why do you build up your secret abominations to make a profit, yet cause widows and orphans to mourn before the Lord? Why does the blood of their fathers and their husbands cry to the Lord from the ground for vengeance upon your heads? Behold the sword of vengeance hangs over you! And the time will soon come that He avenges the blood of the saints upon you, for He will not suffer their cries any longer.

The Lord is trying to get our attention through Mormon's biting words. We can read over them quickly, disregarding those parts offending us, or we can let the Holy Spirit speak to our hearts as we ponder them. Do they apply to us today? How should we respond?

The Great Commission

Matthew 28:18-19 [Matthew 28:19, 20 KJV]
Go ye therefore and teach all nations, baptizing them in the name of the Father and of the Son and of the Holy Ghost, teaching them to observe all things whatsoever I have commanded you and lo, I am with you always, even unto the end of the world. Amen.

Mormon 4:86-88 [Mormon 9:23-25 LDS]
Go into all the world and preach the gospel to every creature. He that believes and is baptized shall be saved, but he that does not believe shall be damned. These signs shall follow them that believe in my name. They shall cast out devils. They shall speak with new tongues. They shall take up serpents. And if they drink any deadly thing, it shall not hurt them. They shall lay hands on the sick, and they shall recover, and I will confirm all my words to all who believe in my name, doubting nothing, even to the ends of the earth. [Mark 16:14-19]

ADDITIONAL SCRIPTURES for Jesus Christ the Rock of Ages

Deuteronomy 32:4, 15, 18	Samuel 22:2, 3, 32, 47
Psalms 18:2, 31, 46	Psalms 28:1
Psalms 31:2, 3	Psalms 42:9
Psalms 61:2	Psalms 78:35
Psalms 89:26	Psalms 92:15
Psalms 94:22	Matthew 7:34
Romans 9:33	I Corinthians 10:1, 3-4
Ephesians 2:19-22	I Peter 2:6-8
I Nephi 3:185, 186 RLDS [same as 13:35, 36 LDS]	II Nephi 3:66 RLDS [same as 18:14 LDS]
II Nephi 9:52 RLDS [same as 18:14 LDS]	Helaman 2:74 RLDS [same as 5:12 LDS]

The Church That Christ Built Has the Following Components:

The Corner Stone is Jesus Christ

The Foundation is the Priesthood: Elders,
Seventies, High Priests, Evangelists, Bishops,
Patriarchs, Apostles, Teachers, Deacons, Priests.

The PRINCIPLES of the GOSPEL are THE WAY to SALVATION.

The Door of the Church is Baptism by water and The Spirit.

The Steps to the door are Faith and Repentance.

The Window above the door represents Laying on of
Hands, Resurrection of the Dead and Eternal
Judgment.

The Windows around the Church represent The Gifts
Of the Spirit which must be part of Christs Church:

Wisdom, Knowledge, Dreams, Visions, Faith, Healing,
Miracles, Prophecy, Discerning of Spirits, Tongues,
And Interpretation of Tongues.

(1 Cor. 12:8 - 12; Acts 2:17)

ROCK OF REVELATION

THE CHURCH THAT CHRIST BUILT
Jesus said, "I will build my Church" (Matthew 16:19).
Reproduced with the permission of Price Publishing House, Independence, Missouri

91

Jesus said, "Now learn a parable of the fig tree: When its branches are still tender, and it begins to put forth leaves, you know that summer is near. So likewise, my elect who see all these things shall know that Christ is near even at the door. But no one but my father knows the day or the hour not even the angels of God in Heaven."

Matthew 24:41-43
Mark 13:45-47
Luke 21:29-33,
D & C 45:5d

...so likewise, my elect who see these things ...

92

Chapter 7

A History of the Restoration of Christ's Church, Part 3
Note: Some scripture is paraphrased in this chapter to clarify meaning.

What do the scriptures say about the restoration of Christ's church in the Last Days?

SIGN 19
Zion (Independence, Missouri) is the gathering place of safety for the Saints during the Tribulation.

Doctrine & Covenants 57:1a, b
"Listen, elders of my church who have assembled yourselves together according to my commandments, in this land which is the land of Missouri. I have appointed and consecrated the land for the gathering of the Saints. Therefore, this is the land of promise and the place for the city of Zion," says the Lord your God.

ZION

Much of the early history of the church was concerned with the eminent return of Jesus Christ. The Saints were instructed to gather to Zion and prepare a community where God's people would find safety in the Last Days. They may have expected Christ to return in their lifetime. If so, they failed to look at ALL of the prophetic signs that must take place before He comes. Pioneers of the "Center Place" were in Missouri to lay the foundation for Zion and to build a church that provided the spiritual conditions required for Christ's return. The guidance given them is applicable today.

Luke 12:34, 35; 38-41; 45-47 [Luke 12:31-47 KJV]
Seek to bring forth the kingdom of God and all these things shall be added to you. Fear not little flock, it is your Father's good pleasure to give you the kingdom.

Be dressed and have your lights burning so you may be like friends who wait for their Lord when he returns from his wedding and immediately open the door for him when he knocks. Those servants, whom the Lord finds watching when He comes, shall be blessed. He shall prepare himself and make them sit down to eat and He will serve them. I say these things to you so you know the coming of the Lord is like a thief in the night. It is like a man who owns a house but fails to watch his goods. A thief comes when he is not expected and steals his things. The thief divides the spoils among his fellows saying, "If the man of the house knew when I would come, he would have watched and not have allowed his house to be entered and his goods stolen."

Then Christ said to them, "Be ready, for the Son of Man will come at an unexpected hour."

Jesus Christ is about to return. His return will be preceded by the warning signs He provided and by the Great Tribulation[38]. It is our job to be aware of these warning signs, watch for their fulfillment, stand fast with our eyes on Christ during the tribulation, and prepare for His return.

Preparation

The first step in preparation is the most basic; we must develop the closest possible relationship to/with the Lord. This happens through daily prayer, meditation, reading of scripture, and communing with other people who know Him. The Saints who do this will not be afraid of things to come. They will be ready and able to reach and help others. God will provide for their needs.

Doctrine & Covenants 85:20a, 21a, b, 22a, b
Behold, I will hasten my work in its time. I give you, the first laborers in this last kingdom, a commandment. Assemble together, organize, prepare and sanctify yourselves, having purified hearts and clean hands and feet so I may testify to your Father and God that you are clean from the blood of this wicked generation. I will fulfill this great and lasting promise when I will.

I give you a commandment. You shall continue in prayer and fasting from this time forth and you shall teach one another the doctrine of the kingdom....

I send you out to testify and warn the people and every man who has been warned must warn his neighbor, so they are left with no excuse.... He who seeks me early shall find me and he shall not be forsaken.

The second step is to heed the warning voice of the Lord. Numerous scriptures in the Doctrine & Covenants were given to the Saints as warning for the times to come. These are important today.

WARNING

Doctrine & Covenants 63:9a-d, 10a [1830, Kirtland, Ohio]
I, the Lord, am angry with the wicked; I am holding my Spirit from the inhabitants of the earth. I have sworn in my wrath and decreed wars upon the face of the earth, the wicked shall slay the wicked, fear shall come upon every man, and the Saints shall hardly escape. Nevertheless, I, the Lord, am with them. I will come down from Heaven and from the presence of my Father, consuming the wicked with unquenchable fire. This is not immediately, but soon. Therefore, seeing that I, the Lord, have decreed all these things upon the face of the earth, it is my will that my saints should be assembled upon the land of Zion. It is my will every man become righteous and faithful and lift his warning voice to the inhabitants of the earth declaring both by word and by flight, that desolation shall come upon the wicked....

---

[38] The Great Tribulation is described in a later chapter on the Antichrist

94

Doctrine & Covenants 81:3a, b [1832, Independence, Missouri]

I give you a new commandment that you may understand my will concerning you, or in other words, I give you direction on how you may act before me, for it has to do with your salvation. I the Lord am bound when you do as I say, but when you do not, you have no promise.

Doctrine & Covenants 83:2a [April 30, 1832]

This is the word of the Lord. The city New Jerusalem shall be built by the gathering of the Saints, beginning at this place....

WARNING

Doctrine & Covenants 98:4c [1833, Kirtland, Ohio]

My indignation is soon to be poured out without measure upon all nations and this I will do when the cup of their iniquity is full. [See D & C 85:19-20.]

Purchase of Lands for the New Jerusalem

Doctrine & Covenants 58:7d

It is wisdom that there should be lands purchased in Independence for the place of the storehouse and also for the house of printing.

Doctrine & Covenants 83:1b, c, 2a, b

[A revelation of Jesus Christ to His servant Joseph Smith, Jr., and six elders as they prayed] The word of the Lord, concerning His church, established in the Last Days for the restoration of His people, as He has spoken by the mouth of His prophets for the gathering of His Saints, is to stand upon Mount Zion, which shall be the city New Jerusalem. This city, which shall be built beginning at the Temple Lot, appointed by the finger of the Lord, in the western boundaries of the state of Missouri, will be dedicated by the hand of Joseph Smith, Jr. and others with whom the Lord is well pleased.

This is the word of the Lord. The city New Jerusalem shall be built by the gathering of the Saints, beginning at the place of the temple, which shall be reared in this generation. For verily, this generation shall not all pass away until a house shall be built unto the Lord and a cloud shall rest upon it, which cloud shall be the glory of the Lord which shall fill the house.

Doctrine & Covenants 100:5b

Let all the churches send up wise men, with their moneys, and purchase lands even as I have commanded them.

Doctrine & Covenants 102:8b, c

...I sent wise men to fulfill that which I commanded concerning all the lands in Jackson County and the adjoining counties round about that can be purchased. It is my will these lands be purchased and after they are purchased my Saints should possess them according to the laws of consecration, which I have given. I will hold the armies of Israel [Saints in Missouri] guiltless in taking possession of their own lands, which they have previously purchased with their money. I will hold the armies of Israel

guiltless of throwing down the towers of my enemies that may be upon them and scattering their watchmen and avenging me of my enemies to the third and fourth generation of them that hate me. [See D & C 58.11-15.]

Directions Given to the Saints Concerning Organized Gatherings

Doctrine & Covenants 28:2c-g [September 1830, Fayette, New York]
As it is written, "Whatsoever you shall ask in faith, being united in prayer, according to my command, you shall receive." You are called to bring to pass the gathering of my elect, for my elect hear my voice and do not harden their hearts. Therefore the decree has gone forth from the Father that they shall be gathered into one place, upon the face of this land, to prepare their hearts and be prepared in all things against the day when tribulation and desolation are sent forth upon the wicked.

"The hour and the day are soon at hand when the earth is ripe and all the proud and wicked shall be like stubble. I will burn them up so wickedness shall not be upon the earth," declares the Lord. "The time is almost here. The time of which the apostles spoke must be fulfilled, for as they spoke so shall it come to pass. I will reveal myself from Heaven with power and great glory, with all the hosts thereof, and dwell in righteousness with my people for a thousand years. The wicked shall not stand."

Doctrine & Covenants 45:6d, e
And the remnant [of the church] shall be gathered to this place and they shall look for me and behold I will come. They shall see me in the clouds of Heaven, clothed with power and great glory, with all the holy angels. He who does not watch shall be cut off.

Doctrine & Covenants 45:10b-d
And at that day when I shall come in my glory, the parable shall be fulfilled which I spoke concerning the ten virgins. They who are wise and have received the truth, have taken the Holy Spirit for their guide and have not been deceived, shall not be cut down and cast into the fire but shall endure and the earth shall be given to them for an inheritance. They shall multiply and grow strong and their children shall grow up without sin to salvation, for the Lord shall be in their midst and His glory shall be upon them and He will be their King and their law giver.

Doctrine & Covenants 45:12-14 [March, 1830, Kirtland, Ohio]
I the Lord said, "Gather out from the eastern lands...Go to the western countries, call upon the inhabitants to repent and inasmuch as they do repent, build up churches for me, and with one heart and mind, gather your riches so you may purchase an inheritance which shall be appointed to you. It shall be called the New Jerusalem, a land of peace, a city of refuge, a place of safety for the saints of the most high God. The glory of the Lord shall be there and the terror of the Lord also and the wicked, filled with fear, will not come to it. It shall be called Zion."

"And it shall come to pass among the wicked that every man who will not take his sword against his neighbor must flee to Zion for safety. And there shall

be gathered into it people out of every nation under Heaven and they shall be the only people who are not at war with one another."

"And it shall be said among the wicked, 'Let us not go to battle against Zion for the inhabitants of Zion are terrible and we cannot win.'"

"And it shall come to pass the righteous shall be gathered out from among all nations and shall come to Zion singing, with songs of everlasting joy."

Doctrine & Covenants 58:12b [August, 1831, Jackson County, Missouri]
Let the work of the gathering be not in haste, nor by flight. Let it be done as it shall be counseled by the elders of the church at the conferences, according to the knowledge which they receive from time to time. [See D & C 57:1-6; 63:13; 97:4; 98:4; 106:2; 128:1-8.]

The Storehouse, a Sharing of Resources

Part of God's plan for Zion included a storehouse where surplus funds were collected to assist the poor. This has precedent in the Old Testament.

Genesis 41:56
The famine was over all the face of the earth and Joseph opened all the storehouses and sold to the Egyptians.

Deuteronomy 28:8
The Lord shall command a blessing upon you in your storehouses and in all that you set your hand to.

Latter Day scripture elaborates on the storehouse.

Doctrine & Covenants 42:9b, 10a, b
Every man shall be made accountable to me as a steward over his own property or that which he has received by consecration, inasmuch as is sufficient for himself and family. If there is residual property in the hands of the church or its members, more than is necessary for their support, after the first consecration, it should be consecrated to the bishop. It shall be kept to administer to those who have not, so every man who has need may be amply supplied and receive according to that need.

Therefore, the residue shall be kept in my storehouse, to administer to the poor and the needy, as appointed by the high council of the church and the bishop and his council. This is for the purpose of purchasing lands for the public benefit of the church, building houses of worship and building up the New Jerusalem, which is hereafter to be revealed. My covenant people may then be gathered in one in that day when I shall come to my temple. And I do this for the salvation of my people.

Doctrine & Covenants 42:14b
If you obtain more than you need for your support, you shall give it to my storehouse so all things may be done according to that which I have said.

Doctrine & Covenants 77:1c
…There must be an organization of my people to regulate and establish the affairs of the storehouse for the poor of my people, both in this place and in the land of Zion…

Doctrine & Covenants 94:5a, b
And if Zion does these things, she shall prosper and spread herself, becoming very glorious, very great and very terrible. The nations of the earth will honor her and say, "Surely Zion is the city of our God. Surely Zion cannot fall, neither be moved out of her place, for God is there and the hand of the Lord is there and He has sworn by the power of His might to be her salvation and her high tower." [See D & C 81:4e, f, g; and D & C 82:2b.]

Today we hear very little about the storehouse. However, oblation funds contributed by members of the church and administered by the Bishops still assist in meeting some of the needs of the poor within the church.

"Behold! Look at the revelations of God; for the time is coming, at that day, when all these things must be fulfilled."

Mormon 4:44

SIGN 20
God's Temple will be built in Independence, Missouri.

The Temple

On August 3, 1831, Joseph Smith, Jr. placed a stone on the northeast corner of a lot chosen by God for the building of His temple. This land is adjacent to the Saints' Auditorium and across from the historic Stone Church in Independence, Missouri. The land is not owned by the Community of Christ. It belongs to the Church of Christ, headquartered on the temple lot.

> **Doctrine & Covenants 57:1d [July 1831, President Joseph Smith Jr.]**
> *The place which is now called Independence is the Center Place and the spot for the Temple [39] is lying westward upon a lot which is not far from the courthouse.*

> **Doctrine & Covenants 58:13 [August 1, 1831]**
> *Let my servant Sidney Rigdon consecrate and dedicate this land and the spot of the temple unto the Lord.*

> **Doctrine & Covenants 83:2a, b [September 22, 23, 1832]**
> *This is the word of the Lord: "The city New Jerusalem shall be built by the gathering of the Saints, beginning at this place. The temple shall be reared in this generation for this generation shall not all pass away until a house shall be built unto the Lord. And a cloud shall rest upon it, which cloud shall be the glory of the Lord, which shall fill the house."*

> **Doctrine & Covenants 94:3, 4, 5 [July 23, 1833]**
> *I say to you that it is my will that a house should be built for me in the land of Zion, similar to the pattern, which I have given you. [There is no reference in the D & C to this pattern so it is possibly the pattern for the Kirtland temple.] Let it be built speedily by the tithing of my people. Behold, this is the tithing and the sacrifice, which I, the Lord, require at their hands so there may be a house, built to me for the salvation of Zion.*

The purpose of the Temple is defined.

> **Doctrine & Covenants 94:3c, d, 4a, b, 5a-d**
> *[The Temple] is to be a place of thanksgiving for all Saints and a place of instruction for all those who are called to the work of the ministry, in all their several callings and offices. There they may be perfected in the understanding of their ministry in theory, principle, doctrine, and all things pertaining to the kingdom of God on earth. The keys of which kingdom have*

---

[39] The first temple built by the Saints was in Kirtland, Ohio. It was dedicated March 27, 1836 and is owned by the Community of Christ/Reorganized Church of Jesus Christ of Latter Day Saints. A second temple, begun in Nauvoo, Illinois, was not finished. Toward the end of the twentieth century, the Church of Jesus Christ of Latter Day Saints, known as the Mormon Church, completed this temple. A third building called the Temple stands in Independence, Missouri, across the street from the spot designated by the church founders. It is owned by the Community of Christ. The Mormon church has numerous temples around the world.

been conferred upon you…. And inasmuch as my people build a house for me, in the name of the Lord, and do not allow any unclean thing to come into it so it is not defiled [40], my glory shall rest upon it. Yes, my presence shall be there for I will come into it and all the pure in heart shall come into it and see God.

But if it is defiled I will not come into it, and my glory shall not be there for I will not come into unholy temples [41].

Doctrine & Covenants 94:5a, b
If Zion does these things, she shall prosper and spread herself and become very glorious, very great and very terrible. The nations of the earth shall honor her and shall say, "Surely Zion is the city of our God and surely Zion cannot fall, nor be moved out of her place. God is there and the hand of the Lord is there and He has sworn by the power of His might to be her salvation and her high tower."

Therefore, says the Lord, "Let Zion rejoice, for this is Zion, THE PURE IN HEART. Therefore, let Zion rejoice while all the wicked shall mourn for my vengeance is speedily coming upon the ungodly and will be like the whirlwind and who shall escape it! The Lord's scourge shall pass over by night and day and the report about it will confound all people."

Doctrine & Covenants 109 and 110
By an act of the World Conference, sections 109 and 110 were removed from the Doctrine and Covenants and moved to its appendix. Later they were removed entirely from the book (the sections are online centerplace.org). A portion of the deleted section is relevant here:

Doctrine & Covenants 109:4
…And again, the Lord says, "Let the work of my temple and all the works which I have appointed to you be continued and not cease. Let your diligence, your perseverance, patience and your works be redoubled. You shall not lose your reward," says the Lord of hosts…."Let all the records be put in order that they may be put in the archives of my Holy Temple, to be held in remembrance from generation to generation," says the Lord.

In spite of these reminders, work had not yet begun nine years after the people were instructed to build a temple. Pride and the unusual religious beliefs of the Saints created animosity among other residents of Independence, Missouri. Severe persecution and mob attacks began to terrorize members of the church. On June 27, 1844, the prophet Joseph Smith Jr. and his brother were murdered and members of the church were forced into exile. The temple was not built.

In 1864, a small group of people, who left the church after the prophet's death, returned to Independence and purchased eight acres of land, including the designated temple lot. That land is now the site of a small denomination known as the Church of Christ.

---

[40] Since the building of this edifice, representatives of the Jesus Seminar and other liberal, controversial organizations and speakers have been invited to make use of the Community of Christ Temple.

[41] The preamble to section 94 given August 2, 1833, in Kirtland, is found in the 1966 edition to the D&C.

Members of this church consider themselves stewards of the temple lot until the various Latter Day Saint churches are united again. The doctrinal differences between the churches (Community of Christ and the LDS church) have not been reconciled and the Church of Christ is unwilling to sell this property.

When the rest of the Saints returned to Independence from exile, they soon found themselves in the midst of the Great Depression. In spite of this economic difficulty, with great sacrifice on the part of the people, the auditorium, the sanitarium (the hospital) and Herald House printing company were completed.

As years passed, members of the RLDS church waited anxiously to see the building of the temple in Independence. In 1984, an additional revelation was given concerning this mission.

> ### Doctrine & Covenants 156:3
> *[Apr. 3, 1984, President Wallace B. Smith]*
> *The Spirit prompts me to say further by way of guidance to the church: My servants have been diligent in the work of planning for the building of my temple in the Center Place. Let this work continue at an accelerated rate, according to the instructions already given, for there is a great need of the spiritual awakening that will be engendered by the ministries experienced within its walls.*

Lacking access to the specific site, church leaders chose to build an impressive structure on property opposite Christ's designated location.

Recent History in Independence

An incremental movement away from the gospel foundations of the church began about 1945 or 1950. New church leaders, many educated at liberal seminaries, introduced new theological doctrines that began to change the basic beliefs of the Reorganized Church of Jesus Christ of Latter Day Saints. At first, the changes were almost unnoticeable, but little by little, the original church became hard to recognize.

Before the turn of the 21st century, new church leaders changed the name of the church to the Community of Christ. The message of the gospel was revised; salvation through faith, repentance, and baptism are no longer emphasized, and the Stakes of Zion[42] were eliminated. Crucial information about Jesus was minimized in church school curriculum, and a whole generation of young people failed to receive basic information about Christ and His church. The new objective of the leaders became worldwide peace and justice. The call to prepare Zion was almost forgotten. The Community of Christ does not resemble the Reorganized Church of Jesus Christ that the Lord restored.

It should not surprise us those directions, for gathering, community building, and the storehouse, are inadequately fulfilled. The "gathering place" is not currently prepared for an influx of church members. Early church revelation concerning the Center Place and the work of preparing for Zion is not relevant to the Community of Christ.

---

[42] Stakes of Zion, D & C 98:4i, 104:11, 15, 108:3, 125:10.

As a result, many conservative members of the original RLDS church chose to leave the new denomination. Several attempts were made to reunite the people, but many differences in the original beliefs of the church and the new direction of the Community of Christ made this impossible. Instead, disaffected members organized "Restoration Churches" in many parts of the country. They attempted to obtain the rights to the original name, 'Reorganized Church of Jesus Christ of Latter Day Saints,' but the leadership of the Community of Christ was unwilling to have another body make use of it.

It is unknown how God will fulfill the signs concerning Zion, the gathering, and the temple in the Last Days. Leaders of the Community of Christ are selling much of the land that was purchased through commandments of God and the monetary sacrifices of past generations.

Property that was sold includes the following.

The Sanitarium
(Commanded to Build, D & C 127:1a-c, 2a-e, 3, 4a. Also, see 172:3, 4)

Herald House
(Commanded to Build: D & C 48:2a, 57:1e, 2g, 4a; 58:7d, 11b, c, 91:3a-c)

Land
(Commanded to Purchase: D & C 45:12c; 48:a; 58:11c, 12; 13a; 63:8c; 98:9f, g, 10b; 100:5a, b; 102:8b, c, 122:6f)

(Announced March 2010: <u>The Church sold the Groves</u>, its care center for seniors in Independence, Mo.)

I am unaware of any commands by God to sell any of these properties. Thankfully, the Lord has His own plan and timetable. It does not depend on us. Anyone who wishes to participate or gather to Zion must follow God's leadership instead of man's misguided direction. God does not change even though men continue to try to modify His plans. The following verses are very important.

WARNING

Doctrine & Covenants 105:9-11
"I tell you, darkness covers the earth and gross darkness the minds of the people and all flesh has become corrupt before my face. My vengeance comes speedily upon the inhabitants of the earth, a day of wrath, a day of burning, a day of desolation, of weeping, of mourning and of lamentation and as a whirlwind it shall come upon all the face of the earth," says the Lord.

"AND UPON MY HOUSE IT SHALL BEGIN AND FROM MY HOUSE IT SHALL GO FORTH," says the Lord.

"IT WILL BEGIN FIRST AMONG YOU WHO HAVE PROFESSED TO KNOW MY NAME AND HAVE NOT KNOWN ME, AND HAVE BLASPHEMED AGAINST ME IN THE MIDST OF MY HOUSE," says the Lord.

"Therefore, see to it that you don't trouble yourselves concerning the affairs of my church in this place, Purify your hearts before me and then go into all the world and preach my gospel to every creature who has not received it. And he that believes and is baptized shall be saved and he that does not believe and is not baptized shall be damned."

Zion shall be redeemed in spite of man's sins.

Genesis 7:67, 70 [I.V. only]
I [Christ] will come in the Last Days when there is wickedness and vengeance… to a place, which I shall provide, a holy city, where my people may prepare themselves, and be looking forward to the time of my coming.

Doctrine & Covenants 97:4 a, c, d
…Zion shall be redeemed, although she is chastened for a little season. Therefore let your hearts be comforted, for all things shall work together for good to those who walk uprightly and in the sanctification of the church. I will raise up to myself a pure people who will serve me in righteousness and all that call on the name of the Lord and keep His commandments shall be saved. Even so, Amen.

Zion shall not be moved out of her place!

Contrary to some opinions, God indicates that the area of Independence, Missouri, is still the location of Zion. D & C 94g is emphatic. Zion shall not be moved out of her place! Failures of men and women will not prevent Him from completing His work, and Zion will be a place of righteousness and of safety for the Saints during the turmoil of the Last Days.

God can overcome all difficulties, but He will do it only for an obedient people. He will not hold us accountable for that which other people fail to do, but He will certainly hold us accountable for that which we fail to do. We may be unable to change the grievous mistakes made by those in positions of authority, but it is our task to help each other prepare for the work to which we are called, to study the scriptures, to pray for discernment and spiritual guidance, and to warn our neighbors. The scriptures provide strong reassurance.

Doctrine & Covenants 98:4f-i
Therefore, let your hearts be comforted concerning Zion for all flesh is in my hands. Be still and know that I am God. ZION SHALL NOT BE MOVED OUT OF HER PLACE even though her children are scattered. The pure of heart who remain, and the pure in heart who return, shall come into their inheritances. They and their children shall sing songs of everlasting joy and will build up the waste places of Zion. All these things will take place so the prophets will be fulfilled.

And behold, THERE IS NO OTHER PLACE APPOINTED THAN THAT WHICH I HAVE APPOINTED. Neither shall there be any other place appointed than that which I have appointed for the gathering of my Saints until the day comes when there is no more room for them. Then I have other places, which I will appoint for them, and THEY SHALL BE CALLED STAKES for the strength of Zion[43].

God's people can look forward to a place of safety and peace in the Latter Days.

Doctrine & Covenants 64:8a
Zion shall flourish and the glory of the Lord shall be upon her and she shall be an ensign [example, banner, standard] to the people.

Doctrine & Covenants 94:5c-g
"Let Zion rejoice for this is Zion, the Pure in Heart. Therefore, let Zion rejoice while all the wicked mourn, for behold, vengeance is coming speedily upon the ungodly, like a whirlwind and who shall escape it? The Lord's scourge shall pass over by night and by day and information about it will distress everyone. Yet it will not stop until the Lord comes; the indignation of the Lord is kindled against the abominations and wickedness of man.

Zion shall escape if she observes all things I have commanded but if she does not observe the things I have commanded, I will visit her with sore affliction, pestilence, plague, sword, vengeance and with devouring fire. Let this be read for their hearing. I the Lord have accepted their offerings and if Zion sins no more, none of these things will come upon her and I will multiply many blessings upon her and upon her generations forever and ever," says the Lord your God. Amen.

WE HAVE BEEN WARNED!

God intends to gather His people to the place He provides in preparation for the Great Tribulation and Christ's return. How this will be accomplished is unknown.

Doctrine & Covenants 97:4a-d, [October 1833]
...Zion shall be redeemed although she is chastened for a little season. Therefore, let your hearts be comforted for all things shall work together for the sanctification of the church and for the good of those who walk uprightly. I will raise up to myself a pure people who will serve me in righteousness. All who call on the name of the Lord and keep His commandments shall be saved. Even so, Amen.

Doctrine & Covenants 140:5c [April 7, 1947]
The work of preparation and the perfection of my Saints goes forward slowly and zionic conditions are no further away nor any closer than the spiritual condition of my people justifies. My word shall not fail; neither will my promises. The foundation of the Lord stands sure.

The Saints will gather to the Center Place before and during the Tribulation.

This becomes a test of faith in an unsafe world. Do we believe in a God who is always in charge, whose promises never fail, and whose purposes WILL be accomplished?

---

[43] Stakes of Zion were eliminated by the Community of Christ.

III Nephi 10:1-8 [III Nephi 21:23-29 LDS]

If they [the Gentiles] will repent and listen to my words, and not harden their hearts, I will establish my church among them, and they shall become part of the covenant [made with the House of Israel] and be numbered among the remnant of Jacob to whom I have given this land [the Americas] for an inheritance. And they shall assist my people, the remnant of Jacob. All those of the House of Israel who come, will build a city, which will be called the New Jerusalem.

They shall assist my people who are scattered upon the face of the land in order to gather them into the New Jerusalem. And the power of Heaven shall come down among them and I will also be in their midst and the work of the Father shall begin at that day when this gospel shall be preached among the remnant of this people.

...At that day the work of the Father will begin among all the dispersed of my people, yes, even the tribes which have been lost which the Father led away out of Jerusalem [in Israel].

The work shall begin among all the dispersed of my people and the Father will prepare the way for them to come to me that they may call on the Father in my name. Then the Father's work will begin among all nations, preparing the way so His people may be gathered home to the land of their inheritance. And they shall go out from all nations and they shall not go out in haste, nor by flight, for the Father says, "I will go before them and I will be their rearward. And then all that is written shall come to pass."

Doctrine & Covenants 45:13

"And it shall come to pass, among the wicked, that every man who will not take up his sword against his neighbor must flee to Zion for safety, and people from every nation shall be gathered, and they shall be the only people who are not at war with one another. And it shall be said among the wicked, 'Let us not go up to battle against Zion, for the inhabitants are terrible and we cannot defeat them.'"

I've gone to prepare a place, for you.

Be ready and waiting for my return.

I am coming back soon.

Love,

Jesus

"I am coming back soon."

Revelation 3:11, 22:12

"I will come in the Last Days when there is wickedness and vengeance... to a place, which I shall provide"

Doctrine and Covenants 36:12c, f RLDS
Moses 7:60 LDS

Jesus said, "Now learn a parable of the fig tree: When its branches are still tender, and it begins to put forth leaves, you know that summer is near. So likewise, my elect who see all these things shall know that Christ is near even at the door. But no one but my father knows the day or the hour not even the angels of God in Heaven."

Matthew 24:41-43
Mark 13:45-47
Luke 21:29-33,
D & C 45:5d

...shall know that Christ is near...

Chapter 8

What do the scriptures say about God's covenants with the Jewish people in the Last Days?

Note: Some scripture is paraphrased in this chapter to clarify meaning.

Covenants Defined and Illustrated

Covenant Relationships

- Understanding God's covenants with the Jewish people
- The purpose and importance of those same covenants
- Helping readers, who have been baptized in the name of Jesus Christ and adopted into His family, to understand the personal covenants they now have with God

To understand fully what will take place in the Last Days, we must first know:

- What is a covenant?
- Who is involved?
- What impact does a covenant have on the lives of those within a covenant relationship?

Many covenant relationships are sacred, i.e. God and Man, husband and wife, parents, and children are sacred covenant relationships.

Some covenant relationships are criminal. The Mafia is a covenant organization. Members are bound by blood and anyone who tries to leave the organization is killed. Gangs may evolve into covenant criminal organizations with their own initiation practices loosely following older traditions.

Reduced to its simplest terms, a covenant is a solemn, unbreakable contract or a binding promise between two or more parties in which each party promises lifetime loyalty to the other.

Covenant relationships may be based on friendship between individuals or families who choose to celebrate their close association with a covenant that binds them in mutually beneficial ways. The custom of selecting godparents for children is an example. One family promises to care for the children of another should the parents be incapacitated or die.

Covenants are made to benefit, mutually, all parties involved in the pledge. Historically, groups would covenant together for protection. This often included an exchange of names, weapons, coats, blood, possessions, and even lives. If the covenant was broken, the offended party was bound through a covenant oath to kill the offender(s). In these relationships, the covenant was so important that it could be broken only by death.

Because of this, very few covenants were broken. Today, we are still influenced by covenants, although they may be called by different names. Remnants of ancient contracts are still recognizable. This Information is essential in order to have a basic understanding of God's covenants with Israel, as well as His covenants with Christians.

Marriage is a covenant.

This covenant is between a husband, a wife, and God. The couple exchanges promises, names, and properties, and integrate their lives. Although marriages are now easily broken, something dies within each individual when divorce takes place.

Priesthood Ordination is a covenant.

> ### DOCTRINE & COVENANTS 83:6e-g [September 22, 23, 1832]
> *"All who receive this priesthood receive me," says the Lord "for he who receives my servants receives me and he that receives me receives my Father. He who receives my Father receives my Father's kingdom. Therefore, all that my father has shall be given to them who receive me. This is according to the oath and covenant of my Father, which he cannot break neither can it be moved. Whoever receives this covenant, then turns from and breaks it, shall neither have forgiveness of sin in this world nor in the world to come."*

Baptism is a covenant.

This covenant is a sacred, eternal promise between God and the person who enters the water. As part of this covenant, the Lord promises salvation and eternal protection if we are faithful to the end (Matthew 10:19; 24:13; Mark 13:13). We take the name of Christian and promise Him a lifetime of loyalty. Christ clothes us with His righteousness and provides for our earthly needs. We recognize everything we have is a gift from Him and even our lives belong to the Lord. Incredibly, as a result of the baptism covenant, Christ chooses to live within our hearts.

A broken covenant with God results in spiritual death unless we repent, asking the Lord's forgiveness. It is essential to remember we continue to sin even after baptism. Regrettably, our part of the covenant is often broken but incredibly, Christ's death paid the price for our sinfulness. When we repent, His sacrifice covers the covenant requirement. Through Him we are justified (declared righteous) and sanctified (made holy). Although all of us will die physically, death no longer prevails. Through Christ, we have eternal life.

Taking Communion, the Renewal of Our Baptismal Covenant

Each member of the Reorganized Church of Jesus Christ of Latter Day Saints has a covenant with Christ. Each communion service provides an opportunity to renew our covenant.

The terms of this covenant include:

- remembering Christ's sacrifice (His body and His blood)
- accepting His name as our own (Christian)
- remembering Him, always
- keeping His commandments in order to retain His spirit

The communion prayers reiterate the terms of the covenant.

Before receiving the communion bread, we hear these words:

Doctrine & Covenants 17:22d
O God, the eternal Father, we ask thee in the name of thy Son, Jesus Christ, to bless and sanctify this bread to the souls of all those who partake of it, that they might eat in remembrance of the body of thy Son and witness unto thee, O God, the eternal Father, that they are willing to take upon them the name of thy Son and always remember Him and keep His commandments which He has given them, that they may always have His spirit to be with them. Amen.

Before drinking the communion wine, these words are read:

Doctrine & Covenants 17:23b
O God, the eternal Father, we ask thee in the name of thy Son, Jesus Christ, to bless and sanctify this wine to the souls of all those who drink of it, that they may do it in remembrance of the blood of thy Son which was shed for them, that they may witness unto thee, O God, the eternal Father, that they do always remember Him, that they may have His Spirit to be with them. Amen.

The Blessing of Children is a covenant.
It is between the parents of the child and the Heavenly Father.

A life in covenant relationship with God and others has important components.

- **LOVE**
  The strength of the covenant is love. Love that is shared will strengthen the relationship. However, one-sided love may break the covenant bond.
- **SACRIFICE**
  There is a cost to covenant relationships. Covenant relationships require sacrifice. Christ gave His life so that we might live. We must die to self in order to serve Him. The sacrifice may require our time, money, energy, worldly goods, pride, ego, or even our lives.
- **OBEDIENCE**
  The responsibility of a covenant relationship is obedience to the terms of the covenant. Humility is required as the terms of the covenant are fulfilled. We must also develop a broken heart and a contrite spirit.

- **INFLUENCE**

  The power of the covenant is its ability to influence others for good, bringing men and women to Jesus Christ, producing a lifelong commitment to love and serve God and our fellow beings.

- **BENEFIT**

  The benefit of the covenant is a life lived for Christ in the presence of His guiding Spirit. He protects, teaches, admonishes, and is with us each moment of our Christian lives[44].

The Father's primary covenants with the Israelites state the following:

Jeremiah 31:33-34

- He will be their God.
- They will be His people.
- They give him their obedience.

Joshua 1:1-4

- He has given His people the land from the wilderness of Lebanon to the great Euphrates River and all the land of the Hittites to the great sea [Mediterranean] which shall be their coastline.

Old Testament Covenants: In the writings of the Old Testament, God made numerous binding covenants with specific people. The first of these was Enoch.

(Summary)

Genesis 7:1-78 I.V. only

ENOCH, seven generations after Adam, was a righteous man who walked closely with the Lord. It was he who established the original city of Zion that was later removed from earth to be with God. By the time of Enoch's birth, the world was already torn between good and evil. The Lord and Enoch spoke about the wickedness and misery caused by human sin and Enoch was deeply troubled. In the midst of his grieving, he saw a vision of Noah, Noah's family and the ark, which would be built. He 'saw' the ark in God's own hand and 'witnessed the rest of earth's people swallowed by the flood.' This disturbed Enoch greatly and he cried to the Lord, asking mercy for Noah and his descendants. Therefore, the Lord made a covenant with Enoch, swearing an oath promising, after Noah, there would never again be a worldwide flood. God also promised that a remnant of Noah's children would always be found among nations for as long as the earth remained. Finally God said, "Blessed is he whose descendants shall give birth to the Messiah."

The righteousness of Enoch and his people reached a level of spiritual perfection never duplicated. Therefore, the entire city and its people were lifted from earth. In order to fulfill God's covenant, Enoch's son Methuselah remained in the land. Methuselah fathered Lamech, who fathered Noah. Abram (later called Abraham) was a descendant of Noah through Shem, one of Noah's sons. Through Noah, all the kingdoms of the earth would develop.

---

[44] Contributed by Charles Deibert, Priest, Community of Christ, Reynoldsburg Congregation

(Summary)
Genesis 8:14-23 [Genesis 6:7-18 KJV]

NOAH was directed to build the ark. The ark was filled with animals who endured the rain and the flood until they landed safely on a mountain. In verse 23, he received God's covenant promise: "I will establish my covenant with you even as I have sworn to your ancestor, Enoch, that from his posterity all nations will come."

(Summary)
Genesis 9:15, 17-25 [Genesis 9:8-16 KJV]

God established His covenant, with Noah, concerning Noah's descendants, reiterating these promises ten times. He promised never again to destroy the earth with a flood, setting a rainbow in the sky to remind men of His promise and their commitment to keep His commandments. God said, "This is My Everlasting Covenant: When your posterity embraces the truth and looks upward, then Zion shall look downward. All the Heavens shall shake with gladness and the earth shall tremble with joy. Then the general assembly of the church of the first-born (Jesus Christ) shall come down out of Heaven and possess the earth. It shall remain in place until the end comes." (Genesis 9:22, 23 I.V. only)

(Summary)
Genesis 11:15; [Genesis 25:11 I.V. only]

ABRAM / ABRAHAM

About 500 years separated the flood from the time of Abram who inherited the covenants God made with Enoch and Noah. The Father also made a variety of new covenants with Abram. One specific covenant promised Abram and his posterity all of the land later occupied by the Twelve Tribes of Israel. This was to be an everlasting inheritance. (Genesis 15:9)

(Summary)
Genesis 15:9-21

This scripture illustrates how this covenant was made. Abram was instructed to sacrifice a cow, a goat, a ram, one turtledove, and a young pigeon. The animals were divided in half, each piece lying against another. The birds were placed next to them. Abram watched over the carcasses all day, driving away the fowls that wanted to feed on them. When the sun went down, he fell into a deep sleep. When all light disappeared, a smoking firepot and a blazing torch passed between the animal parts. Through this ritual, the Lord made a covenant with Abram, saying, "I have given this land, from the river of Egypt to the great river Euphrates, to your descendants as an everlasting covenant." (See Genesis 14:40)

Although throughout time, many other people have occupied the land of Israel, God's promise has never been withdrawn. This land will always belong to the Children of Israel.

(Summary)
Genesis 12: 2, 6 (Gen, 12:2, 7 KJV)

The Lord directed Abram to leave his country and his father's house. In addition, He said, "I will make a great nation of you and I will bless you and make your name great. You shall be a blessing and **I will bless them that bless you and curse them that curse you.** In you, all the families of the earth will be blessed... and the Lord said to Abram, "I give this land to your posterity." (The Covenant requirement was an exchange of lives. Abram literally gave his life to follow a God that no one else was aware of at the time. Christ gave His life for the salvation of all, including Abram.)

This Old Testament covenant contains an important phrase that remains true today. God's covenant with Abram and his offspring says, "I will bless them that bless you and curse them that curse you." People overlook or ignore this scripture. In ignorance and prejudice, they persecute God's chosen people. This will not go unpunished. God takes His covenants seriously. He does not modify covenants through time. He does not take them from the Jews to bestow them on Christians. He will not forget His promises or His people.

The Lord said to Abram, "Remember the covenant which I made with you, for it shall be an **Everlasting Covenant** and you shall remember the days of Enoch, your ancestor. I give you and your children all the land, which you see FOREVER. And I will make your offspring as numerous as the dust of the earth."

The Covenant requirement was an exchange of worldly possessions. Abram left the land of his fathers and received the promise of the land of Israel for his posterity.

Genesis 14:40 [I.V. only]
God blessed Abram, giving him riches, honor and lands for an everlasting possession. [All given] according to the covenant, which He made.

Genesis 15:21 [Genesis 15:18 KJV]
In that same day the Lord made a covenant with Abram saying, "I have given the land, from the river of Egypt to the great river Euphrates to your offspring."

The above covenant and those that followed were passed from generation to generation through the lineage of Judah and his eleven brothers.

Genesis 17:2-28 [Genesis 17:1-23 KJV]
I will make my covenant between me and you. I will greatly multiply your future generations and I will make you a father of many nations.

Your children will be known among all nations and your name shall be changed to Abraham for I have made you a father of many nations; I will make you very fruitful and some of your offspring will be kings. [The Covenant requirement was an exchange of names. Abram became God's Son, Abraham.]

Sarai [Abraham's wife] will be renamed Sarah. I will bless her and give you a son by her and she shall be the mother of nations, kings and people.

I will establish a covenant of circumcision with you and all generations that follow you. Every male child among you will be circumcised. This shall be a token of the covenant between us. [The covenant requirement, shedding of blood, was fulfilled by circumcision and later by the blood of Christ.]

114

Covenant Terms

Genesis 17:12
You will keep all my covenants that I have given you.

Genesis 17:13
I will give you and your children after you a land where you are a stranger, the land of Canaan, for an everlasting possession.

(Summary)
ISHMAEL, Father of the Arab Nations[45]
Abraham and Sarah had no children. Therefore, Sarah gave her bondwoman Hagar to Abraham, and she bore a son.

(Summary)
Genesis 16:12, 13 [Genesis 16:11, 12 KJV]
An angel of the Lord spoke to Hagar saying, "You are expecting a child and shall call his name Ishmael.... He will be a wild man. His hand will be against every man and every man's hand against him and he shall dwell in the presence of all his brothers."

When Sarah finally became a mother, there was great jealousy between the two women because Sarah's son Isaac was the legitimate son of Abraham. Sarah insisted Hagar and her son be cast out. While in the desert without food or water, an angel spoke to Hagar:

(Summary)
Genesis 21:16 [Genesis 21:17, 18 KJV]
"Fear not, Hagar, God has heard the voice of your son. Lift him up and hold him by the hand for I will make of him a great nation."

Ishmael, though first born, was not the legitimate heir of Abraham. Therefore, he was not heir to the covenant promises nor was he a Hebrew patriarch. However, he is recognized as the father of the Arab nations. The Arabs believe Ishmael, not Isaac, was the son Abraham prepared for sacrifice.

To this day, Arabs can be described as a thorny people, quick to anger and take offense. A common expression in the Middle East is, "Me against my brother. My brother and I against our neighbor; my neighbor and I against the rest of the world."

(Summary)
Genesis 22:1-22 I.V; [Genesis 22:118 KJV]
ISAAC, the Second Hebrew Patriarch
As the legitimate son and heir of Abraham and Sarah, Isaac was next in line to inherit God's covenant blessings for his descendants. When Isaac was nearly grown, God directed Abraham to sacrifice his only heir (approximately 1882 B.C.)[46]. Distraught,

---

45 The magazine *Midnight Call*, March 2007, provides a different genealogy for the Arab nations. It indicates that Abraham is a descendant of Peleg, whereas the Arabs descended from Joktan. If this is true, Ishmael cannot be the father of the Arab nations. However, most Arabs I've consulted accept him as their founding father and believe it was he, not Isaac, who was nearly sacrificed by Abraham.

46 Thomas Robinson, *The Bible Timeline*, Thomas Nelson Publishers, Nashville, Tenn. 1992

Abraham prepared to do God's will, but before his son was slain, God substituted a ram for the sacrifice, a type and shadow of things to come. In this same location, almost 2000 years later, another lamb was sacrificed, Jesus Christ, God's only Son.

Mount Moriah was in the land later named Jerusalem. The imposing mound on which the ram's sacrifice took place now rests beneath the Dome of the Rock, the second-most holy site in the Muslim world. This stone juts upward from a floor of rock, extending unevenly to many parts of the Old City and outside the city walls to Golgotha, the place of Christ's crucifixion.

Genesis 17:25 [Genesis 17:19 KJV]
I will establish my covenant with your son Isaac. It will be an everlasting covenant with all his children and children's children after him.

(Summary)
Genesis 26:2-4
God reaffirmed His covenant with Abraham to Isaac, Abraham's son. The Lord appeared to Isaac and said, "Do not go to Egypt. Dwell in the land where I tell you. Stay in this land and I will be with you, will bless you, and will give all these countries to you and your children. Your offspring will multiply as the stars in the Heaven and through them all the nations of the earth will be blessed."

Isaac, son of Abraham, had twin sons of his own named Esau and Jacob. Esau was the firstborn, entitled to the blessing and inheritance of the birth position. Jacob was the second child. As Isaac lay dying, Jacob pretended to be Esau and stole the birthright (covenant blessing) from his twin brother. He became the next person through whom the birthright and covenant descended.

(Summary)
Genesis 26:31-33; 27:1-36
Although the blessing was stolen, it could not be withdrawn.

(Summary)
Genesis 28:3, 4, 12-15
JACOB (ISRAEL), the Third Hebrew Patriarch
Jacob's blessing: May God Almighty bless you and make you fruitful and multiply you that you may inherit the land that God gave to Abraham.

(Summary)
Genesis 28:13-15
Jacob's Dream: Jacob saw a ladder stretching to the Heavens with angels of God ascending and descending. And the Lord stood above saying, "I am the Lord God of Abraham and the God of Isaac. I will give you the land where you lie and your offspring shall be as numerous as the dust of the earth, spread abroad to the west, the east, the north and south. In you and in your progenitors all the families of the earth shall be blessed. Behold, I am with you and will keep you in all the places where you go. I will bring you again into this land for I will not leave you until I have done that which I have told you."

116

(Summary)
JACOB is renamed ISRAEL. Even though Isaac blessed Jacob by mistake, God honored His covenant and called Jacob by a new name. In Genesis 35:9-14, God said, "Your name is no longer Jacob but you will be called Israel (exchange of covenant names). Be fruitful and multiply. A nation and a company of nations shall come from you and kings shall be among your offspring. I pass on to you and your offspring the land which I gave Abraham and Isaac."

Genesis 46:2-4
God spoke to Israel in a dream and said, "I am the God of your father. Do not be afraid to go down into Egypt, for there I will make you a great nation."

The covenants between God and the descendants of Abraham are permanent. God will never break them. God's covenants with Israel are reaffirmed many times in both the Old and New Testaments. Therefore, it is a mistake to overlook or take them lightly. Jacob was a thief and a liar. Yet he received the first son's blessing from his father. Therefore, through Jacob, God honored His covenant with Abraham and Isaac.

Jacob (Israel) had twelve sons appropriately called the Children of Israel. Nine of the sons planned to murder Joseph the youngest who was his father's favorite. Instead, they sold him into slavery. These men were stubborn, willful, prone to murmur against God, and often influenced by the sins of the cultures around them. God even called them and their descendants a "stiff-necked" people who obstinately repeated the mistakes of their past. Through willful disobedience, they challenged the grace and mercy of God and at numerous times lost His protection and the possession of the Promised Land. In spite of everything, God CHOSE these people. His covenants with all twelve sons remain firm to this day.

(Summary)
The TWELVE SONS of JACOB / ISRAEL
The names of Jacob's sons by Leah were Reuben, Simeon, Levi, Judah, Issachar, and Zebulun; his sons by Rachel were Joseph and Benjamin. The sons of the handmaids were Dan, Naphtali, Gad, and Asher. Levi was set aside to become the first in a tribe of priests called by his name. The children of Israel were prolific. Their descendants included three kings: David, then Solomon, and finally the greatest, Jesus the Christ.
These twelve men and their offspring are called, the Children of Israel. Before his death, Israel spoke prophetically to each of his sons and then to Ephram and Manasseh, the sons of Joseph.

(Summary)
JUDAH[47] was Jacob's fourth son. The birthright or covenant blessing should have been given to one of his older brothers.

(Summary)
Genesis 49:2-6
Because of poor judgment and behavior, the older men disqualified themselves. Therefore, the covenant blessing was passed to Judah, whose descendants include Jesus of Nazareth.

---

[47] Judah is called Judas in Matthew 1:2. Do not confuse him with the apostle Judas who betrayed Christ.

(Summary)
Genesis 49:8
When it was time for Judah's blessing, Jacob said, "Judah, your brothers will praise you. Your hand shall be on the neck of your enemies; your father's children shall bow down before you. Judah is a lion's cub... the scepter shall not depart from him and he will keep a firm grip on the staff of command until Shiloh [the ultimate ruler-Jesus Christ] comes and the nations obey Him."

(Summary)
JOSEPH was the eleventh son born to Israel. He was not one of Christ's ancestors, but he and his descendants are mentioned here because of their connection with the Book of Mormon. According to this book, descendants of Joseph's son Ephram eventually migrated to Central America, where two tribes, the Nephites and the Lamanites, emerged. That story will be briefly explained later in this chapter.

(Summary)
Genesis Chapters 37-50 I.V.
When Joseph's brothers sold him, he was taken to Egypt. There he endured enslavement, character assassination, and many years of imprisonment. In spite of this, he eventually became the ruler of the country, second only to the Pharaoh. In this position, he was able to reunite with his family, save them from starvation during a famine, and make a home for them in Egypt.

Joseph's Blessing from Jacob

Genesis 49:22-26
Joseph is a fruitful bough by a well whose branches run over the wall. The archers have sorely grieved him and shot at him and hated him but his bow was very strong and the arms of his hands were made strong by the hands of the mighty God of Jacob. The God of thy father shall help thee and the Almighty shall bless thee with blessings of Heaven above, blessings of the deep that lies under it, the blessings of the breast and of the womb. The blessings of thy father have prevailed above the blessings of my progenitors to the utmost bound of the everlasting hills and they shall be on the head of Joseph and on the crown of the head of him that was separate from his brothers.

The Blessing of Ephraim and Manasseh, Joseph's Sons

Genesis 48:18-20, 22 [Genesis 48:11-20 KJV]
Joseph presented his sons to his father, Jacob, called Israel. He placed Ephraim in his right hand toward Israel's left hand and Manasseh in his left hand toward Israel's right hand. Israel stretched out his right hand and laid it instead upon Ephraim's head [the youngest] and his left hand upon Manasseh's head, guiding them deliberately, for Manasseh was the first born.... Then he said, "The Angel that redeemed me from all evil, bless the lads. Let my name be named on them and the name of my fathers, Abraham and Isaac. Let them grow into a multitude in the midst of the earth."

Joseph was dismayed that Ephraim was blessed before his older brother. His father, however, refused to change the position of his hands.

Genesis 48:25 [Genesis 48:19 KJV]

Israel replied, "I know it, my son. Manasseh will become a people and he shall also be great but truly, his younger brother shall be greater than he. His seed shall become a multitude of nations." [See Lehi in I Nephi, B. of M.]

(Summary)
Exodus 6:8

MOSES was also one of the descendants of the children of Israel. In about 1570 B.C., 800 years after Enoch, God chose him to lead the Hebrew people out of Egypt to the land of their heritage.

Exodus 32:13

The children of Israel will inherit the land forever.

(Summary)
Exodus 3:17-23

God instructed Moses to depart from Egypt into a land flowing with milk and honey, the land (Canaan, later called Israel) which He gave to Abraham, Isaac, and Jacob.

(Summary)
Numbers 14:1-45

The Israelites lacked trust in God's ability to fulfill His promises, and because they provoked Him repeatedly, they were not permitted to enter the Promised Land. Instead, they were forced to roam forty years in the wilderness. Most of the people who left Egypt died. Only Joshua, Caleb, and the children born in the desert were permitted to enter and live in the land of milk and honey.

(Summary)
Numbers Chapter 22, Chapter 23, and Chapter 24

The children of Israel wandered in the wilderness, at one point pitching their tents in the plains of Moab near the Jordan River by Jericho. The people of Moab were afraid of the strength of the Israelites, and their king sent for the prophet Balaam to curse them. Balaam sought God and discovered the children of Israel were a chosen people. God would not permit them to be cursed. (See the remarkable story of Balaam's donkey, Numbers 22:21-35.)

(Summary)
Numbers 24:14-19

The Moabite king was angry at Balaam's refusal to curse the Israelites, so the prophet informed him of the Latter Days and the future regarding the Israelites and Moabites. Verse 17 tells us that Balaam fell into a trance and prophesied the Second Coming of Jesus Christ: "Come, I will tell you what these people shall do to your people in the latter days.... I shall see Him but not now; I shall behold Him but not yet. There shall come a Star out of Jacob,[48] and a Scepter shall rise out of Israel, and it shall smite the corners of Moab and destroy all the children of Sheth.... Out of Jacob He that shall have dominion will come and shall destroy those who remain in the city."

---

[48] The "Star out of Jacob" and "He that shall have dominion" are references to Jesus Christ. The scepter represents his future kingship and power. In verse 14, Balaam indicates that this prophesy will happen in the latter days or after the Second Coming of Christ when he returns to destroy his enemies during the battle of Armageddon.

Meanwhile, God used the children of Israel's time in the wilderness to teach them responsibility as His chosen people. The Lord also warned that if future generations forsake their covenant, serving other gods, they will suffer severe punishment. Each time He said this, God also said, "The House of Israel shall know that I am the Lord their God."

(Summary)
Deuteronomy 29:12-29
Toward the end of the Hebrews' desert experience, Moses instructed those still living to make a covenant with the Lord on "this day." They would be God's people and He would be their God. This fulfilled the promise to their fathers, Abraham, Isaac, and Jacob. Moses warned that if they forsook the covenant, God's anger would be rekindled and they would be destroyed.

(Summary)
Deuteronomy 30:1-5
This verse records another promise to the children of Israel: God said, "And it shall come to pass when all these things have come upon you and you are scattered among all the nations where you have been driven by the Lord your God, you shall recall God's blessings, and curse of which you were warned."

Deuteronomy 30:19
God told the people, "…I have set before you life and death, blessing and cursing; therefore choose life that both you and your offspring may live."

Deuteronomy 30:2, 3, 5
"And you and your children shall return to the Lord your God and shall obey His voice according to all I command and do this with all your heart and soul. Then the Lord your God will turn your captivity and have compassion on you. He will return and gather you from all the nations where He has scattered you… and will bring you into the land, which your fathers possessed. You will possess it and He will do good things for you and multiply you above your fathers."

Deuteronomy 31:2,
Moses revealed he was 120 years old. The Lord did not permit him to cross the Jordan River into the Promised Land, but God assured Moses, He the Lord, would go before the people and they would possess the land.

(Summary)
JOSHUA succeeded Moses as leader of the Israelites. In 1228 B.C., the Israelites successfully occupied most of Canaan, an area much larger than the current land of Israel. Joshua divided the region among the tribes and inspired the people to renew their covenant with God. Nine tribes received an inheritance of land in Canaan. Two tribes accepted land on the other side of the Jordan River. The Levites (priests) received no inheritance. They were given instead a place within cities to live and cattle for their substance. Other needs of the priests were cared for by each of the tribes.

Joshua 1:1-4

God said to Joshua, "Arise, take all these people over the Jordan [river] into the land which I give the children of Israel. Every place that the sole of your foot touches, I have given to you from the wilderness of Lebanon to the great river Euphrates, all the land of the Hittites and to the great sea which shall be your coast."

The descendants of Ephraim and Manasseh (sons of Joseph/Egypt) also received an inheritance of land (Joshua 14:3-4 and Chapters 14-22). Much later, Lehi, a descendant of Ephraim, was told by God to leave Jerusalem with his family to avoid its coming destruction. He and his family eventually settled in the new world.

(Summary)

The Descendants of Ephram and the Book of Mormon Story: In the blessing Joseph received, he was described as a fruitful bough by a well whose branches run over the wall. (RLDS scholars interpreted this to mean that some of Joseph's descendants, called branches, would cross a great body of water as they traveled to a different land.) Many generations after Joseph's death, Lehi, a descendant of Ephram, left Jerusalem with his family before it was destroyed by the Babylonians (approximately 600 B.C.). After wandering in the wilderness for many years, Lehi and his family crossed the ocean with God's guidance, eventually arriving in Central America. (See the story in First and Second Nephi in the Book of Mormon.) Two groups of people descended from two of Lehi's sons. The Nephites descended from Nephi and the Lamanites descended from Nephi's older brother Laman. Both groups inhabited Central America for hundreds of years, but wars between them eventually destroyed the Nephite civilization. Descendants of the Lamanites met the first European explorers who landed on their shores.

I Nephi 1:53 [I Nephi 2:19 LDS]

And the Lord spoke to me saying, "You are blessed Nephi, because of your faith, for you have sought me diligently, with lowliness of heart. Inasmuch as you shall keep my commandments, you shall prosper and shall be led to a land of promise, a land which I have prepared for you which is choice above all other lands."

I Nephi 5:211-213 [I Nephi 18:22-25 LDS]

I, Nephi, guided the ship and we sailed toward the appointed location. After we had sailed for many days, we arrived and went forth upon the land and pitched our tents, calling it the Promised Land.

Ancient Israel

The First Kings of Israel, Saul, David and Solomon

By 1025 B.C., Saul was crowned king. His reign was followed by David who authored the book of Psalms. David is known as the boy who fought the giant, Goliath. He was obliged to fight the enemies of Israel, but as a man of war, he was not permitted by God to build the sacred temple.

About five hundred years separated Joshua's entrance into the Promised Land and the building of the first temple. David's son, King Solomon, received the privilege of building God's house, constructing it on the same mount where Abraham almost slew Isaac many years before. It required seven years to complete the building, and it stood in this location until destroyed by the Babylonians 416 years later. The temple is fully described in I Kings, Chapter 6.

The Kingdoms of Israel and Judah

After Solomon's death (between 922 and 926 B.C.), the nation of Israel split into two parts. The small southern kingdom of Judah included the city of Jerusalem. It was occupied by the tribe of Judah, which gave the kingdom its name. The tribe of Benjamin and some of the Levite priests settled there as well.

The larger kingdom, Israel, the land to the north, is where most of the remaining tribes finally settled. In the intervening years, many Israelites forgot their covenant and turned to other gods and interests. This eventually contributed to rivalry and war between the kingdoms of Israel and Judah, leaving both nations vulnerable to enemies. It is the responsibility of covenant partners to protect each other. Had they returned to the God of Israel, their covenant would have protected them against invaders.

The Jews descended from the tribe of Judah. Their rich literature and culture reach back to the dawn of recorded history. From the time of Adam, men encountered their creator, who required obedience to His laws, but at the same time provided for man's protection and needs.

Deuteronomy 5:6-21 THE TEN COMMANDMENTS

- I am the Lord thy God, which brought you out of the land of Egypt, from the house of bondage. You shall have no other gods before me.
- You shall not make any graven image, or likeness of anything that is in Heaven above, or in the earth beneath, or in the waters beneath the earth. You shall not bow down yourself to them, nor serve them; for I, the Lord thy God, am a jealous God, visiting the iniquity of the fathers upon the children... and showing mercy to thousands that love me and keep my commandments.
- You shall not take the name of the Lord your God in vain.
- Keep the Sabbath day and sanctify it, as the Lord, your God has commanded you.
- Honor your father and your mother.
- You shall not kill.

122

- You shall not commit adultery.
- You shall not steal.
- You shall not bear false witness against your neighbor.
- You shall not desire your neighbor's wife nor his house, his field, his manservant, or his maidservant, his ox, his ass, or anything that is your neighbors.

> **Deuteronomy 6:4, 5**
> *Hear, O Israel; the Lord our God is one Lord. And you shall love the Lord thy God with all your heart, and with all your soul, and with all your might.*

The Hebrews

The people who followed Moses from Egypt were given free agency, the ability to choose for themselves, but their choices were frequently outside the will of God. Throughout the years, the Israelites were often disobedient. Prophets continued to interact with the Creator, bringing His Word to the Hebrew nation, warning of terrible consequences if they continued to disobey the Lord. In spite of these prophetic warnings, both kingdoms (Israel and Judah) were involved in various forms of paganism, including the worship of Baal. This was a common failing of the early Israelites. They were surrounded by other cultures that often enticed them away from God. Still, in times of peril, they would repent and call on the Lord.

Two prophets, Amos and Hosea, repeatedly chastised the Hebrews for backsliding. They were reminded of numerous times, when they were obedient, God intervened on their behalf, but when they were prosperous, it was easy to forget their special status as a covenant people. Both prophets warned that there would be no salvation for either kingdom unless the moral and social decay of the citizens changed. These warnings, if heeded, would have saved Israel and Judah from numerous disasters.

It took centuries to fully instill the concept of one God in the thinking of the whole Hebrew nation. For this, they suffered persecution, poverty, enslavement and death in order to become the people God wanted them to be.

The Consequences of Broken Covenants with God

The Bible indicates that over centuries the people were severely disciplined because of their rebelliousness. Each time this happened, they lost their covenant protection and were subject to invasion by powerful enemies who conquered their lands and enslaved their people. The Assyrians were the first invaders. Then they were conquered and displaced for seventy years by the Babylonians. The Greeks followed and finally the Romans. A Jewish wit suggested, "If we are God's chosen people, why couldn't He have chosen someone else."

The Assyrian Conquest

By the time of the Assyrian invasion, in 721 B.C., the northern kingdom called Israel no longer held ten distinct Hebrew [49] tribes. Their locations and identities disappeared. Some people migrated elsewhere and were absorbed into new communities. Some

---

[49] Abba Eban, My People - The Story of the Jews, Behrman House, Inc., New York, New York, 1968

integrated with the kingdom of Judah. On occasion, foreign settlers intermarried with the native population, bringing pagan traditions. Few of the people retained their original heritage or worshipped the God of Abraham. By 700 B.C., the northern kingdom of Israel ceased to exist. In its place, a new community arose. These occupants were known as Samaritans, named after their capital, Samaria. This marked the end of Hebrew history and the beginning of Jewish history. The word, Jew, is an abbreviation of Judah.

Three tribes (Judah, Benjamin, and Levi) maintained their identity as a people, and continued to occupy the southern kingdom of Judah. Influenced by neighboring tribes, they began to worship false gods. Between 639 and 622 B.C., the prophets Zephaniah, Jeremiah, Nahum, and Habakkuk, condemned the religious corruption and paganism spreading throughout the kingdom. Influenced by their words, Josiah, the young Hebrew king, broke Judah's ties to the Assyrian religion. He restored the Law of Moses and asserted Judah's independence. However, at his death, Egypt took control of the land and Judah's freedom was lost.

The Babylonian Conquest

Before the Babylonian captivity, God sent some of the same prophets to warn the Jews again, that God would not tolerate their continued disobedience. Isaiah, Zephaniah, Jeremiah, Habakkuk and Micah preached repentance, warning that the people must return to the one real God or suffer. Like their forefathers, throughout the centuries, they failed to listen. Therefore, in 588 B.C.[50], Jerusalem was once again besieged and overthrown. Babylonian King Nebuchadnezzar II captured King Jehoiachin of Judah and his family, carrying them into exile. Judah's population was enslaved and Solomon's temple destroyed. Captivity lasted seventy years. At the end of that time, some Jews were permitted to return to Jerusalem to rebuild the temple and fortify its walls. This temple was much smaller, and had none of the grandeur of their former place of worship.

The Greek Conquest

In 169 B.C., the Greeks stormed the new temple in Jerusalem and stripped it once again of its treasures. The Greek ruler, Antiochus IV, forbade the practice of Judaism, including observing the Sabbath, circumcision, or owning the sacred scrolls. In an attempt to force the people to abandon their belief in God, he also brought pigs and idols into the temple. A family with five sons rallied the Jews to revolt against the Greeks to preserve their heritage. This small army, inspired by the slogan "Whoever is for the Lord, follow me," began a rebellion against incredible odds. The rebels were called the Maccabees, meaning, "hammer."

The rebellion lasted three years, but the Maccabees were victorious. In 164 B.C., the Jews reentered the temple, finding it totally desecrated. The eternal light that hung in the temple, unused for years, held only enough oil to last one day. Miraculously, the lamp continued to burn for eight days until more oil was obtained (I Maccabees 4:36-

---

[50] Thomas Robinson, The Bible Timeline , Thomas Nelson Publishers, Nashville, Tenn. 1992

51)[51]. This event is celebrated as the Feast of Hanukkah, the Festival of Lights. (I Macc. 4:52-59; II Macc. 10:1-8)

The Roman Conquest and King Herod

The Roman Republic began to grow in 184 B.C., and by 64 B.C., it incorporated the lands formerly belonging to Syria. Israel and Jerusalem were tiny troublesome parts of the new empire. Roman protectorates ruled the area, but the Jews tried to maintain life as usual. In 40 B.C., the Roman Senate appointed Herod (the Great) as the protectorate and king of Judea. Herod, who was half-Jewish, was under appointment as governor of Galilee.

We remember Herod as a vicious murderer, but he was also a skillful architect who made significant contributions to the cities of ancient Israel. He planned and rebuilt much of Samaria, constructed impressive towers on the Mediterranean coast, and designed and supervised the building of the city Caesarea Maritima, which became a major Roman port and administrative center for Palestine. Herod also developed a huge stone harbor for shipping and designed the city's sewers flushed out by tides of the sea. In 18 B.C., he repaired and enlarged the second Jewish temple in Jerusalem. Although it was smaller than Solomon's majestic structure, much of its beauty was restored. Unfortunately, Herod's zealous ambitions created many enemies. He was always prepared to kill in order to protect his throne. When travelers from distant countries inquired about a baby who was born "King of the Jews," Herod immediately tried to discover where the child could be found. Sending an army throughout the area, he executed all boys in Bethlehem under the age of two (Matthew 3:16). Nevertheless, he remained unaware the real heir to the throne of Israel had escaped.

Christ in Herod's Temple

Mary and Joseph took the infant Jesus to the temple in Jerusalem for circumcision[52] and blessing before fleeing from Herod into Egypt. At the age of twelve, Jesus sat within the temple walls discussing scripture with the elders. As an adult, He often taught in the outer courts. He chastised the hypocrisy of scribes and Pharisees and cleansed the temple of moneychangers. A few days before His death, He said to the apostles, "I tell you, not one stone on this temple shall be left. All of it shall be torn down" (Matthew 24:2).

In A.D. 70, Christ's prophecy concerning the destruction of the temple was fulfilled. The Jews provoked Rome for the last time. Soldiers destroyed the temple, tore down the walls surrounding Jerusalem, and massacred or scattered all of its citizens. This exile lasted 1,978 years (A.D. 70 to 1948). The common prayer of the people became "Next year in Jerusalem."

---

[51] Four books called Maccabees were written in Hebrew and translated into Greek. These books describe Jewish oppression and persecution from 222 to 164 B.C. The first two books are regarded as canonical by Roman Catholics, but Protestants consider all of them to be apocryphal.

[52] Circumcision (a traditional Jewish religious ceremony involving surgical removal of penile foreskin) is performed on Jewish boys eight days after their birth. A prayer is offered for the child, who becomes part of Abraham's Covenant.

Abba Eban's, *The Story of the Jews, a History*, records: "In the final act of Roman oppression, 500,000 Jews died or were sold as slaves." Destruction was followed by ruthless suppression of Jewish intellectual life. New laws deprived the people of every vestige of their religion; circumcision, keeping the Sabbath, and any observance of Jewish law was forbidden. Crimes punishable by torture and death included giving or receiving rabbinical ordination and any study of Jewish lore. Authorities were aware conferment of spiritual authority would revive a sense of community. However, new pupils were secretly ordained and the spark of Jewish identity was not quenched.

The Jews after the Exile from Jerusalem

Eban continues, "A few determined Jews remained hidden in Israel after 70 A.D. Many were rabbis or teachers. They sought a means to adapt Jewish life to the changing and troubled conditions of their world. It was necessary to consolidate a people decimated by wars, emigration and religious conversions. The old national institutions were replaced by a new focus on loyalty. The memory of the Temple and the glory of Israel were somehow to be sustained throughout each exiled generation. An invitation was issued to anyone who had studied to come and teach and anyone who had not studied to come and learn. These activities strengthened the resolve to maintain the identity of the exiles."

The initial movement was highly successful, but the time of renewal and intellectual growth was followed by centuries of fear, repression, persecution, eviction, torture, and death. From the sixth century on, the Children of Israel were continually harassed and compelled to move from place to place. They were either forced into Christian baptism or uprooted from the soil. Though they had no political home, at times they settled temporarily in peaceful and prosperous surroundings. However, in much of Europe and the Middle East they continued to represent an unwelcome entity. Poverty, numerous abuses, and hardship drove them from one country to another. For almost nineteen hundred years, the Chosen People fled individuals and governments determined to terrorize and kill them. Small groups settled where they could, but they were seldom warmly received. They had no civil rights, were subjected to special restrictions, and they were forced to live in primitive conditions. Thousands of Jewish books, including the Talmud, were burned. Even when they converted to Christianity, they were often accused of unfounded crimes, tortured, and put to death. Anti-Jewish laws were enacted in country after country, and the repression of these people was used as an example to vacillating Christians.

During Crusades, intended to liberate the Holy Land from other aggressors, tens of thousands of European Jews were murdered and their communities destroyed. The Inquisition, which began in Spain in 1464, was not abolished until 1834. In all, some 400,000 people, including many Jews, were tried for crimes against the church. In Spain and Portugal, about 30,000 people were put to death.

Old Testament books of Ezekiel Chapter 16 and Hosea Chapters 1-3 equated the Jews and the city of Jerusalem to an adulterous woman still loved by her husband. God was compared to the jealous husband whose patience was tried repeatedly, over centuries, as the people wavered between Him and other gods. His anger caused tremendous suffering among the Jews as He worked to perfect them and return the people to himself. The behavior of this stiff-necked people is not unlike the behavior of many worldly Christians today. However, the children of Israel have been chosen by God for a high purpose, and He will not rest until this purpose is fulfilled. In the latter days, God will bring all twelve tribes back to the nation of Israel, and there they will learn to seek the Lord their God. This is one of the most important signs of the Last Days. (See Jeremiah 31:31-36; Ezekiel 36:8-33; Zechariah 12:9-10.)

"Yet I am their sanctuary."

Ezekiel 11:16

The Jewish people in the Twentieth Century

Anti-Semitism, which already existed in much of the world, grew in alarming proportions at the beginning of the twentieth century. During the Great Depression, many of the world's problems were again blamed on Judah's descendants. The Nazis, under Adolf Hitler, used this pretense to massacre millions of Jewish men, women, and children. They were aided by other nations, including much of the Arab world. Targets also included Romanian Gypsies and outspoken Christian leaders, but none suffered as many losses as the 6 million murdered Jews.

During the Second World War, localized hate groups initiated riots, genocide, and slaughter. Jewish populations were walled inside ghettos. Hitler's armies herded millions of Jewish men, women, and children into overstuffed cattle cars for shipment to concentration camps. Armed guards patrolled outside the trains to prevent escape. Standing for hours, unable to move for the duration of the trip, Hitler's prisoners were without food, water, privacy, or toilet facilities. Jewish babies received no more mercy than adults did. At any opportunity, desperate mothers threw infants out of packed moving trains, hoping someone would find and rescue their child. In concentration camps, rape, torture, and death were daily events. Wherever they were exiled, religious Jews found strength in the promises of God and continued to look forward to a return to their homeland. The words "Next year in Jerusalem" became a sustaining slogan. The only hope for the Jews lay in their covenants with God.

To the great shame of the Christian world, many believers condoned brutality toward the Jews. Anti-Semitism continues within some Christian churches to this day. **No other body of people in the entire history of the world has undergone two thousand years of brutal mass persecution and continued to exist.** In spite of intense suffering and relentless oppression of the Jews, God has always preserved a remnant of His people. The Jews still exist because of their covenant with God, and they have a significant role to play in the Last Days.

> ### Ezekiel 11:16-20
> *God's promise says, "Although I have cast them [the children of Israel] far off among the heathen, and although I have scattered them among the countries, yet I am their sanctuary in the countries where they are. Therefore, I will gather them out from the other people and bring them together out of the countries where they have been scattered, and I will give them the land of Israel. And they shall come here and remove all the detestable things and abominations that are here. And I will give them one heart and I will put a new spirit within them, and I will take the stony heart out of their flesh, and will give them a heart of flesh so they may walk in my statutes and keep my ordinances and do them. And they shall be my people and I will be their God."*

> ### Ezekiel 16:60-62
> *"Nevertheless, I will remember my covenant with you [all the children of Israel] in the days of your youth and I will establish with you an everlasting covenant. Then, you shall remember your ways and be ashamed… and you shall know that I am the Lord."*

Because God will never break His covenants, all prophecies concerning the Jews in the Last Days will come to pass. As they do, the signs of the times will be fulfilled.

Jewish history and the present state of Israel have a tremendous impact on the world today. Until mankind accepts this tiny nation and the legitimate return of its people, terrorism and war in the Middle East will never be resolved. God has a plan for this land, and although it is not yet understood, His promises in the Old Testament are eternal. Over the next few years, as Israel discovers it must stand alone against a world that is increasingly anti-Semitic, the Lord will remind His people of their covenants and promises. As they repent and remember their covenants, they will play a pivotal role in the Last Days scenario. ISRAEL AND ITS CITIZENS WILL STAND, maligned, battered, and exhausted, but undefeated. The real battle is not fought by human beings. This battle belongs to the Lord.

Israel Today

God made the Israelites a marvelous promise:

> **Joshua 1:9**
> *"Have I not commanded you? Be strong and of good courage; be not afraid, neither be dismayed; for the Lord your God is with you wherever you go."*

God's covenants with the Children of Israel will be fulfilled in the Last Days.

(Summary)
Joshua 1:1-4
At the death of Moses, the Lord said to Joshua, "arise, go over the Jordan River and take all these people with you to the land, which I have given them. From the wilderness and Lebanon, even to the great Euphrates River, all the land of the Hittites, and to the great sea toward the going down of the sun. This shall be your coast."

These verses established the legal right of the children of Israel to all land from the wilderness of Lebanon to the great Euphrates River and all the land of the Hittites to the great sea, which will be Israel's coastline forever. This right is based on Israel's covenant relationship with God and on God's promises, which are part of this covenant.

All covenants between God and man are eternally irrevocable!

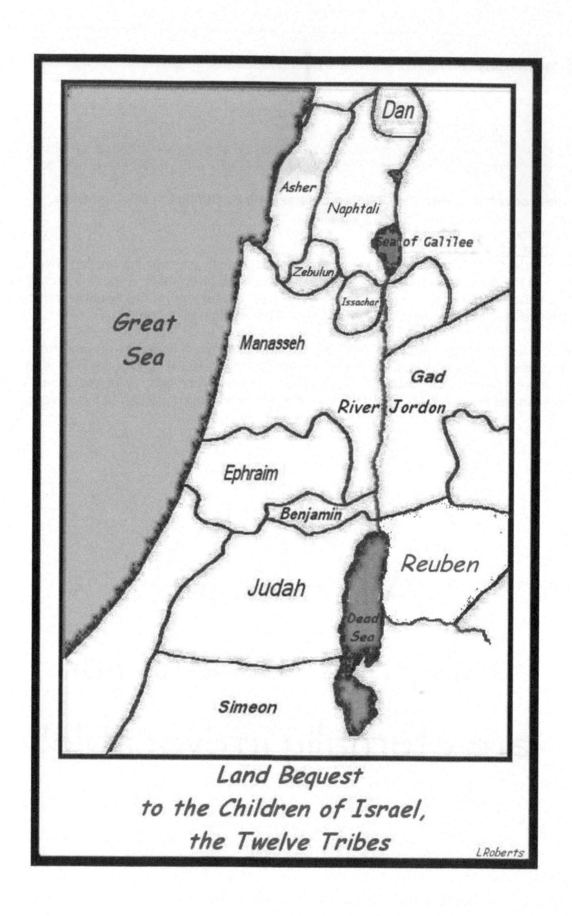

Land Bequest
to the Children of Israel,
the Twelve Tribes

L Roberts

"Arise, go over the Jordan River and take all these people with you to the land, which I have given them."

Joshua 1:2

Jesus said, "Now learn a parable of the fig tree: When its branches are still tender, and it begins to put forth leaves, you know that summer is near. So likewise, my elect who see all these things shall know that Christ is near, even at the door. But no one but my father knows the day or the hour not even the angels of God in Heaven."

Matthew
24:41-43
Mark 13:45-47
Luke 21:29-33,

... even at the door.

Chapter 9

What do the scriptures say about Israel in the Last Days?

Note: Some scripture is paraphrased in this chapter to clarify meaning.

SIGN 21
In the Last Days, the Children of Israel return to their Promised Land.

The scriptures clearly predict that the Jews will return to Israel in the Last Days. The purpose of their return is to fulfill the covenants God made with them, and to find Jesus Christ as their Lord and Savior.

DOCTRINE & COVENANTS 45:3f
[Revelation to Joseph Smith Jr., March 7, 1831]
When that day shall come, a remnant that has been scattered among all nations shall be gathered again, but they shall remain [in the lands where they are] until the times of the Gentiles is fulfilled. I have told you this concerning Jerusalem.

The return of the Jews to Israel is the most challenging and controversial topic in this book. It cannot be addressed in a few sentences or pages. It has impacted the political and moral life of the world today, and increases our appreciation of its importance as a last-day warning sign. Evidence in scripture indicates that the return of the Jews is of great importance to God, and therefore, worth our time to study.

Luke 21:25 [The Times of the Gentiles]
In the generation in which the time of the Gentiles is fulfilled, there shall be signs in the sun, and in the moon, and in the stars. Nations will be in great turmoil, like the sea and the roaring waves. The earth shall be troubled, and also the waters of the great deep.

The times of the Gentiles (Luke 21:25) ended when Israel succeeded in capturing Jerusalem and the Temple Mount during the 1967 Six-Day War. Jordan attacked Israel in an unsuccessful bid to remove the Jews from the land. Instead, Israel became sovereign over all Jerusalem, including the Temple Mount, and the biblical Old City. After almost 1,900 years of exile, the Jewish people, in fulfillment of God's prophetic plan, are returning to Israel in unparalleled numbers from countries all over the world.

Jeremiah 31:7-11
The Lord says, "Sing with gladness for Jacob, and shout among the chief of the nations. Write about, and praise, and say, O Lord, save thy people, the remnant of Israel. Behold, I will bring them from the north country, and gather them from the coasts of the earth, and with them the blind, and the lame, the woman with child who is about to give birth, and a great company shall return here. They shall come with weeping, and I will lead them with supplications. I will cause them to walk by the rivers of waters in a straight way so they will not stumble, for I am a father to Israel.... Hear the word of the Lord, O ye

nations and declare it in the isles afar off saying, 'He that scattered Israel will gather and keep him, as a shepherd keeps his flock.' For the Lord has redeemed Jacob, and ransomed him from the hand of the evil one who was stronger than he."

Ezekiel 34:11-16
God says, "Behold, I will search for my own sheep and seek them out as a shepherd seeks out his flock when he is among his sheep that are scattered. I will deliver them out of all the places where they have been scattered in the cloudy and dark day. I will bring them out from the people, and gather them from the countries, and will bring them to their own land, and feed them upon the mountains of Israel by the rivers, and in the inhabited places of the country."

Ezekiel 36:16-19
The word of the Lord came to me saying, "Son of man, when the House of Israel dwelt in their own land, they defiled it by going their own way and doing unclean things. Therefore, I poured my fury upon them, for the blood they shed upon the land and for their idols that polluted it. I scattered them among the heathen, and they were dispersed through the countries. I judged them according to their ways and the things they did."

Ezekiel 36:21-28
...I had pity for my Holy Name, which had been profaned by the House of Israel, among the heathen, wherever they went. So, I will sanctify my great and Holy Name, which you [the children of Israel] profaned in the midst of them, and the heathen shall know that I am the Lord when it will be done before their eyes. And, I will take you from among the heathen, and gather you out of all the countries, and will bring you into your own land. Then, I will sprinkle clean water on you, and you shall be clean from all your filthiness and your idols. And, I will give you a new heart, and a new spirit, and will take away the stony heart, and replace it with a heart of flesh. And, I will put my spirit within you, and cause you to walk in my statutes, and keep my judgments, so that you shall dwell in the land that I gave to your fathers. And, you shall be my people, and I will be your God.

Ezekiel 37:1-12, 14
The hand of the Lord was upon me, and carried me out in the Spirit of the Lord, and set me down in the midst of a valley, which was full of bones. I walked through the valley, and there were very many bones lying in the open, and they were very dry. And, God said to me, "Son of man, can these bones live?" And I answered and said, "O Lord God, You are the only one who knows."

So, He said to me, "Prophesy over these bones and say to them, O you dry bones, hear the word of the Lord! Behold, I will cause breath to enter into you, and you shall live. And, I will lay sinews upon you, and will bring flesh on you, and cover you with skin, and put breath in you, and you shall live, and you shall know that I am the Lord."

134

So, I prophesied as I was commanded. As I prophesied, there was a noise, the sound of shaking, and the bones came together, bone to bone. When I saw this, the sinews and the flesh came over them, and the skin covered them above, but there was no breath in them. Then God said to me, "Prophesy to the wind. Prophesy son of man and say to the wind, the Lord God says, come from the four winds. Breathe upon these who were slain so they may live." So I prophesied as He commanded me, and the breath came into them, and they lived, and stood up upon their feet, an exceedingly great army. Then He said to me, "Son of man, these bones are the whole House of Israel. They say, 'Our bones are dried, and our hope is lost; we are cut off from our parts.' Therefore, prophesy and say to them, this is what the Lord

God says; Behold, O my people, I will open your graves, and cause you to come up out of them, and bring you into the land of Israel. And, you shall know that I am the Lord when I bring you out of your graves. And, I shall put my Spirit in you, and you shall live, and I shall place you in your own land. Then, you shall know that I the Lord have spoken it and performed it," says the Lord.

Ezekiel 37:21-28
Say to them [the whole House of Israel], "This is what the Lord God says; Behold, I will take the children of Israel from among the heathen, wherever they have gone, and will gather them on every side, and bring them into their own land. I will make them one nation in the land upon the mountains of Israel; and one King shall be king to them all. They shall no more be two nations; neither shall they be divided into two kingdoms any more. Neither shall they defile themselves any more with their idols or any detestable thing, nor with any of their transgressions; for I will save them out of all their dwelling places where they have sinned, and I will cleanse them so they shall be my people, and I will be their God."

"And, David, my servant, [Jesus Christ] shall be king over them; and they all shall have one shepherd. They shall walk in my judgments, and observe my statutes, and do them. They shall dwell in the land where their fathers dwelt. I have given it to Jacob my servant, and they will live there, even they and their children, and their children's children forever; and my servant David[53] shall be their prince forever. Moreover, I will make a covenant of peace with them; it shall be an everlasting covenant with them; and I will place them, and multiply them, and will set my sanctuary in the midst of them forever. My tabernacle will also be with them; yes, I will be their God, and they shall be my people. And, the heathen shall know that I the Lord do sanctify Israel when my sanctuary shall be in the midst of them forever."

---

[53] NIV Study Bible, International Bible Society, Colorado Springs, Co. 1978, "My servant David" is a reference to the coming Messianic ruler, the Christ. Christ is called David because he is a descendant of King David and will once again, in the Last Days, bring Israel into her homeland and establish her as the people of God

<u>I Nephi 7:17-25</u>

After our offspring are scattered, the Lord God will proceed to do a marvelous work among the Gentiles which shall be of great worth to our descendants; it will be as though they are being nourished by the Gentiles, carried in their arms and on their shoulders. And, it shall also be of worth to the Gentiles, and not only to the Gentiles, but to all the House of Israel who will come to know about the covenants of the Father to Abraham, who said, "In your offspring all people of the earth shall be blessed. However, you must know that all the people of the earth cannot be blessed until God makes bare His arm in the eyes of the nations.

Therefore, the Lord God will proceed to make bare His arm[54] in the eyes of all the nations, bringing about His covenants and His gospel to those who are of the House of Israel. Therefore, He will bring them out of captivity, and they shall be gathered together to the lands of their inheritance. And, they shall be brought out of obscurity and out of darkness, and they shall know the Lord is their Savior and their Redeemer, the mighty one of Israel.

These and many other scriptures testify of God's intent to bring the children of Israel back to their homeland in the Last Days. It is fascinating to watch, since this is taking place right now.

The New Country Israel and Events since AD 1900

At the turn of the century, the land called Palestine was sparsely inhabited by a mixture of Arabs, Jews, and Bedouins living together in an uneasy peace. In 1920, the League of Nations placed Palestine under British mandate. The British had allies among the Arab nations, and although both Jews and Arabs lived together in the land for generations, the British and Arabs strongly contested further Jewish settlement in the Middle East. At approximately the same time, the rest of the world suffered through two great wars and a major economic depression. In 1939, pro-fascist countries of Germany, Italy, Japan, Rumania, Bulgaria, and Hungary formed a military alliance, for mutual strength. In Germany, Adolph Hitler, a power-hungry, ruthless demagogue emerged and began to provide convincing, impassioned direction the people desperately sought. He persuaded gullible sympathizers and his allies that the Jews were responsible for the world's grave and deteriorating situation. As Hitler gained control over Germany, he terrorized the Jews. Mandatory armbands, with a visible Star of David, identified them as undesirables in the German population.

During the Second World War (1939-45), as Hitler's armies conquered much of Europe, he ordered the Jewish population deported to concentration camps. There they worked as slaves for the Nazi war machine and were used in bizarre medical experimentation. When no longer of value, 6,000,000 (six million) people of Hebrew descent were killed by firing squad, gas chambers, electric shock, and other means of torture. Crematoriums worked around the clock to destroy evidence of bodies thrown into the fire, dead and alive. The Americans who liberated these camps in 1945 were overwhelmed by the horror of living skeletons wandering aimlessly through filth, mud, mass graves, and unburied dead. Gas chambers and crematoriums provided their own

---

[54] Baring the arm was comparable to girding up the loins symbolizing manly action and fighting strength. Isaiah 52:10 and Ezekiel 4:7

silent testimony. The world expressed horror and shock, but no country welcomed Jewish refugees.

Without a home, the hearts of the Jews turned to their Promised Land. A few Jews continued to live and farm in various parts of Israel after most of their brothers were banished by the Romans. A small Jewish population existed for centuries in Galilee, and colonization that was more formal began in 1856 near Jaffa. During the rest of the nineteenth century, small numbers of Jews continued relocating to various parts of Israel.

After Germany's surrender in 1945, aliyah (the Jewish return) to Palestine expanded.

Seeking a place of their own, "wandering Jews" arrived in their Promised Land in ever-increasing numbers. After the Second World War, the need for a Jewish homeland became an urgent matter. Between April 1945 and January 1948, refugees attempted to reach the Holy Land in sixty-three clandestine, overcrowded ships. Fifty-eight ships were intercepted by the British, and prevented from landing[55]. Some of the refugees reached Israel and began to rebuild their lives. Those who were caught were prevented from entering the Holy Land, while at the same time; they were not welcome to return to their countries of origin.

Speaking as chairman of the Zionist Executive Committee, November 28, 1945, David Ben-Gurion declared, "We, the Jews in the Land of Israel, do not want to be killed; we want to live. But I must tell Ernest Bevin and other members of Parliament (Great Britain) that we are ready to die rather than give up three things:

- Freedom for Jewish immigration
- Our right to rebuild the waste places of our homeland
- The political independence of our people in their own land[56]"

In 1947, defying pressure from Great Britain and the Arab countries, the United Nations divided Palestine, creating designated homelands for both Jews and Arabs. The Jewish portion was renamed Israel. Against bitter opposition, Jewish immigration to the Holy Land increased. The incentive was freedom, and a home that would be their own. By May 1948, 120,000 Jews had immigrated to their new country. In that same year, when the British relinquished their colony, the land became a battleground. The first war between Jews of Israel and their Arab neighbors was fought for control of the land granted to the Jews (May 1948-49). Even though the two groups had clashed before, the decision to divide the country turned existing malevolence into brutal warfare.

Five Arab armies invaded Israel while radio broadcasts warned Arab inhabitants to flee the country, so invading armies could move in quickly. At the time of the invasion, the Jews were badly outnumbered. To the amazement and dismay of the world, they were victorious. All invading armies were defeated, and the new nation of Israel gained more land than the U.N. proposed. At the same time, Egypt gained control of the Gaza Strip, and Jordan obtained the West Bank.

---

[55] David Ben-Gurion, The Jews in Their Land (Garden City, NY: Doubleday, 1966)
[56] David-Ben-Gurion, The Jews in Their Land (Garden City, NY: Doubleday, 1966

The Arab evacuees, who expected to return home after a quick victory, became homeless. At first, Israel tried to make peaceful arrangements with her former inhabitants. Displaced people were invited to return to their own land and resume their lives. For most of these refugees, this was not an option. Their loathing toward Jews was so intense that they preferred to wait for a future Arab military victory before their return. Those who returned became full-fledged, if troublesome, citizens of the new country. **The remaining Arab refugees had no place to go. Huge Arab nations that promoted the war surrounded them, but refused the refugees the courtesy of a new home in any of their countries. Miserable refugee camps were created immediately outside the borders of Israel. The displaced people living in the camps [57] became known as Palestinians.**

©R.S. Blain Photography and Graphics

Insane hatred for the Jews created a fanatical desire for revenge[58] among Palestinians. This was fueled by Arab countries, which induced hostility, and manipulated the exiles toward ridding the world of the nation of Israel. Today, schools in refugee camps teach children to glorify in jihad (Arab holy war). Children dream of becoming suicide bombers for Allah. Encouraged, these people continue to destroy themselves in order to wipe out the Jewish homeland.

---

[57] Ibid

[58] The Haj by Leon Uris, Doubleday & Company, Garden City, New York, 1984 provides an excellent look into Arab thought during this period of history

Bare Facts about the Modern Nation of Israel

Israel is one of the smallest nations in the world. It consists of approximately 8,040 square miles, the exact size changing whenever boundaries fluctuate between Israel and Arab nations. This tiny country is half the size of Jordan, and like Lebanon, is completely dwarfed by its huge neighbors. Israel occupies a narrow strip of land on the coast of the Mediterranean Sea. This strip forms a strategic land bridge between the Mediterranean and the Arab countries to the east of it. Compared with Its neighbors it is tiny, but throughout much of history, whoever controlled this parcel of land also controlled commerce, in most of the mid-east. Its location is exposed, and vulnerable to attack. Egypt, Lebanon, Syria, Jordan, and Saudi Arabia at its southernmost tip are within a two-hour drive of Jerusalem. Iraq, Iran, Turkey, Russia, Afghanistan, and Pakistan are no farther away than an hour by air. These surrounding countries repeatedly harass and invade the Jewish homeland. Israel has no friends in the vicinity!

For thousands of years, wars have been fought over the land of the Jews. Commerce is no longer the point of contention; religion, ethnicity, bigotry, and greed are! Today, Israel is the most highly contested piece of ground in the world. It is hard to believe a country so small has so much international attention. Its existence is a major thorn in the side for its much larger, wealthy, Arab neighbors. Arab Muslims are determined to kill all Jews and turn the nation of Israel into an Arab/Palestinian state. Therefore, Israel's existence is a major concern for the rest of the world.

> **Ezekiel 38:18-20, 23-SOON GOD WILL SHATTER HIS SILENCE!**
> *"It shall come to pass, when the enemy from the north shall come against the land of Israel, my fury shall come up in my face," says the Lord God. "In my jealousy and in the fire of my wrath, I speak. In that day, there shall be a great shaking in the land of Israel. The fishes of the sea, and the fowls of the Heaven, and the beasts of the field, all creeping things that creep upon the earth, and all the men that are upon the face of the earth, shall shake at my presence. And the mountains shall be thrown down, and the steep places shall fall, and every wall shall fall to the ground…. Thus, I will magnify myself, and sanctify myself. I will be known in the eyes of many nations, and they shall know that I am the Lord."*

"I will be known in the eyes of many nations, and they shall know that I am the Lord."

Ezekiel 38:23

Middle East

In the above image, the State of Israel is shown in black at the left of the arrow. She is located on the border of the Mediterranean Sea and is surrounded by Afghanistan, Africa, Egypt, Ethiopia, Saudi Arabia, Lebanon, Somalia, Syria, Iraq, Iran, Turkey and more. Notice the size of the Arab nations that surround her. It is ludicrous to believe that Israel is a threat to her huge, oil-rich neighbors. NOTICE: THE SHAPE AND SIZE OF ISRAEL MAY HAVE CHANGED BY THE TIME OF THE PRINTING OF THIS BOOK.

Wars and Terrorism in Modern Israel

Because of continual threat of warfare and terrorism, Israel must be constantly alert for aggression from its neighbors. The Palestine Liberation Organization (PLO), created three years before the famous Six-Day War, was dedicated to overtaking Israel and killing the Jews. The organization carried out terrorist attacks in 1964, 1965, and 1966. At that time, the Jews were not in possession of East Jerusalem, the West Bank, the Gaza Strip, the Golan Heights, or the Sinai Peninsula.[59] In 1967, the entire Arab world prepared methodically for the extinction of Israel. The rest of the world was aware of this plan, but looked the other way.

WARS: **The Six-Day War (June 5, 1967)** was an unconventional struggle with a surprising outcome. Badly outnumbered again, Israel won an incredible victory and succeeded in occupying additional land, including the city of Jerusalem and the Temple Mount. As a goodwill gesture, they immediately offered to return the Sinai to Egypt and the Golan Heights to Syria. This offer was met with the Arab League's famous "Three NOs": no peace, no recognition, and no negotiation[60]. **The Yom Kippur War (October 6-22, 1973)** was an additional attempt by the Arab nations to eliminate the Jews. Although severely outnumbered, Israel defended itself successfully again.

TERRORISM: Arab terrorism has increased since 1973, and is more difficult to control. Suffering is enormous on the part of all combatants.[61] The current membership of the United Nations blames the nation of Israel for the instability within the region and at the same time refuses to recognize acts of aggression by the Palestinians and the Arabs. The U.N. also insists that Israel's "apartheid" wall (a concrete protection barrier that separates the combatants) must be removed. Arab nations continue to create bitter hostility among Palestinian refugees, especially the young. Schools are terrorist recruiting grounds. Students are trained as suicide bombers, encouraged to die to reclaim Israel as Palestinian territory. With the promise of gifts of young virgins in the afterlife, the youth become walking death traps threatening the entire Jewish population. Conflicts rage, and after sixty years, the nation of Israel remains a battleground. Burned-out tanks lie along the roadsides leading to Jerusalem, and Palestinians continue to live in squalid camps along the borders of Israel.

A Homeland for the Palestinians

If the Palestinians wanted a viable state of their own, they could have negotiated it with Israel long ago. However, land for the Palestinians has always been a political issue rather than one of genuine concern for a homeless people. The total number of displaced Palestinians who fled Israel in 1948 is estimated to be 650,000 individuals. Most who left the country are no longer alive, but the number of Palestinians now wishing to enter Israel exceeds five million, far more than the tiny country can accommodate.

---

[59] Michael Boren, Six Days of War: June 1967 and the Making of the Modern Middle East (Oxford University Press, 2002) N.Y., N.Y; Internet: Wikipedia, www.wikipedia.org, "Israel, Occupied Territories."

[60] Ibid

[61] Some Arab mothers actually encourage their children to become suicide bombers. This is considered an honor for the family.

The Palestinians are Arab Muslims.

They share a common language, culture, and religion with the large Arab nations surrounding them. Saudi Arabia, Syria, and Iran are oil rich and sparsely populated. These nations have an abundance of unoccupied land that could easily have accommodated all of the disfranchised people. Much of the land is desert, but the Arabs, including the Palestinians, have always lived in desert lands. Despite this logic, none of these huge nations (the original invaders of Israel) welcomes the refugees into their countries or makes efforts to improve the lives of the people they displaced. Instead, the exiled people are forced to live in squalid refugee camps that breed violence and terrorism against the Jews. The Palestinian refugees are unsuspecting pawns. They are led, blindly and deviously, by the rest of the Arab world, which continues to use them in the fight against Israel.

The book, *Lessons from the Land of the Bible*, by Clarence H. Wagner[62] says, "Palestine originally included the region now occupied by Jordan, plus all the land west of the Jordan River. In 1948 the area west of the river became Israel, the West Bank, and Gaza." Arab propaganda states 'Israel usurped all of Palestine, leaving the Palestinian people with nothing'. **This is not the case.** "In 1946, when Transjordan achieved independence and became Jordan, Palestine was artificially redefined to include only the area west of the Jordan River, thereby reducing it to 20% of its original size. In 1947, the U.N. divided that 20% into an Arab state and a Jewish state. This did not change the fact Jordan was/is still part of Palestine [63] with over 70% of its population being Palestinian Arab. When Jordan ignored the U.N. partition and annexed the West Bank in 1949, Palestinian Arabs under the Jordanian umbrella controlled 82.5% of the Palestine Mandate given to the Jews, while the Jewish state held a bare 15.5%. Jordan remains a Palestinian/Arab state in territory and by population now occupying 80% of the original Palestine. Despite Arab claims, Israel did not usurp all of Palestine nor were the Arabs left without a Palestinian state[64]."

The Big Mistake

After the Six-Day War of 1967, in which the Jews were victorious, Israel occupied Gaza and part of the West Bank. They began building small kibbutzim, or community settlements, as protective barriers between Israel's larger cities and the surrounding Arab nations. These outreaching communities were vehemently opposed by neighboring Arab states. Coercing the United Nations and the United States, the Arabs demanded that Israel remove the settlers. On August 20, 2005, Israel, buckling under pressure, forcibly removed the Jewish settlers and destroyed the Jewish homes, businesses, and farms. This violent expulsion of the Jews, provisioned the land for Palestinian refugees to move in and build homes. At the same time, it was supposed to encourage and improve peaceful relations between them and Israel. IT DID NOT! There were immediate overt acts of aggression toward the Jews who fought back, as Palestinian terrorist organizations (Hamas and Fatah) reclaimed the land! Refugees who wanted homes were caught in between. Armed camps and those who govern them broke the rules of the original U.N. agreement, and instead immediately agitated

---

[62] Clarence H. Wagner Jr., Lessons from the Land of the Bible, New Revised Edition Jerusalem, Israel , Published by Bridges for Peace, Faith Publishing, 1998).

[63] Facts and Logic About the Middle East, FLAME, Gerardo Joffe, President, San Francisco, Ca. 2008., www.factsandlogic.org.

[64] Ibid

142

venomous hostilities and terrorism against Israel. Today (August 31, 2011), turmoil continues within the Palestinian communities. The refugees who want peace continue to live in constant fear.

Gaza's proximity to all parts of Israel places extremists in excellent positions to execute murderous attacks on the Jewish settlements and cities. The West Bank offers the same opportunities. In spite of negotiation promises, communities in Israel are frequently bombarded and heavily damaged by enemy missiles fired from Gaza and the West Bank. Jewish soldiers are often kidnapped, tortured, and killed. In retaliation for these attacks, the Jews fight back; terrorists and Palestinian refugees lose their lives and the world continues to blame the Jews.

Tragically, Palestinians continue to live as exiles because of their political value as pawns for the Arab nations. Anti-Semitism and propaganda successfully cloud real issues. Palestinians are portrayed as victims of a mighty and aggressive Israel, yet the avowed goal of these "victims" and most of their Arab brothers continue to be complete eradication of Israel and the death of every Jew. They are assisted in this by much of the world that still denies the Jewish right to live as a free people. Incredibly, most of the global community condemns Israel instead of the Arab nations. Arab and rogue countries that are members of the United Nations encourage young Palestinians to fight and die as martyrs, for a cause that will never be successful. The years of poverty, hatred, and bloodshed were avoidable. Now the situation is so complex that only the return of Jesus Christ will resolve these issues.

The Islamic religion plays a major part in the current world crisis. The ultimate goal of radical Muslims is far more than Jewish genocide. Their intent is to create a totally Muslim world. They are determined to convert all of the world's people to Islam and are committed to doing this by any means possible. Christians and countries that support Israel are regarded as mortal enemies of Allah. Many Muslims in the United States and elsewhere live peacefully with their neighbors. **HOWEVER, THE MILITANT FORCES WITHIN THIS RELIGION ARE A THREAT TO PEACEFUL EXISTENCE OF ALL PEOPLE EVERYWHERE.**

An amazing set of DVD's titled "Against All Odds Israel Survives" is distributed by Questar. These document miracles of biblical proportions in this land since 1948.

Israel welcomes her refugees.

In today's unsettled, warlike atmosphere, new immigrants continue to make their aliyah (immigration or return) to the nation of Israel. This places a great economic hardship on the country because of the terrorist situation. Israel, which had been fully self-supporting, now needs financial assistance. The cost of self-protection hurts the whole economy, yet the tiny nation continues to welcome thousands of new Jewish refugees as they return to their homeland. The country is assisted with funding from many American Jews and from groups such as the International Fellowship of Christians and Jews (IFCJ)[65]. Immigrants are provided with basic needs: food, shelter, and classes to learn the Hebrew language. Day care is provided for children so parents can work. Appropriate jobs and housing are located as quickly as possible. The talents of the new people benefit the country and help it grow.

It is hard to fathom that while Israel continues to adopt and resettle persecuted, poverty-stricken Jews from around the world, wealthy Arab states refuse to assist their Palestinian brothers.

The Bible indicates there will be wars and bloodshed in the land of Israel until Christ returns. None of it, the wars, the bloodshed or the violence will stop the return of God's people to their homeland.

The Father will gather them together again and give them Jerusalem for the land of their inheritance.

III Nephi 9:71

---

[65] Information about the International Fellowship of Christians and Jews can be obtained at info@ifcj.org or www.ifcj.org or (800) 486-8844

SIGN 22
The Tribes of Judah and the House of Israel will be reunited.

Jeremiah 3:17, 18
At that time, they shall call Jerusalem the throne of the Lord and all nations shall be gathered into it, to the name of the Lord, to Jerusalem; neither shall they walk any more after the imagination of their evil hearts.

DNA marking[66] is proving to be one of the most exciting scientific developments in recent years. Among its many benefits, it is helping to identify some of the tribes of Israel that have been missing for thousands of years. The three tribes listed below have recently been discovered in very unlikely places. DNA markings will hasten the discovery of all twelve tribes.

The B'nei Ethiopia, Children of Cush is a Hebrew tribe that was discovered in Africa just before the turn of the twenty-first century. Until very recently, they were unaware that Hebrew people still existed outside their own community. Like other observant Jews, they had faithfully maintained their unique religious and cultural heritage throughout their forced exile from Israel. The excitement in learning that the Jewish nation exists in Israel awakened their desire to return to the land of their fathers. Because they were persecuted in Africa, making aliyah (return) to Israel was a welcome option. With the help of relief organizations, many of them made a successful return to the Holy Land, integrating into a completely new culture[67].

Early in 1998, Beta Yisrael (House of Israel), a group of "lost" Jews, was discovered in Ethiopia. They were found in the Kwara region[68] of the country. The international rescue committee's DNA program has undisputed proof that they are descendants of the tribe of Daniel.

The B'nei Menash, Children of Manasseh, were located[69] in India. With the help of the International Fellowship of Christians and Jews (IFCJ), this impoverished community is making its aliyah to Israel.

The IFCJ coordinates and finances the return of displaced Jews to the land of Israel. Its president, Rabbi Yechiel Eckstein, made an "eye-popping" statement in his November 2007 newsletter. "Tens of thousands of Jewish people from Asia, Africa, South America and Russia are calling out for help in making their long awaited aliyah to Israel.... These scattered groups trace their Jewish lineage to the ten original tribes of Israel lost after Israel's conquest by Assyria[70] in 722 B.C.E." The Jews returning to Israel from Russia, the Ukraine, South and Central America, Europe, Asia, the Arab countries, and the United States are welcomed with open arms. This migration has never before taken place in all of world history. Israel will soon be one of the most successfully integrated

---

[66] DNA Markings-see http://en.wikipedia.org/wiki/DNA
[67] Newsletter: SHORESH, The International Fellowship of Christians and Jews, Chicago, Ill. 2005-2009, info@ifcj.org or www.ifcj.org.
[68] Ibid
[69] Ibid
[70] Ten Lost Tribes-Wikipedia http://en.wikipedia.org/wiki/Ten-Lost-Tribes.

countries in the world. This is one of the most important indications that we are indeed in the Last Days[71].

It is also exciting to discover the growing number of Messianic Jews. Small clusters of believers, descendants of the earliest Jewish Christians, have existed since the time of Christ. Other Jews found Jesus through the centuries. Many places in the world have Messianic congregations, and at present, young Messianic Jews actively seek Jewish converts throughout the United States, Europe and Israel. One of these groups, Jews for Jesus, recently completed large and successful evangelistic programs [72] in New York City, Chicago, and other American cities (2006-07).

On Sunday, March 2, 2008, the History Channel ran a documentary on the Lost Ark of the Covenant. The exciting thing about the documentary was an interview with an African tribe who believe they are descendants of the Lost Tribes. Their oral history indicates they were guided by Jeremiah and other priests to their present location, not far from Egypt. Their DNA is convincing and so are their customs, which are quite similar to ancient Hebrew practices. At present, they have no plans to migrate to Israel.

Latter Day Saints believe some American Indian tribes are also descendants of Jacob through his son Joseph and grandson Ephram. Recent DNA tests by National Geographic and various forensic bodies seem to disprove this theory. However, there are numerous American Indian tribes, and it is unlikely that tests have been performed on all of them. Actual descendants of Ephram may still be identified, adding to the known tribes of the Children of Israel.

> ### III Nephi 9:71 [20:33 LDS]
> *The Father will gather them [the Jews] together again and give them Jerusalem for the land of their inheritance. [See III Nephi 10:5-8, 21:26-29 LDS.]*

> ### Jeremiah 3:17, 18
> *At that time they shall call Jerusalem the throne of the Lord… In those days the House of Judah shall walk [again] with the House of Israel,…*

> ### Ezekiel 37:22
> *I will make them one nation in the land upon the mountains of Israel, and one king [Jesus Christ] shall be king to them all. They shall no more be two nations; neither shall they be divided into two kingdoms any more.*

God fulfills His covenants.

In the midst of struggle, the Jewish people are returning to their homeland. The rest of the tribes are beginning to follow. God is fulfilling His covenant with the Twelve Tribes of Israel, and today, the land literally "blooms like a rose" (Isaiah 35:1, 2). Innovative farming techniques are reclaiming the desert; groves of fruit trees grow along the Dead Sea, oranges blossom, bearing fruit, early in the year. Until the terrorist attacks, Israel

---

[71] "Lost Tribes of Israel," NOVA, www.pbs.org/wgbh/nova/transcripts/2706israel.html, and Ten Lost Tribes, Wikipedia http://en.wikipedia.org/wiki/Ten_Lost_Tribes.

[72] Information about this Messianic body can be obtained by writing to Jews for Jesus, 60 Haight Street, San Francisco, CA 94102-5895.

grew most of the food required by its population. It is the only place in the mid-east where tourists from the west can safely eat fresh fruit and vegetables[73].

Psalm 85:12
The Lord shall give that which is good; and our land shall yield her increase.

Isaiah 29:29 [29:17 KJV]
"Behold," says the Lord of hosts, "I will show the children of men that in a very little while Lebanon shall be turned into a fruitful field and the fruitful field shall be esteemed as a forest."

Isaiah 35:1, 2
The wilderness and the solitary places shall be glad, and the desert shall rejoice and blossom as the rose.

Ezekiel 36:35
And they shall say, "This land that was desolate has become like the Garden of Eden; and the waste and desolate and ruined cities are fenced and inhabited."

Cities in Israel are modern, progressive, and technologically advanced. During times of peace, communities are clean and beautiful; the museums and gardens are some of the best in the world. History and archeology are alive in the twenty-first century. The integrated nation is determined to survive. Terrorism and bombing of cities in Israel take an enormous toll on the population; however, the potential for future greatness is evident in the heart of Israel's current pandemonium. In recent years, the citizens have suffered severe economic hardship, but they are prepared to fight for their existence, so the country maintains its military and civilian strength.

Unfortunately, Jerusalem is the target of many missile attacks. Since the turn of the twenty-first century, the beautiful city has become Israel's poorest metropolis. It is divided between Jewish and Palestinian populations and more than 300,000 Israelis fled the area after 1967. More recent information, provided by the Jerusalem Institute for Israel Studies, indicates an additional 17,200 Jews left the city in 2006 and 10,900 Arabs moved in. Demographic trends and increased violence led the state to construct a 465 mile barrier surrounding and dividing Jerusalem. This creates new challenges, but God has not changed His mind. His city will be reborn!

Isaiah 52:1
Awake! Awake! Put on thy strength O Zion. Put on thy beautiful garments, O Jerusalem the holy city. Henceforth the uncircumcised and the unclean shall no more come into you.

I Nephi 4:33
And after they are restored, they shall no more be confounded neither shall they be scattered again. [See Isaiah 4:1-5; 60:1-22; Zechariah 1:17; 2:1-13]

---

[73] Arab countries us fresh human waste as fertilizer. People from the west often become deathly ill when eating uncooked fruits and vegetables in these countries.

"Awake! Awake! Put on thy strength O Zion."

Isaiah 52:1

SIGN 23
In the Last Days the Jews Will Control all Israel Including Jerusalem and the Temple Mount.

Genesis 13:13 [I.V. only]
The Lord said to Abram, "Remember the covenant which I made with you for it shall be an Everlasting Covenant and you shall remember the days of Enoch, your ancestor."

Genesis 13:14 [13:15 KJV]
I give you and your children all the land, which you see forever …

Genesis 14:40 [I.V. only]
God blessed Abram and gave him riches and honor and lands for an everlasting possession, according to the covenant, which He had made.

Ezekiel 11:16-20, God's Promise to the Children of Israel
"This is what the Lord God says: 'Although I have cast them [the Children of Israel] far off among the heathen, and although I have scattered them among the countries, yet I am their sanctuary in the countries where they are.' Therefore, God says: 'I will gather them out from the other people, and bring them together out of the countries where they have been scattered, and I will give them the land of Israel, and they shall come here and remove all the detestable things and abominations that are here. I will give them one heart, and I will put a new spirit within them, and I will take the stony heart out of their flesh, and will give them a heart of flesh so they may walk in my statutes and keep my ordinances and do them. They shall be my people, and I will be their God.'"

Joel 3:16-18
[In that day] the Lord shall roar out of Zion and utter His voice from Jerusalem, and the Heavens and earth shall shake. But, the Lord will be the hope of His people and the strength of the children of Israel, and they shall know I am the Lord their God dwelling in Zion. My mountain, Jerusalem, shall become holy, and no strangers shall pass through her anymore. The mountains shall drop down new wine and the hills shall flow with milk. All the rivers of Judah shall flow with waters, and a fountain shall come forth out of the house of the Lord and shall water the valley of Shittim.

Zechariah 2:4, 5
…Jerusalem shall be inhabited as a town without walls for the multitude of men and cattle therein. For I will be like a wall of fire round about her and will be the glory in the midst of her.

Zechariah 14:9-11
Then the Lord shall be King over all the earth. In that day, there shall be one Lord and His name one. And the land shall become as a plain from Geba to Rimmon [the area south of Jerusalem], and it shall be lifted up and inhabited within the walls and gates of Jerusalem. And men shall dwell in it, and there shall be no more utter destruction. Jerusalem shall be safely inhabited.

III Nephi 9:67-69, 71 [20:29, 33 LDS]

"I will remember the covenant which I have made with my people. I will gather them together in my own due time and will give them again the land of their fathers for an inheritance, which is the land of Jerusalem [Israel], which is the Promised Land to them forever," says the Father.

"Then, when the fullness of my gospel is preached to them and they believe in me, that I am Jesus Christ the Son of God, and they pray to the Father in my name,... the Father will gather them together again and give them Jerusalem for the land of their inheritance. Then, they shall break forth in joy and sing together, for the Father has comforted His people, and He has redeemed Jerusalem."

(Fulfillment)

The fulfillment of these prophecies is taking place in incremental stages. From AD 70 until 1967, most of the city of Jerusalem, including the Temple Mount, was unavailable to the Jews. After the Six-Day War, the entire city of Jerusalem, the remaining portion of the West Bank (land west of the Jordan River) and the Gaza Strip became part of Israel. At that time, the Jews also regained control of the Temple Mount and the Western Wall[74]. This wall is the holiest spot in the world for Israelites. It is the last remaining vestige of the Jerusalem temple where Jesus walked, taught, and prayed. It draws tourists from all nations, Jewish visitors who come to pray, and Christians who are seeking the history of their faith. In an uneasy agreement, Muslims retain their holy mosque, the Dome of the Rock[75], which rests above the wall on the Temple Mount. There is still considerable controversy about the division of Jerusalem. However, all areas, which were given by God to the Twelve Tribes of Israel, will eventually be theirs.

Joel 3:20, 21

Judah shall dwell forever and Jerusalem from generation to generation. I will cleanse their blood that I have not yet cleansed, for the Lord God dwells in Zion.

"I will remember the covenant which I have made with my people."

Ezekiel 16:60, III Nephi 20:29 (III Nephi 20:1-46)

---

[74] Robert Van Kampen, author of *The Sign of Christ's Coming* and *the End of the Age*, says, "Because the seventy week prophecy of Daniel which specifies 'Your people' (Israel) and 'Your holy city' (Jerusalem), the prophecies of the seventieth week could not be fulfilled until Israel took possession of her land and regained control of God's holy city. Therefore, it was not until 1967 that the greatest and last historical 'barrier' to the second coming of Christ was completely removed."

[75] The Dome of the Rock covers a huge rock where Jews believe Abraham almost slew Isaac, and Muslims believe their prophet was taken to Heaven. This building is one of the world's most beautiful pieces of architecture. It is decorated, inside and out with intricate mosaics, elaborate cut stone, and the floors are embellished with priceless Persian rugs. The fate of this beautiful structure in the Last Days is unknown

SIGN 24
The Temple will be rebuilt on the Temple Mount.

The Jewish temple must be rebuilt on the Temple Mount in Jerusalem before the return of Christ. Work on the temple has not yet begun, but skilled Jewish artisans have already recreated the necessary implements required in the Old Testament for temple services and daily sacrifices. Actual building of the temple must be delayed until the mosque, the Dome of the Rock, is somehow removed or agreement is reached between the Jews and Muslims to build the temple in a different location on the mount.

For centuries, the Jews believed Solomon's temple and the second temple were in the same location as the Dome of the Rock which is the third-most holy site in the Arab world; Mecca the first and Medina the second. Deliberate destruction of the mosque in order to build a Jewish temple is not a viable option. It would cause major worldwide turmoil, destroy a magnificent piece of Persian architecture, and possibly damage the rock, which has religious significance for Judaism, Islam, and Christianity. However, recent archeological discoveries indicate the temple was actually located a hundred or so yards distant from the dome. On August 30, 2007, what appeared to be the remains of the second temple were discovered during the installation of pipes in the compound. In October 2007, archeologists confirmed the discovery of temple artifacts in this location[76]. The new location is directly west of the Golden Gate. IF this discovery is accurate, the two buildings could exist side by side. Because of extreme animosity between Muslims and Jews, it is quite unlikely to happen.

Today the controversy over the mount is so intense that the entire world watches in suspense. Religious Jews want to rebuild their temple above the rock covered by the mosque. Israel technically is in possession of and militarily controls the Temple Mount, but the Arabs care for the mosque and conduct daily worship. The Arabs, of course, oppose any construction on the mount, fearing possible destruction of their own magnificent building. This is the fundamental (and realistic) reason why Arabs opposed the recent opening of an ancient tunnel next to the Wailing Wall. This tunnel is directly beneath part of the mosque. A zealot could detonate explosives, severely damaging the dome. Such an act would create a huge Arab reprisal and be condemned by the rest of the world.

The February 2007 riot over repairs to a footpath leading to the mount demonstrates the insanity of partisans in this cultural battle. I have walked this dirt path. It is an entrance to the mount seldom used by anyone other than Christian tourists. Arabs use formal gates and Jews rarely enter the enclosure for fear of stepping on the unknown place where the Holy of Holies housing the Ark of the Covenant was located[77]. The tourist path, near the Eastern Gate, is badly in need of repair, and work was progressing. It is not a plausible spot for an attack on the Dome of the Rock or on worshippers at this shrine. The Arabs are aware of this, but the issue has political value. The repairs are being used to create more unrest among the Palestinians and to gain sympathy from an uninformed world. These riots also keep unwelcome tourists away from the mount. The

---

[76] Jerusalem District archeologist Yuval Baruch announced the discovery of second temple artifacts in August 2007. It was reported in papers worldwide, including the New York Times and the Moscow Times.

[77] The Holy of Holies was the location of God's place in the temple. Once a year the high priest was permitted to open the veil and enter this spot. A rope was attached to his leg so that in the event he displeased God while there and was killed, he could be pulled from under the veil by priests who waited on the other side.

path may or may not receive needed repair. Nevertheless, a new Jewish temple will eventually be built somewhere on the Temple Mount. This may not happen until the tribulation.

As of August 2011, the obstacles to rebuilding the temple are unresolved. Something very significant must take place before work can begin. If the newly found location of the temple is correct, the Antichrist, who will bring temporary peace to the world might persuade both Arabs and Jews to place the new temple near the Eastern Gate opposite the Mount of Olives. This is the gate Christ entered, on a donkey, and it is the gate (now firmly sealed[78]) where ancient tradition indicates He will enter once more. According to scripture, the temple must exist in Jerusalem during the reign of the Antichrist. He will desecrate it during the tribulation by entering the Holy of Holies, sitting on the Mercy Seat, and declaring himself to be God (II Thessalonians 2:3, 4). Much more important, Jesus Christ will return to this temple. [Mal. 3:1-4 and III Nephi 11:4-7]

Malachi 3:1-4
Behold, I will send my messenger who will prepare the way before me. Then the Lord, whom ye seek, will suddenly come to His temple. He is the messenger of the covenant in whom you delight….

But who can endure the day of His coming? And who shall stand when He appears? He is like a refiner's fire and launderer's soap. And He shall sit as a refiner and purifier of silver, and He shall purify the Levites and refine them as gold and silver. Then they will be able to bring offerings of righteousness to the Lord. Then the offerings of Judah and Jerusalem will be acceptable to the Lord as in the days gone by and as in the former years.

---

[78] The Eastern Gate was sealed many centuries ago by an Arab conqueror in an attempt to prevent the return of Jesus Christ.

SIGN 25
The Gospel in the Bible and Book of Mormon will be taken to the Jews.

This sign is still unfulfilled. The next few years will be unprecedented for those who watch expectantly as prophecy from the scriptures unfolds. In spite of all peace treaties, we will witness more destruction and warfare in Israel. This devastation may be one of the motivations bringing secular Jews back to God. It may also introduce them to Jesus Christ, their Savior.

> ### Isaiah 9:6
> *Speaking to the Jews, Isaiah said, "A child is born for us. A son is given to us, and the government will be on His shoulders. He will be called Wonderful Counselor, Mighty God, Everlasting Father, and Prince of Peace. There will be no end to the increase of His government and peace. He will reign on David's throne, and over His kingdom to order it, and to establish it with justice and righteousness from now and forever."*

> ### Romans 11:26, 27
> *When the fullness of the Gentiles comes [last days] all Israel shall be saved. As it is written there shall come out of Sion [Zion] the Deliverer, and He shall turn away ungodliness from Jacob [Israel] for this is my covenant to them, and I shall take away their sins.*

The Book of Mormon, Second Witness of Christ to the Children of Israel and the People of the World

God declares in the Doctrine & Covenants that during the Last Days the gospel message will reach the Jews through this book. Joseph Smith, its translator, was unfamiliar with the Hebrew language, including its poetry and unique sentence structure. At the time he worked, ancient Hebrew was a "dead" language, unspoken for centuries. The Book of Mormon, as originally translated in English, was filled with archaic words and phrases that puzzled Western readers. However, Hebrew scholars reading the original translation discovered that it is consistent with the ancient form of the Hebrew language. Ancient Hebrew sentence structure and poetic form are found throughout the text of the Book of Mormon. Verses below are from modern translations.

> ### I Nephi 3:16, 17, 19 [10:11-14 LDS]
> *Lehi, Nephi's father, spoke many things to his sons concerning the Gentiles and the House of Israel saying they could be compared to an olive tree whose branches were broken off and scattered upon all the face of the Earth. Then Lehi said, "Therefore, it is necessary that we [a branch of the Jews through Ephram] should be led with one accord into the land of promise [the Americas], fulfilling the word of the Lord, that we should be scattered upon all the face of the earth. ...After the House of Israel is scattered, and after the Gentiles have received the fullness of the gospel; the natural branches of the olive tree, or the remnants of the House of Israel, will be gathered together again and grafted in, and come to the knowledge of the true Messiah, their Lord and their Redeemer."*

I Nephi 4:16-29 [15:13-18 LDS]

[Nephi continued the thoughts of his father] *"And now, the thing which our father means, concerning the grafting in, of the natural branches through the fullness of the Gentiles is, in the latter days. When our posterity has dwindled in their belief for many years and generations, and after the Messiah is born to the children of men, then the fullness of the gospel of the Messiah will come to the Gentiles and they will bring it to the remnant of our descendants. At that day, the remnant of our children shall know they are of the House of Israel and the covenant people of the Lord. They shall come to the knowledge of their forefathers, and also to the knowledge of the gospel of their Redeemer which was taught to their fathers by Christ. They shall come to the knowledge of their Redeemer and the very points of His doctrine that they may know how to come to Him and be saved."*

"At that day, they will rejoice and give praise to their everlasting God, their rock and salvation. They will receive the strength and nourishment from the true vine[79] [Jesus Christ], and will come into the true fold of God and they shall be remembered again among the House of Israel. They shall be grafted in, being a natural branch of the olive tree, into the true olive tree."

"This event will not take place until after the Jews are scattered by the Gentiles. Then the knowledge of the Lord shall come by way of the Gentiles so the Lord may show His power to them because He was rejected by the House of Israel. Therefore, our father was not speaking of our descendants alone but also of all the House of Israel, pointing to the covenant that must be fulfilled in the latter days, which is the covenant the Lord made with our father Abraham, saying, 'In your seed, all the people of the earth shall be blessed.'"

III Nephi 2:105, 107-109 [III Nephi 5:22, 24-26 LDS]

In as much as the children of Lehi kept His commandments, the Lord blessed them and prospered them according to His word.... As surely as the Lord lives, He will gather from the four quarters of the earth all the remnant descendants of Jacob who are scattered abroad, upon all the face of the earth. As He covenanted with all the house of Jacob, that covenant will be fulfilled in His own due time, and all the house of Jacob will be restored to the knowledge of the covenant, that He has with them. Then, they shall know their Redeemer, who is Jesus Christ the Son of God. They shall be gathered in from the four quarters of the earth into their own lands, from where they were dispersed. As the Lord lives, so it shall be. Amen. [See III Nephi 7:36; 9:50; 13:24-44; Mormon 2:39-42.]

III Nephi 9:69-72, 78 [III Nephi 20:30-34, 40 LDS][80]

The time will come when the fullness of my gospel shall be preached to them [the Jews]. They shall believe I am Jesus Christ the Son of God, and shall pray to the Father in my name. Then shall their watchmen lift up their voices, and with one voice, they shall sing, for they shall see eye to eye. Then, the

---

[79] In John 15:5 Christ says, "I am the vine, ye are the branches."

[80] RLDS and LDS church scholars continue to discover new insights about the Book of Mormon's relationship to the Israelites. This research provides strong evidence that this book is of Hebrew origin. In time this information may influence Jews and other Christians to read the Book of Mormon.

Father will gather them together again and give them Jerusalem for the land of their inheritance. They shall break forth in joy and sing together, for the Father has comforted His people, and He has redeemed Jerusalem.

They shall say, "How beautiful upon the mountains are the feet of Him that brings good tidings to us, that publishes peace... that publishes salvation, that says to Zion, 'Your God reigns!'"

Doctrine & Covenants 17:2c, d [April 6, 1830]
...The Book of Mormon..., contains the fullness of the gospel of Jesus Christ to the Gentiles and to the Jews.

Doctrine & Covenants 18:3b, c [March 1830, Manchester, New York]
I command you that you shall not covet your own property, but impart it freely, so the Book of Mormon which contains the truth and the Word of God to the Gentiles may also go to the Jews, of whom the Lamanites are a remnant, so they may believe the gospel and not look for a different Messiah to come.

Doctrine & Covenants 45:9a-d [March 7, 1831, Kirtland, Ohio]
The Jews shall look upon me and say, "What are these wounds in your hands and feet?" Then they shall know that I am the Lord for I will say to them, "These wounds are the wounds with which I was injured in the house of my friends. I am He who was lifted up. I am Jesus who was crucified. I am the Son of God." And, they shall weep because of their iniquities, and they shall lament because they persecuted their King.

Doctrine & Covenants 87:3c, 4 [March 8, 1833, Kirtland, Ohio]
...The Word may go forth to the ends of the earth, to the Gentiles first and then to the Jews; and then the day will come when the arm of the Lord shall be revealed in power to convince the nations, the heathen nations, and the house of Joseph, of the gospel of their salvation. For, it shall come to pass in that day, that every man shall hear the fullness of the gospel in his own tongue and in his own language. They will hear this through those who are ordained to this power by the administration of the Comforter. It will be shed forth upon them for the revelation of Jesus Christ.

One major barrier that still keeps Jews from hearing or accepting the gospel of Jesus Christ is they clearly remember persecution by Christians throughout the centuries. We cannot deny that numerous people who called themselves Christians were involved in heinous crimes against these people. Jews were forced from their homes and their belongings confiscated; they were expelled from myriad countries, and tortured and killed during the Inquisition. The crusades, pogroms, ritual murder, and finally the Holocaust of the twentieth century make it difficult for Jews to believe the teachings of Jesus. Whole families died in Nazi gas chambers. Others were killed by firing squads. Women and girls were raped, and babies were used for target practice. Living human beings were used for horrific experiments. Evidence of Hitler's crimes against the Jews is preserved in former concentration camps, and in Holocaust museums in the United States, and in Israel. Even today, in many countries, God's chosen people are persecuted. Many immigrate to Israel to avoid further victimization. Even the United States is not exempt from anti-Semitism. Hate messages are painted on synagogues, people are demeaned, and property is destroyed. Neo-Nazis have reemerged, and it is still not safe to be Jewish anywhere in the world.

There is no excusable justification for barbaric, intolerant, and prejudiced behavior. Prejudice is fueled by ignorant misinformation and spreading malicious lies. Jews, especially, have been used as convenient scapegoats for society's problems. Blind hatred caused millions of Jewish deaths, especially during the Second World War. Abominable behaviors continue to spread fear as anti-Semitism rears its ugly head again, a worldwide offense against God.

One widely quoted rationale is 'the Jews killed Jesus'. This is as ludicrous as it is offensive. The four gospels describe Christ's arrest, trial, and crucifixion. The high priest, arresting officers, or crowds that cried, "Crucify Him" **did not represent all the Jews of that day,** or any of the Jews since that time. It certainly did not represent the Jewish thousands who chose to follow the Lord as disciples. The total number of Jews involved in Christ's arrest, imprisonment, trial, and crucifixion is infinitesimal compared with the Jewish population then or today.

Paul is quoted in I Thessalonians 2:14, 15, saying, "The Jews killed Jesus." This scripture was and is misinterpreted. Paul, himself a Jew, was guilty of persecuting Christ's followers, but after his conversion, he realized even though Christ had enemies among the Jews, Christ's friends and the growing crowds who followed Him were Jewish. Therefore, the entire ethnic group could not possibly be responsible for the Savior's death. No court would convict them of this charge.

The scripture in the Inspired Version and King James Bible reads this way:

> **I Thessalonians 2:14, 15**
> *Paul says, "For you, brothers, became followers of the churches of God which in Judea are in Christ Jesus; for you also have suffered similar things from your own countrymen, even as they have of the Jews; who both killed the Lord Jesus, and their own prophets, and have persecuted us."*

The New Testament in the Complete Jewish Bible[81], used by Messianic Jews, was translated from the ancient Greek original in 1989. The scripture reads this way:

> **I Thessalonians 2:14, 15**
> *Paul says, "For, brothers, you came to be imitators of God's congregations in Y'hudah [Judea] that are united with the Messiah Yeshua [Jesus] You suffered the same things from your countrymen as they did from the Judeans who both killed the Lord Yeshua and the prophets, and chased us out too."*

---

[81] The Complete Jewish Bible, an English Version by David H. Stern, Jewish New Testament Publications, Inc. Clarksville, Maryland, USA-Jerusalem, Israel, Copyright 1998.

Old Testament Scriptures foretold the death of Christ.

Isaiah 53:1-12

Who has believed our message? To whom has the arm of the Lord been revealed? He will grow up before Him, like a tender plant and like a root out of dry ground. He has no form, nor comeliness that attracts us. When we see Him, He has no beauty that we should desire him.

He is despised and rejected of men; a man of sorrows acquainted with grief, and we hid our faces from Him. He was despised, and we did not esteem Him. But surely, He has borne our grief and carried our sorrows. Yet we esteem Him stricken, smitten of God and afflicted. He was wounded for our transgressions. He was bruised for our iniquities. The penalty, for our peace, was upon Him, and with His stripes, we are healed.

All we like sheep have gone astray. Everyone has turned to his own way and the Lord has laid on Him the iniquity of us all.

He was oppressed, and He was afflicted. Yet, He did not open His mouth. He was taken from prison and from judgment. Who can speak of His descendants? He was cut off out of the land of the living. He was stricken for the transgressions of my people. He made His grave with the wicked and with the rich in His death, though He had done no violence or spoken any deceit.

It was God's will to cause Him to suffer and to put Him to death. The Lord shall make His soul an offering for sin, and He shall see His seed and prolong His days, and the will of the Lord will prosper in His hands.

After the suffering of His soul, He will be satisfied by the knowledge that His death justified many. He shall bear their iniquities. Therefore, I will divide Him a portion with the great, and He shall divide the spoil with the strong, because He has poured out His soul unto death, and He was numbered with the transgressors, and He bore the sins of many and made intercession for the transgressors.

Psalm 22:14-18

I am poured out like water, and all my bones are out of joint. My heart is like wax. It is melted in the midst of my bowels. My strength is dried up like a potsherd; and my tongue cleaves to my jaws, and you have brought me into the dust of death. Dogs have surrounded me. The assembled wicked have enclosed me. They pierced my hands and my feet. I may tell all my bones; they look and stare upon me. They part my garments among them and cast lots upon my vesture.

NO ONE MURDERED JESUS CHRIST. According to the above scriptures, Jesus went to the cross obediently, predetermined by God's plan and GAVE His LIFE for the sins of mankind; for you, for me and for the Jews. He is the source of salvation for all who accept Him and He alone will judge the Jewish people. Unfortunately, many churches fail to teach their congregation basic facts about Jesus. It is amazing how many Christians are appalled when I share the following:

- Jesus Christ is a Jew, born to Mary and Joseph from the lineage of David and Judah whose ancestor Jacob was the father of the Twelve Tribes of Israel (See Matthew 1).
- The Apostles were also Jews.
- If it were not for the Jews, we would have no Old or New Testament.
- The writers of both Testaments were Jewish. Much of the New Testament is specifically addressed to Jews.

The prophets and patriarchs of the Bible were Hebrews. This includes Moses, Joshua, David, Isaiah, Jeremiah, Ezekiel, Daniel, and other prophets quoted from Christian pulpits. Jacob/Israel, son of Isaac, son of Abraham, fathered twelve sons, one of whom was Judah. Judah's descendants are called Jews. In later years, some members of the other eleven tribes assimilated with Judah's offspring, and were also known as Jews. Jesus' entire ministry was ONLY addressed to Jews. In Matthew 15:23 Christ says, "I am only sent to the lost sheep of the House of Israel." Non-Jews first heard of Christ's message through Paul and Christ's other Jewish disciples. All of the first Christians were Jews. Through the ministry of the Apostles (who were Jews), many additional Jews were converted to Christ. They became the first Christians but also remained Jews by birth and heritage. Their conversion changed their understanding of God. They found a risen Savior, Jesus Christ. Today, they are Messianic [82] Jews. If it were not for Messianic Jews, Christianity would not have survived the first century. Peter and Paul, both Jews, took Christ's message to the Gentiles[83].

---

[82]Messianic (from the word Messiah) Jews are Jewish men and women who accept Jesus Christ as their Savior.
[83]The term Gentile pertains to anyone who is not Jewish.

Top left, modern Jerusalem viewed from the Old City walls. Top right, the ruins of steps outside the Old City walls, one of the many places Jesus taught. Bottom left, Author and husband on ruins of steps to the temple. These steps led directly to the temple lot. Bottom right, Ms. Roberts in downtown Jerusalem.

Jesus said, "Now learn a parable of the fig tree: When its branches are still tender, and it begins to put forth leaves, you know that summer is near. So likewise, my elect who see all these things shall know that Christ is near, even at the door. But no one but my father knows the day or the hour not even the angels of God in Heaven."

Matthew 24:41-43
Mark 13:45-47
Luke 21:29-33

But no one knows the day or the hour ...

PART 2

Chapter 10

What do the scriptures say about the Antichrist and the Great Tribulation in the Last Days?

Note: Some scripture is paraphrased in this chapter to clarify meaning.

Signs of the Last Days

Part one of this book described the warning signs Christ gave to prepare His people for the coming ordeal. Part 2 addresses things still to come. Recommendations for additional reading are included at the end of this book.

This section of the book contains an overview of some of the things that will happen in the near future. It includes the following:

- The Antichrist (the man of perdition or lawlessness, an evil world leader) will be revealed;
- This leader will sign a covenant with Israel to bring peace in the Middle East;
- A period (possibly 7 years) called the Great Tribulation will begin as soon as the covenant is signed;
- In the middle of the tribulation period (possibly 3 ½ years) the Antichrist will break his covenant with the Jews;
- Christians and Jews will be persecuted and killed during this horror. (Revelation 20:4);
- The Antichrist will enter the Holy of Holies in the temple, desecrating it by his presence.
- He will sit on God's Mercy Seat above the Ark of the Covenant and declare himself to be God;
- The war of Armageddon will follow the tribulation;
- The Great Day of the Lord, Christ's Second Coming will be manifest;
- The Antichrist and False Prophet will be slain;
- Satan will be bound for a thousand years;
- Enoch's City of Zion will return and God's Millennium will begin.

Now is the Time for __ALL__ God's People to Stand to Serve the Lord!

Mark 1:13

Philippians 4:13

Buckle on Your Full Armor
You will need it.

Ephesians 6:10-18

©RSBlain Photography and Graphics

Endure until the Very End

Matthew 10:19; Mark 13:13;

II Nephi 7:10 (II Nephi 10:6 LDS); D. & C. 16:4d

Mormon 4:25-26

Behold what is said in the scriptures: 'Man shall not smite, nor judge for judgment is mine,' says the Lord. 'And vengeance is mine also, and I will repay. And he who breathes out wrath and strife against the work of the Lord and against God's covenant people [the House of Israel] and say, 'We will destroy the work of the Lord and He will not remember His covenant which He has made with the House of Israel,' are in danger of being hewn down and cast into the fire. The eternal purposes of the Lord shall roll on until all His promises shall be fulfilled'.

Zechariah 8:3

I have returned to Zion and will dwell in the midst of Jerusalem. And Jerusalem shall be called a city of truth. And the mountain of the Lord of Host, the Holy mountain.

We Will Know the Beast!

Most of the information about the Antichrist and the Great Tribulation is found in the Book of Revelation. John was given a vision but it was written in coded symbols so its interpretation would not be clear until the Last Days. Other portions of scripture also provide insights into this period. The books of Daniel and Isaiah also speak profoundly about the times to come. Many theologians and writers provide their own interpretation of the end times but they seldom agree with one another. I have chosen to let the scriptures speak for themselves, and have tried to put them in an order that may help our understanding. Most of these things will become clear during the Tribulation period. Already in the twentieth and twenty-first centuries, events and technological developments are lifting the curtain on some of these mysteries. Though our understanding is incomplete, we must trust Jesus, never letting our faith in Him fail.

II Thessalonians 2:3, 4, 7-10 [I.V. only]

Let no man deceive you by any means. There shall come a falling away first and then the man of sin will be revealed. The son of perdition who opposes and exalts himself, above all that is called God or that is worshipped, so that he as god sits in the temple of God, showing himself to be god.... Now, the mystery of iniquity is already at work, and it is Satan who is now at work, and Christ allows him to work, until the time is fulfilled when he shall be taken out of the way. And then that wicked one shall be revealed whom the Lord shall consume with the spirit of His mouth, and shall destroy with the brightness of His coming. Yes, the Lord, Jesus, whose coming is not until after there is a falling away because of the work of Satan who with all power, and signs and lying wonders, and who deceived the unrighteous who perish; because they did not receive the love of truth, so that they might be saved.

SIGN 26
The Man of Lawlessness and Perdition (Antichrist) will be revealed.

Soon, very soon, and just before the tribulation, this relatively unknown yet powerful and charismatic man will appear as a new world leader. There will be no warning. He has no former political history, and his background is very obscure. Nevertheless, millions of people around the world will be drawn to him, and he WILL PROMISE AND DELIVER WORLD PEACE. He will make a covenant with Israel to restore harmony and provide protection for them against their enemies (Daniel 9:27). Nations and their people will be ecstatic, because wars have exhausted them. Most governments will agree to any terms as long as peace and security are obtained.

DO NOT BE FOOLED!
The world leader who achieves this peace will be the Antichrist!

The Bible calls him contemptible and vile (Daniel 1121; Revelation 13:1-10). When he signs the agreement with Israel, we will know his identity and know, without doubt, that the Great Tribulation is beginning! This covenant of peace will be warmly received by much of the world, but Isaiah warns it is actually a Covenant with Death (Isaiah 28:15, 18).

Scriptures indicate THE ANTICHRIST IS EVIL INCARNATE. Salvation is lost to anyone who reveres him and accepts his number, 666.

The scriptures describe the Antichrist in this manner:

- He is a vile person who will obtain the kingdom by flatteries. (Daniel 11:21-45)
- His origin is hell. (Revelation 17:8)
- He will come in his own name. (John 5:44)
- He will be admired and lauded. (Revelation 13:3, 4)
- He will come to do his own will. (Daniel 11:36)
- He will declare war on many nations, and defeat many countries. (Daniel 11:40)
- He will persecute the world's Jews and Christians. (Revelation 13:7)
- He will destroy all who oppose him. (Daniel 8:24)
- His power comes from Satan, with whom he has an alliance, and he will collaborate with a man called the False Prophet. (Revelation 13:11-15; 16:13)
- He will receive a deadly head wound, that will be healed. (Rev.13:3)
- He will require everyone to wear the mark 666, in order to buy or sell. (Revelation 13:16-18)
- He will demand that the whole world worship him. (Revelation 13:15)
- Those who do not worship him will be murdered. Many will be beheaded. (Revelation 20:4)
- He will overcome the city of Jerusalem. (Daniel 9:26)
- He will announce that he is God and will sit in the Holy of Holies in the Temple of God. The whole world will be forced to bow down to him. (II Thessalonians 2:3, 4)

First Half of the Great Tribulation

For about three and a half years, the Antichrist will consolidate his power. He will make war with all his enemies, and force other nations to give him their allegiance. Satan, called the "dragon" (Revelation 12:8) is the strength behind this beast. Together they will attempt to conquer the world while murdering all who oppose them.

Daniel 8:24, 25
His [the Antichrist's] power shall be mighty but not by his own hand, [Satan is the source of the Antichrist's power]. And he shall be horribly destructive and he shall prosper and destroy the mighty and the holy people [the Jews in Israel]. And through his policy, he shall cause deceit to prosper in his hand. He shall magnify himself in his heart and by peace shall destroy many [he will bring peace to the Mideast but at the same time will kill many Christians and Jews].

Daniel 11:21
...A vile person shall appear [the Antichrist], but they will not give the honor of the kingdom to him. Then he shall come in peaceably and obtain the kingdom through flatteries.

Daniel 11:36
And the king [Antichrist] shall do according to his [own] will. He shall exalt and magnify himself above every god, and speak hideous things against the God of gods. He shall prosper until his rage has accomplished all he determined to do... and he shall magnify himself above all.

Daniel 11:38
He shall honor the God of forces, [Satan and demonic minions], the god whom his fathers did not know. He will honor him with gold and silver and with precious stones and pleasant things. He will do this in the strongholds of a strange god whom he shall acknowledge [Satan] and increase with glory. He will cause them to rule over many and shall divide the land for gain.

Daniel 11:40-42
And at the time of the end, the king of the south shall push him [the Antichrist] and the king of the north shall come against him [the Antichrist] like a whirlwind with chariots and with horsemen and many ships. He [the Antichrist] shall enter into the countries and shall conquer and pass through them. He shall enter into the glorious land [Israel] and many more countries shall be overthrown; but Edom and Moab and the chief of the children of Amman [modern Jordan] shall escape. However, the land of Egypt shall not escape.

Daniel 11:43, 44
He shall have power over the treasures of Egypt. Libya and Ethiopia shall be at his steps. But the tidings out of the east and the north shall trouble him. Therefore, he shall go forth with great fury to destroy all of them. And he shall plant the tabernacles of his palace between the seas and the glorious holy mountain [Mount Zion in Jerusalem]. Yet, he shall come to his end and no one will help him.

...At that time, there shall be a period of trouble unlike the nation [Israel] has ever experienced ...

What do the scriptures say about the wrath of God?

While the Antichrist pursues his goals, the God of Heaven and earth is also busy. The Wrath of God is full! Angels guarding the seven seals of a book, seven angels holding trumpets and the angels entrusted with seven gold vials filled of the wrath of God are at hand and ready to complete their missions. The purpose of each is to bring mankind to repentance.

Zephaniah 2:3
Seek ye the Lord, all you meek of the earth who have wrought His judgment; seek righteousness, seek meekness so perhaps you shall be hid in the day of the Lord's anger.

The Seven Seals

(Summary)
Revelation 5:2, 5
And I, John, saw a strong angel, and heard him proclaim with a loud voice, "Who is worthy to open the book, and loose the seals thereof"? ...And behold, the Lion of the tribe of Judah, the Root of David, took the book and the seven seals that held it. And the angels sang a new song, saying, "Thou art worthy to take the book and open the seals for you were slain, and by your blood you have redeemed us to God out of every kindred, and tongue, and people, and nation; and have made us kings and priests for our God; and we shall reign on earth."

The seven Seals in the Book of Revelation can only be opened by Jesus Christ. When He opens these seals of the book, the whole world will be transformed.

(Summary)
Revelation 6:2 [THE CONQUERER]
When the first seal is opened, a white horse and a man with a bow are revealed. A crown is given to this man and he is sent forth to conquer. He is followed by six other horsemen.

(Summary)
Revelation 6:3 [WAR]
When the second seal is opened, a red horse follows. He who sits upon it is given power to take peace from the earth so men will kill one another. He is given a great sword.

(Parallel)
Matthew 24:29, 30
And you shall hear of wars and rumors of wars.... Nation shall rise against nation, and kingdom against kingdom.

(Summary)
Revelation 6:5, 6 [FAMINE]

As the third seal is opened, a man on a black horse rides forth. He carries a pair of balances in his hand, and a voice cries, "A measure of wheat for a penny and three measures of barley for a penny; and hurt not the oil or the wine.

(Parallel)

Matthew 24:30
...There shall be famine and pestilences, and earthquakes in diverse places.

(Summary)
Revelation 6:7, 8 [DEATH]

The fourth seal reveals a pale horse whose rider is named Death. He is followed by Hell, and they receive power over one fourth of the world, to kill with sword, and with hunger, and with the beasts of the earth.

(Summary)
Revelation 6:9-11 [SOULS of the MARTYRED SAINTS]

When the fifth seal is opened, it reveals, under the altar, the souls of those who are slain for the Word of God and for the testimony, which they hold. They are crying out for vengeance, but the Lord tells them to wait a bit longer for the rest of the Saints who will yet be martyred.

Now it is the Lord's turn!

(Summary)
Revelation 6:12-17 [UNNATURAL DISASTERS]

When the sixth seal is broken, a great earthquake will occur. The sun will become black and other Heavenly signs further alarm earth's population.

(Parallel)

Matthew 24:34 [24:29 KJV]
And immediately after the tribulation of those days, the sun shall be darkened, and the moon shall not give her light, and the stars shall fall from Heaven, and the powers of Heaven shall be shaken.

(Parallel)

Joel 2:10
The earth shall quake before them; the Heavens shall tremble; the sun and the moon shall be dark, and the stars shall withdraw their shining.

(Parallel)

Zephaniah 1:15
That day is a day of wrath, a day of trouble and distress, a day of wasteness and desolation, a day of darkness and gloominess, a day of clouds and thick darkness. [See Joel 2:30, 31; Revelation 8:12.]

(Summary)
Revelation 7:1-17 THE SAINTS ARE SEALED

After six of the seals were opened, John saw four angels standing on the four corners of the earth, holding the four winds of earth that they do not blow on the earth, the sea, or any tree. Then another angel appeared from the east, with the seal of the living God. He cried with a loud voice to the four angels to whom it was given to hurt the earth and sea, saying, "Do not hurt the earth or sea, or any of the trees, until we have sealed the servants of our God on their foreheads. And he sealed one hundred and forty four thousand people, twelve thousand from each of the twelve tribes of Israel.

Then John beheld a great multitude of people from all nations, kindreds and tongues, standing before the throne, and before the Lamb. They were clothed with white robes and held palms in their hands. They cried with a loud voice, saying, "Salvation to our God who sits upon the throne, and to the Lamb." The angels and elders fell on their faces before the throne and worshipped God, saying, Amen; blessing, and glory, and wisdom, and thanksgiving, and honor, and power, and might be unto our God forever and ever.

John was told the people he saw came out of the Great Tribulation, and have washed their robes, and made them white in the blood of the lamb. Therefore, they are before the throne of God to serve Him day and night in His temple. He who sits on the throne dwells among them. They will never hunger or thirst any more. The sun shall not light on them nor any heat, for the Lamb which is in their midst shall feed them, and shall lead them into living fountains of waters; and God shall wipe away all tears from their eyes.

Revelation 8:1-6 [SMOKING CENSER]
After the seventh seal was opened, there was silence in Heaven for about half an hour. Then John saw seven angels standing before God, and they were each given a trumpet.

And another angel came and stood at the altar carrying a golden censer. He filled it with incense to offer it with the prayers of all the saints upon the golden altar, which stood before the throne. The smoke of the incense, which came with the prayers of the saints, ascended up before God out of the angel's hand. And the angel took the censer, and filled it with fire from the altar, and cast it to earth; and there were voices, and thunder, lightning and another earthquake.

Seven Trumpets

Revelation 8:6, 7
And the seven angels with trumpets prepared to sound. The first angel sounded, and there followed hail and fire mingled with blood, which were cast upon the earth; and the third part of trees and all green grass were burned up.

Revelation 8:8, 9
The second angel sounded, and a great mountain burning with fire was thrown into the sea; and a third part of the sea became blood. A third of the sea creatures died, and a third of the ships were destroyed.

Revelation 8:10, 11
The third angel sounded a great star named Wormwood fell from Heaven, burning as a lamp. It fell upon a third part of the rivers, and upon the fountains of waters. Many men died because the water became bitter.

Revelation 8:12

The fourth angel sounded, and a third of the sun, moon and stars were darkened, and day and night were shortened by a third.

(Parallel)

Joel 2:30, 31

I will show wonders in the Heavens, and in the earth, blood, and fire, and pillars of smoke. The sun shall be turned into darkness, and the moon into blood, before the great and terrible day o f the Lord comes.

The Three Woes

Revelation 8:13

And I, John, beheld and heard an angel flying through the midst of Heaven, saying with a loud voice, Woe, woe, woe, to those who inhabit of the earth because of the other voices of the trumpet of three angels which are yet to sound. [Note: This is repeated from above, because it is relevant to the woes.]

Woe #1
The fifth angel sounded; a star falls from Heaven and the fifth angel receives a key to the bottomless pit.

Revelation 9:1-11

John saw a star fall from Heaven to earth; and an angel was given the key of the bottomless pit. And he opened the bottomless pit, and there arose a smoke out of it, as the smoke of a great furnace; and the sun and the air were darkened by reason of the smoke from the pit.

And out of the smoke came locusts upon the earth, and they were given the power of scorpions. They were commanded that they should not hurt the grass of the earth, nor trees, or any green thing, but only those men who do not have the seal of God on their foreheads. They should not kill them, but they should be tormented for five months, and their torment will be like a scorpion, when he strikes a man. And in those days, men shall seek death but not find it. They shall desire to die, but death will flee from them.

The shapes of the locusts were like horses prepared for battle; and on their heads were crowns of gold, and their faces were the faces of men. They had hair like the hair of women, and their teeth were as the teeth of lions. They wore breastplates like iron; and the sound of their wings was as the sound of chariots of many horses running to battle. Their tails were like scorpions, and there were stings in their tails; and their power was to hurt men for five months.

They had a king over them, which is the angel of the bottomless pit, whose name in Hebrew is Abaddon, but in Greek it is Apollyon. One woe is past; and, two more woes will come [Revelation 9:12].

Woe #2
An Army of Two Hundred Thousand, Thousand Horsemen.

<u>**Revelation 9:13-20**</u>
When the sixth angel sounded, John heard a voice from the four horns of the golden altar, which stands before God, saying, "Loose the four angels which are bound in the bottomless pit." And the four angels which had been prepared for a year, a month, a day and an hour were freed to kill one third of mankind. They led an army of two hundred thousand, thousand horsemen. The riders had breastplates of fire and of jacinth, and brimstone; and the heads of the horses were like the heads of lions; and out of their mouths came fire, smoke and brimstone. Their power is in their mouths, and in their tails; for their tails were like serpents with heads that were able to bite.

But the remaining people on earth who were not killed by these plagues still did not repent of the works of their hands. They worshiped devils, and idols of gold, and silver, brass, stone and wood, which cannot see, hear or walk. They also did not repent of their murders, nor their sorceries, their fornication, or their thefts.

The second woe, which began when the sixth angel sounded, appears to continue through Chapter 10 and to verse 14 of Chapter 11 in Revelation.

(Summary)
<u>**Revelation 10:8-11**</u>
John, the writer of Revelation, saw another mighty angel descend from Heaven. He was clothed with a cloud and a rainbow was on his head. His face was so bright it appeared to be the sun, and his feet were as pillars of fire. His right foot was upon the sea, and his left foot on the earth, and in his hand, he held a little open book. He cried with a loud voice, like a lion roaring, and when he cried, seven thunders uttered their voices.

John was about to write, when a voice from Heaven said to him, "Those things which the seven thunders uttered are sealed. Do not write them." Then the angel standing on the sea and earth lifted up his hand to heaven and swore by Him who lives forever and ever, who created heaven, and the things therein, and the earth, and the things therein, and the sea, and the things there in that TIME SHOULD BE NO LONGER. When the seventh angel sounds, the mystery of God will be finished, as He declared to His servants the prophets.

And John heard a voice from Heaven, which said, "Go and take the little open book from an angel. John requested the book from the angel who said, "Take it, and eat it up; and it shall bitter in your belly, but sweet as honey in your mouth, and it was. Then the angel directed him to prophesy before many peoples, and nations, and tongues, and kings.

God's Two Witnesses

John's prophecy concerns two witnesses of God that have power to shut Heaven so it does not rain. The men, clothed in sackcloth, will prophesy to the Jews and the Antichrist near the Wailing Wall in Jerusalem.

(Summary)
Revelation 11:3-6

And I (God) will give power to my two witnesses, and they shall prophesy a thousand two hundred and three score days (about 3 1/2 years[84]) clothed in sackcloth. They shall stay by the Wailing Wall in Jerusalem, and have the power to prevent rain, turn water into blood, and smite the earth with plagues. Anyone who tries to hurt them will be devoured by fire from their mouths. The Antichrist will make war with these witnesses and at the end of God's specified time the witnesses will be killed.

Revelation 11:7

When they have finished their testimony, the beast [Antichrist] that ascended out of the bottomless pit shall make war against them, and overcome them and kill them.

(Summary)
Revelation 11:8-12

For three and a half days, their bodies will lay prostrate in the streets while followers of the Antichrist celebrate their demise. But suddenly the earth will bulge and groan expanding as cracks appear in its surface and the spirit of life will reenter the witnesses. They will rise to their feet as a great voice from Heaven says to them "Come up here"! The ground will heave and roll as their horrified enemies watch the risen witnesses ascend into Heaven. At the same hour there was a great earthquake, and a tenth of the city will fall beneath them, and seven thousand terrified people die.

Revelation 11:14

The second woe is past; and the third woe comes quickly.

Woe # 3
Time comes to an end; the Great Dragon persecutes the woman.

Revelation 10:7

In the days of the voice of the seventh angel, when he begins to sound his trumpet, the mystery of God will be finished, as He has declared to His servants the prophets.

Revelation 11:15-19

And the seventh angel sounded; and there were great voices in Heaven, saying, "The kingdoms of this world are become the kingdom of our Lord, and of His Christ; and He shall reign forever and ever." And the twenty four elders which sat before God, fell on their faces and worshipped Him, saying, "We give thee thanks, O Lord God Almighty, which are, and was, and are to come, because you have taken your great power, and have reigned."

And the nations were angry, and your wrath has come, and the time of the dead, so they should be judged. And you will give rewards to your servants the prophets, and to the saints, and those who fear your name, small and great; and you will destroy them who destroy the earth.

---

[84] These witnesses are represented by two candlesticks and two olive trees that stand before the altar of God. (See Revelation 11:4.)

And the temple of God was opened in Heaven, and there was seen in His temple the ark of His testament; and there were lightnings, and voices, and thunderings, and an earthquake, and great hail.

Revelation 12:1-8
And a great sign appeared in Heaven, in the likeness of things on the earth; a woman clothed with the sun and the moon under her feet and upon her head is a crown of twelve stars.

And the woman who is expecting a child, cried, travailing in birth pains, and brought forth a male child, who was to rule all nations with a rod of iron; and her child was caught up to God and His throne.

But there appeared another sign in Heaven; and behold, a great red dragon, having seven heads and ten horns, and seven crowns upon his head. His tail drew a third of the stars out of Heaven, and cast them to the earth. And the dragon stood before the woman who had given birth to the child, prepared to eat it after it was born. But the woman fled into the wilderness where God prepared a place for her, and would feed her for a thousand two hundred and three score years.

And there was a war in Heaven. Michael and his angels fought the dragon and his angels. But the dragon did not prevail against Michael, or the child, or the woman who was the church of God, who was delivered of her pains, and brought forth the kingdom of our God and His Christ. [**The woman is identified as the church of God, Revelation 12:7. The child is the kingdom of God and Christ, Revelation 12:7. The dragon or serpent is the devil or Satan, Revelation 12:8.**]

Revelation 12:9-11 [I.V.]
And a loud voice in Heaven said, "Now the salvation, and strength, and kingdom of our God and the power of His Christ is come, for the accuser of our brothers is cast down, for he accused them day and night before our God. But they overcame him by the blood of the Lamb, and by the word of their testimony…. They kept their testimony even to death, and did not love their own lives more than they loved the Word of God. Therefore, rejoice O Heavens, and you who dwell in them."

Revelation 12:12-17
Then John heard another voice saying, "Woe to the inhabitants of the earth, and they who dwell upon the islands of the sea, for the devil has come down to you. He is full of wrath because he knows that he has only a short time, for when the dragon saw that he was cast down to earth, he persecuted the woman, which brought forth the man-child. Therefore the woman was given two wings of a great eagle, so that she might flee into her place in the wilderness, where she is nourished for a time, and times, and half a time, from the face of the serpent.

And the serpent cast water like a flood from his mouth, so that he might cause her to be carried away in the flood. But the earth helped the woman, and opened its mouth, and swallowed up the flood caused by the dragon.

Therefore, the dragon was furious with the woman, and went to make war with the remnant of her children who keep the commandments of God, and have the testimony of Jesus Christ.

Revelation 13:1
And I, John saw another sign, in the likeness of the kingdoms of earth; a beast [Antichrist] rose up out of the sea, and he stood upon the sand of the sea. He had seven heads and ten horns; and upon his horns, ten crowns; and upon his heads was the name of blasphemy. And I saw one of his heads had a deadly wound which was healed; and all the world wondered after the beast.

Revelation 13: 2-10
…And the beast, which I saw, was like a leopard, and his feet were as the feet of a bear, and his mouth like the mouth of a lion; and the dragon [Satan] gave him his power, and his seat, and great authority.

And I saw one of his heads had a wound that should have killed it, but the deadly wound was healed; and the entire world wondered about the beast. And people worshiped the dragon [Satan], which gave power to the beast; and they worshiped the beast, saying, "Who is like the beast? Who is able to make war with him"? And he was given a mouth to extol himself and blaspheme; and power was given to him to continue forty-two months [3 ½ years]. And he opened his mouth in blasphemy against God, to blaspheme His name, and His tabernacle, and those who dwell in Heaven.

And it was given to him to make war with the saints and to overcome them; and he had power over all kindreds, and tongues, and nations. And those, whose names are not written in the book of life of the Lamb slain from the foundation of the world, shall worship him. If any man has an ear, let him hear. He that leads into captivity shall go into captivity; he that kills with the sword must be killed with the sword. Here is the patience and the faith of the saints. [The Beast of Revelation 12, 13, and 17 are the same. Later in this chapter, Revelation 17:9-15 will provide some insight into the beast.]

The Antichrist will make war with the Saints.

Revelation 13:7-9
It was given to him to make war with the Saints and to overcome them; and power was given him over all kindreds, tongues and nations. And, all who dwell upon the earth, whose names are not written in the Lamb's book of life… shall worship him. If any man has an ear, let him hear.

This will be a wretched and desperate time for people who call themselves Christian but do not closely follow Jesus Christ. Compromising Christians and many "Christian" churches will undergo terrifying persecution, to get their attention, in order to bring them back to God. However, the Saints who flee to Zion will live in safety, and the Holy Spirit will be with believers who are outside Zion's sanctuary, facing the wrath of the Beast. Make no mistake; those who have a close personal relationship with Christ may still face persecution. Many of God's people will be killed, but they know to whom they belong. They know where they are going, and if they face death they know that time on earth is

NOT THEIR REAL LIFE. It is only a probationary period. They look forward to living with Christ when He returns.

(Summary)
Revelation 13:11-14
I, John, saw another beast come out of the earth. He had two horns like a lamb but he spoke as a dragon and performs miracles such as making fire come from Heaven to earth in the sight of men. (The second beast is called the False Prophet. He assists the Antichrist in many ventures subduing many people with satanic powers. Finally, he commands the creation of an image of the beast, which was wounded by a sword and lived).

And he (the Antichrist) causes everyone, small and great, rich and poor, free and bond to receive a mark on their right hand or on their foreheads so no one can buy or sell unless they have the mark or the name of the Beast or the number of his name. Here is wisdom. Let those who understand count the number of the Beast for it is the number of a man and his number is six hundred three score and six (666).

In order to purchase food or other necessities, the Antichrist will force all people to wear his mark, represented by the number 666. People who sell these things must also wear this mark. However, those who accept this emblem will suffer God's wrath forever.

Revelation 14:9, 10
...If any man worship the beast and his image, and receive his mark in his forehead or in his hand, that man shall drink of the wine of the wrath of God, which is poured out without mixture into the cup of His indignation. He shall be tormented with fire and brimstone in the presence of the holy angels, and in the presence of the Lamb.

There are many theories about the number 666. Although all of them are thought provoking, we cannot know its exact meaning until this takes place. According to Biblical numerology, six is the number that represents man. Some writers suggest that three sixes may be man trying to imitate the trinity of God (the Antichrist, the false prophet and Satan). Whatever it is, those who lack this mark will be especially easy for the Beast to identify (Revelation 13:16-18).

When this proclamation is put into effect, the Antichrist will have the ability to control almost every man and woman on the planet. All those who revere him and accept his number (666) will LOSE their salvation. Those who do not worship him will be arrested, tortured, or targeted for murder. Many will be beheaded (Revelation 20:4).

The Second Half of the Great Tribulation

By this time, the Antichrist will be a person of almost unlimited resources and authority. He will take revenge against God and God's people. The source of his power is Satan himself. Power will be given to this beast (Revelation 17:7-14) over all races and nations. With the aid of a false prophet (Revelation 13:11) and a speaking image of himself (possibly televised, Revelation 13:15), the Antichrist and the False Prophet will perform many miracles. These signs and wonders will cause great confusion, enabling the unholy trinity, to wreck havoc on earth for an additional period. Nothing will be withheld. They will lie, destroy, deceive, perform incredible miracles, murder, and

174

blaspheme against God, His temple, and the inhabitants of Heaven. Except for those whose names are written in Christ's Book of Life, most people on earth will obey them. All who oppose them will find their lives threatened by the forces of hell (Revelation 13:8).

The Antichrist will make war[85] against Israel.

The book of Joel describes a battle in the Valley of Jehoshaphat near Jerusalem where Israel is attacked by surrounding nations (all Arab countries). The Antichrist will use the animosity, of these nations, to conquer Israel and this will occur just before the Day of the Lord.

> ### Joel 3:1, 2, 9-14
> *In those days and in that time, I [God] shall bring again the captivity of Judah and Jerusalem. I will gather all nations and bring them down into the valley of Jehoshaphat and will plead with them, for my people and for my heritage Israel, whom they have scattered among the nations and parted my land.*
>
> *Proclaim this among the Gentiles; Prepare war, wake up the mighty men, let all the men of war draw near; let them come up. Beat your ploughshares into swords and your pruning hooks into spears. Let the weak say, "I am strong."*
>
> *Assemble yourselves, come all you heathen, gather yourselves together round about, and cause your mighty ones to come down. Let the heathen be wakened and come up to the valley of Jehoshaphat. There I will sit and judge all the heathen round about.*
>
> *Pick up the sickle, for the harvest is ripe…, the press is full, the fats overflow, for wickedness is very great. Multitudes, multitudes in the valley of decision, for the day of the Lord is near in the valley of decision.*

The Antichrist attacks the Jews in Jerusalem.

Great atrocities will take place during the first half of the tribulation, but nothing will equal the horror of the second half of this period. After three and a half years of false security for Jews in the Holy Land, the Antichrist (or Beast) will invalidate his covenant, breaking his promises with Israel and taking Jerusalem by force. The Jews in Israel will be targeted for incredible persecution. Their army will be outnumbered and citizens will flee for their lives.

Miraculously, in the vast mid-east desert wilderness, God has reserved a place where Jewish refugees will be safe from the Antichrist. During this forced exodus, God intends to bring the Jews back to their covenant with Him. Those who refuse will not re-enter the land of Israel.

---

[85] Over the centuries there have been many Antichrists, men who have fought against God. This confuses many who read the scriptures. However, there is only one Antichrist or Beast who will appear in the Last Days and fulfill the scriptures in this chapter

Isaiah 28:18-20

Israel's covenant with death [with the Antichrist and Satan] will be invalidated [The Antichrist will break it]. Israel's agreement with Hell will not stand. When the overwhelming scourge sweeps by, you [Israel] will be beaten down by it. As often as it comes, it will carry you away. It will sweep through morning after morning, it shall pass over, by day and by night; and it shall deeply trouble those who understand the report, and they cannot hide from it. When you [people of Israel] understand this message, it will cause sheer terror. There will be no place to hide.

Zechariah 14:4-7

Then Christ's feet shall stand in that day upon the Mount of Olives, which is before Jerusalem on the east. And the Mount of Olives shall cleave in the midst thereof toward the east and toward the west, and there shall be a very great valley; and half of the mountain shall remove toward the north, and half of it toward the south. And you shall flee to the valley of the mountains; for the valley of the mountain shall reach to Azal; yes, you shall flee, like you fled from before the earthquake in the days of Uzziah, king of Judah. And the Lord my God shall come, and all the saints with you. And it shall come to pass in that day, that the light shall not be clear, nor dark; but it shall be one day which shall be known to the Lord, not day, nor night; but it shall come to pass, that at evening time it shall be light. [Zechariah 14:1-5, 6-9, 11-16]

Matthew 24:16-20

When you shall see the abomination of desolation, spoken of by Daniel the prophet [the Antichrist defiles the holy temple by sitting within the Holy of Holies on the Mercy Seat of God], concerning the destruction of Jerusalem, then you shall stand in the holy place, [Whoever reads this let him understand]. Then let them who are in Judea, flee into the mountains. Let him who is on the housetop, flee, and not return to take anything out of his house. Neither let him who is in the field, return back to take his clothes. And woe unto them that are with child and to them that give suck in those days! Pray that the Lord will not allow your flight to be in winter or on the Sabbath day. For then, in those days, the Great Tribulations shall come upon the Jews and upon the inhabitants of Jerusalem unlike anything that ever before or ever again shall be sent upon Israel from God, since the beginning of their kingdom until this time; no, nor ever shall be sent again upon Israel.

All these things are only the beginning of sorrows, which shall come, and unless those days are shortened, none of their flesh shall be saved. But for the elect's sake, according to the covenant, those days shall be shortened. Behold these things I have spoken to you concerning the Jews.

Luke 21:19, 20 I.V. [Luke 21:19-21 KJV]

When you see Jerusalem surrounded with armies, know that the desolation of it is close at hand. Let those who are in Judea flee to the mountains, and let them who are in the midst of it, depart out; and those who work the fields must not return to enter the city, for these are the days of vengeance that all things which are written about may be fulfilled.

Petra

It is not my intention to speculate in this book. However, the following theory may be worth considering. Ancient Edom was in the southwestern portion of Jordan and Moab was on the east bank of the Dead Sea, north of Edom. Within this vast desert, fortified by mountains, are the remains of a very ancient, uninhabited metropolis called Petra[86]. Only Bedouin tribes, camels and sheep live in the vicinity. Many Bible scholars theorize that the fugitives from Israel will flee to this area in the Last Days.

Petra is an incredibly beautiful city, lost to history for thousands of years. It is five hours by car from any form of civilization. The journey is difficult by automobile and almost impossible for refugees on foot. In recent years, Petra has become an out-of-the-way tourist destination with a few small hotels (only one during my visit in 1996), limited but comfortable and clean rooms, and rationed water. Surrounded by mountains and desert, the ancient city is hidden between imposing heights. It has only one major entrance, easily defended by a few marksmen standing above on overhanging cliffs. However, today it is vulnerable to attack by air.

Petra's existence was a well-kept secret until the mid-nineteenth century. Then in 1812, Johann Burckhardt, a Swiss explorer, heard rumors about the city. Disguised as an Arab, he was smuggled into its hidden location. The entrance to Petra is through a long, narrow, winding passageway that descends between towering rocks toward an unseen lower level. Rounding a bend, Burckhardt was startled to find bright sunlight, and a huge uninhabited metropolis carved into the walls of flaming red mountains. This unexpected and bewildering sight resembled Greek or Roman architecture chiseled into the rose-colored sandstone by the hand of a giant sculptor.

The magnificent doorways seem to promise elaborate interiors but Petra's elegance is primarily on the outside. Inside each entrance is a primitive cave! The cavity's size depended on its use. Huge caverns accommodated the government of the city, others held various businesses, and smaller chambers served as personal residences. A unique system traps water in the rainy season. Rock troughs cut into the sides of the narrow passageway captured water from the mountains. The troughs run down the sides of the descending passageway and into the city. They empty into a recently discovered system of pipes, aqueducts, hidden cisterns and water filtration systems, which hold water during the long dry desert seasons. It is estimated 30,000 people had ample water on a daily basis. In fact, there was at least one swimming pool in the ancient city, along with sophisticated plumbing for some homes, fountains, and lush green gardens. Some of this is still functional.

Originally, Petra served as an oasis for camel trains crossing the desert. It was abandoned when a better route was found and today the caves are barren. No furnishings survive. The caves of Petra certainly can be reoccupied and hold thousands of people but living in them will be a primitive camping experience. Adequate food, clothing, bedding, and latrine requirements for refugees will require miracles, but God has done it before. Moses led Israelites through the desert for 40 years. Their clothing

---

[86] Movie fans may recall that Petra was a backdrop in the Indiana Jones film *Indiana Jones and the Last Crusade*. It is also the place of safety for Jews in the Left Behind series of books.

did not wear out and they were fed manna from Heaven. At God's command, Moses even struck a mountain to produce flowing water for the Israelites.

Exodus 17:5, 6
The Lord said to Moses, Go before the people... and take your rod in your hand. I will stand before you upon a rock in Horeb; and you shall smite the rock, and there shall come water out of it, so the people may drink. And Moses did so in the sight of the elders of Israel.

Deuteronomy 8:2, 4
You shall remember all the ways which the Lord your God led you these forty years in the wilderness.... Your raiment did not get old upon you, neither did your feet swell, these forty years.

Isaiah 16:1-5, is quoted by people who believe that Petra will be the place of refuge for the Jews. These verses appear to direct Moab (modern Jordan) to welcome future refugees. However, the verses in Isaiah Chapter 15 and the balance of portions of Chapter 16 describe a different scenario. It is possible that verses 1-5 have been taken out of context. However, Jordan or Petra should not be eliminated as the possible place of refuge by this observation. Both are in proximity to Israel and Jordan has been one of her less aggressive neighbors. Wherever refuge is found, it will be an extremely critical and difficult time for the Jews of Israel. The death toll while reaching a place of safety may be high.

The Antichrist will gain absolute control over most of the world.

Scripture scholars agree the total number of years the Antichrist is in power is seven, 3 ½ + 3 ½ years in the first and second half of the tribulation.

The Antichrist will attempt to replace God.

Once Jerusalem is captured, the Antichrist will establish his throne inside the new temple. He will open the sacred veil and sit inside the Holy of Holies upon the Mercy Seat of God. This is the location of the Holy Ark of the Covenant. He will proclaim himself "God" and command the whole world to worship him. (This is the Abomination of Desolation spoken of by Daniel.)

Daniel 11:31
And arms [men with weapons] shall stand in his defense, and they shall pollute the sanctuary of strength [The Holy of Holies in the Temple in Jerusalem]. He [the Antichrist] shall take away the daily sacrifice and they shall place the abomination that makes desolation [The Antichrist will sit on the Holy of Holies].

Matthew 24:33 [24:15 KJV]
Then shall the abomination of desolation spoken of by Daniel the prophet be fulfilled. [This refers to Daniel 11:31, and the Antichrist who will sit on the Mercy Seat of God.]

<u>**II Thessalonians 2:3, 4**</u>
Let no man deceive you by any means, for there shall come a falling away first. And that man of sin will be revealed, the son of perdition; who opposes and exalts himself, above all that is called God or that is worshipped; so that he, as god, will sit in the temple of God, showing himself that he is god.

<u>**Revelation 13:8, 9**</u>
And all that dwell upon the earth shall worship him, even those whose names are not written in the book of life of the Lamb slain from the foundation of the world. If any man has an ear, let him hear.

All those who will not bow down, worship the Antichrist or his image, and accept his mark will be executed. Thereafter, most of the world will worship the beast (Antichrist) and the dragon (Satan) which gave the Antichrist power.

God's people will require incredible faith and **MUST ALWAYS WEAR THEIR FULL ARMOR** in order to withstand unrelenting persecution. This armor is identified in Ephesians 6:10-18, the Helmet of Salvation, the Breastplate of Righteousness, the Belt of Truth, the Shoes of Peace, the Shield of Faith, and the Sword of the Spirit, which is the Word of God. In addition, the Blood of Jesus Christ covers each person who has taken Christ's name through baptism.

But God says:

<u>**Revelation 14:9, 10**</u>
"If any man worship the Beast and his image, and receive his mark in his forehead or in his hand, he shall drink the wine of the wrath of God which is poured out without mixture into the cup of His indignation. He shall be tormented with fire and brimstone in the presence of the holy angels, and in the presence of the Lamb[87]."

Before Christ returns, many treacherous people will attempt to deceive believers and lead them away from God. Some attempts will be successful. Those who refuse to deny Christ will be persecuted. We must hold on to our belief in Jesus Christ and walk with Him until the very end. (Matthew 10:22; Matthew 24:13; Hebrews 3:14)

---

[87] These scriptures describe not only the Antichrist and his False Prophet, but a talking image or picture of him that performs miracles. This thought seemed incredible a few years ago, but in the age of television, computers, mini-screens on telephones, holograms, and technological animation, it is no longer hard to imagine.

Christians!

THIS IS A FUNDAMENTAL TEST OF FAITH.
WE MUST NOT WORSHIP OR BOW TO THE BEAST.
WE MUST NOT ACCEPT
THE MARK OF his UNCLEAN and UNHOLY PRESENCE.

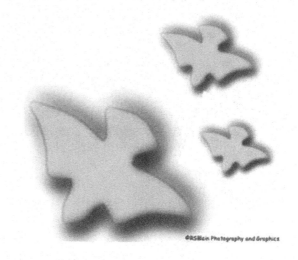

©RSBlain Photography and Graphics

Jehovah,

The great God Almighty,

Creator of Heaven

and Earth,

Is ready to say —

©RS Blain Photography and Graphics

181

For it shall be with them as the days before the flood; for until the day that Noah entered the ark, they were eating and drinking..., and knew not until the flood came and took them all away. So shall the coming of the Son of Man be.

<u>Matthew 24:45</u>

So shall the coming of the Son of Man be.

Chapter 11

What Do the Scriptures Say About
Armageddon and the Return of Jesus Christ?

Note: Some scripture is paraphrased in this chapter to clarify meaning.

Today, scripture is being fulfilled. Therefore, "Blessed are those servants whom the Lord finds watching when he comes...." (Luke 12:40). From the earliest records of the Bible, Christ makes this promise. "**I WILL COME AGAIN**."

Genesis 7:67-69 [I.V. only]

"I will come again in the Last Days, in the days of wickedness and vengeance to fulfill the oath which I made to you concerning the children of Noah. And, the day shall come that the earth shall rest. But, before that day, the Heavens shall be darkened, and the veil of darkness will cover the earth. And, the Heavens shall shake and also the earth. And, Great Tribulations shall take place among the children of men, but I will preserve my people and I will cause RIGHTEOUSNESS TO COME DOWN OUT OF HEAVEN. I will SEND TRUTH FORTH OUT OF THE EARTH to bare testimony of my Only Begotten,

Matthew 24:34 [24:29 KJV]

And immediately after the tribulation of those days, the sun shall be darkened, and the moon shall not give her light, and the stars shall fall from Heaven, and the powers of Heaven shall be shaken.

Matthew 24:38-49

And they shall see the Son of Man coming in the clouds of Heaven, with power and great glory. And anyone who treasures my words, shall not be deceived. For the Son of Man shall come, and He shall send His angels before Him with the great sound of a trumpet, and they shall gather together the remainder of His elect from the four winds; from one end of Heaven to the other.

But as it was in the days of Noah, it shall also be at the coming of the Son of Man: until the day Noah entered the ark, they were eating and drinking, marrying and giving in marriage, and did not know until the flood came and took them all away. It shall be the same at the coming of the Son of Man. Then that which is written shall be fulfilled. In the Last Days, two men will be in the field; one will be taken and the other left. Two women will be grinding at the mill. One will be taken and the other left. What I say to one, I say to all men; "Watch, therefore, for you do not know at what hour your Lord will come."

Matthew 24:42, 43, 51

"When they see all these signs my elect will know that I am near, even at the door. No one but my Father in Heaven knows what day I will come, not even the angels of God in Heaven.... Therefore, be ready! When you least expect me, the Son of man will appear."

Revelation 16:15

Behold, I [Christ] come as a thief. Blessed is he that watches, and keeps his garments, so he does not walk naked and they see his shame.

Doctrine & Covenants 108:5, 6

Hearken and hear O inhabitants of the earth. Listen together, all elders of my church and hear the voice of the Lord. He calls upon all men and commands all men everywhere to repent. For behold, the Lord God has sent forth the angel, crying through the midst of Heaven, saying: 'Prepare ye the way of the Lord, and make His paths strait. For the hour of His coming is at hand, when the Lamb shall stand upon Mount Zion, and with Him a hundred and forty four thousand, having His father's name written in their foreheads'.

Wherefore, prepare for the coming of the Bridegroom! Go, each of you go out to meet Him, for behold, He shall stand upon the Mount of Olivet, and upon the mighty ocean, even the great deep, and upon the islands of the sea, and upon the land of Zion. He shall utter His voice out of Zion, and He shall speak from Jerusalem, and His voice shall be heard among all people. It shall be a voice like the voice of many waters, and as the voice of a great thunder, which shall break down the mountains, and the valleys shall not be found. He shall command the great deep and it shall be driven back into the north countries. The islands shall become one land, and the land of Jerusalem and the land of Zion shall be turned back into their own places, and the earth shall be like it was in the days before it was divided. And the Lord, even the Savior shall stand in the midst of His people, and shall reign over all flesh.

And they who are in the north countries shall come in remembrance before the Lord. Their prophets shall hear His voice and shall no longer wait. They shall smite the rocks, and the ice shall flow down at their presence. And a highway shall be cast up in the midst of the great deep. Their enemies shall become a prey to them, and in the barren deserts, there shall come forth pools of living water. The parched ground shall no longer be a thirsty land.

*They shall bring forth their rich treasures to the children of Ephraim my servants. And the boundaries of the everlasting hills shall tremble at their presence. Then, they shall fall down and be crowned with glory in Zion by the hands of the servants of the Lord, who are the children of Ephraim. And they shall be filled with songs of everlasting joy. This is the blessing of the everlasting God upon the tribes of Israel, and the richer blessing upon the head of Ephraim and his fellows. And the tribe of Judah, after all their pain, shall be sanctified in holiness before the Lord to dwell in his presence day and night forever and ever. **SO ...**

The Good News,

The Great News,

The Shout to the Heavens News Is

Jesus Christ Is Returning Soon!

Before this can happen, the whole world must undergo terrible chastening. The evil of ordinary men will reach its peak and the Antichrist will outdo them all. The parable of the wheat and tares allegorically describes some of the things that will take place during this period (Matthew 13:22-29).

God's Reaping Time

> <u>Matthew 13:36-45 [13:37-43 KJV]</u>
> *The disciples asked Jesus to explain the parable of the tares of the field. He answered saying, "He who sows the good seed is the Son of Man. The field is the world. The good seed are the children of the kingdom, but the tares are the children of the wicked. The enemy that sowed them is the devil. The harvest is the end of the world or the destruction of the wicked. The reapers are the angels or the messengers sent from Heaven. As the tares are gathered and burned in the fire so shall the destruction of the wicked be at the end of this world.*
>
> *In that day, before the Son of Man shall come, He shall send forth His angels and messengers of Heaven. And they shall gather out of His kingdom all things that offend, and those, which do iniquity. They shall be cast out among the wicked and there will be wailing and gnashing of teeth for the world shall be burned with fire. Then the righteous shall shine forth as the Son in the kingdom of their Father.*

"Whoever has ears to hear, let him hear!"

Matthew 11:15, Mark 4:9, Mark:23-25, Luke 8:8, Revelation 3:22

Other writers of the Bible foresaw a reaping time also.

> <u>Joel 3:13-17</u>
> *Put in the sickle [of Heaven] for the harvest [of evil men] is ripe; come [Lord], for the press is full and the fats overflowing. Their wickedness is very great.*
>
> *Multitudes and multitudes [of armies] are in the valley of decision for the day of the Lord is near in this valley. The sun and the moon shall be darkened and the stars shall withdraw their shining. Then the Lord shall roar out of Zion and utter His voice from Jerusalem. The Heavens and the earth shall shake but the Lord will be the hope of His people and the strength of the children of Israel.*

John's Vision

<u>Revelation 14:14-15</u>
I beheld a white cloud and upon the cloud sat one who was like the Son of Man having on his head a golden crown and in His hand a sharp sickle. And an angel came out of the temple crying to Him with a loud voice, "Thrust in your sickle and reap for the time has come for you to reap, for the harvest of the earth is ripe."

<u>Revelation 14:16-20</u>
And He who sat on the cloud thrust in His sickle on the earth and the earth was reaped. And another angel came out of the temple in heaven and he also carried a sharp sickle. And from the altar came a third angel who had power over fire. This angel cried to the one who carried the sickle saying, "Thrust in your sickle and gather the clusters of the vine of the earth for her grapes are fully ripe." And the angel thrust in his sickle, gathered the vine of the earth, and cast it into the great winepress of the wrath of God. **And the winepress was trodden outside the city, and blood came out of the winepress, up to the horses' bridles, by the space of a thousand and six hundred furlongs.**

The nations will be furious that the time of their judgment has come but, **"Those Who Fear GOD Will Glorify Him!"**

The Great Day of the Lord

<u>Isaiah 13:6-11, 14-20, 22</u>
"Howl; for the day of the Lord is at hand; it shall come as a destruction from the Almighty. Therefore, all people shall be faint, and every man's heart shall melt, and they shall be afraid; pangs and sorrows shall take hold of them and they shall be in pain like a woman about to give birth. They shall look in amazement at one another and their faces shall be like flames, for behold, the day of the Lord comes, cruel with wrath and fierce anger to lay the land desolate and God shall destroy the sinners out of it. The stars of Heaven and the constellations shall not give their light. The sun shall be darkened as it goes forth and the moon's light will fail to shine. And I, God, will punish the world for its evil and the wicked for their iniquity. I will cause the arrogance of the proud to cease and the haughtiness of those who are terrible will be laid low.

…Every man shall turn to his own people and everyone will flee into his own land. Every one that is proud shall be thrust through; and every one that is joined to the wicked shall fall by the sword. Their children also shall be dashed to pieces before their eyes; their houses shall be spoiled, and their wives ravished.

I will stir up the Medes against them, for they do not delight in silver or gold. Their bows shall dash the young men to pieces; and they shall have no pity on the fruit of the womb; their eye shall not spare children.

And Babylon, the glory of kingdoms, the excellent beauty of the Chaldees' shall become like God's overthrow of Sodom and Gomorrah. It shall never again be inhabited…. Her time is near and her days shall not be prolonged, for I will destroy her speedily. I will be merciful to my people, but the wicked shall perish."

Isaiah 34:2, 3, 5, 8
The indignation of the Lord is upon all nations and His fury upon all their armies. He has utterly destroyed them and given them up to slaughter. Their slain shall be cast out and their stink shall come up out of their carcasses, and the mountains shall be melted with their blood…. "My sword shall be bathed in Heaven, and it shall come down upon Idumea and upon the people of my curse for judgment. The sword of the Lord is filled with blood. It is made fat with lambs and goats, with the fat of rams, for the Lord has a sacrifice in Bozrah [88] and a great slaughter in the land of Idumea…. It is the day of the Lord's vengeance and the year of recompense for the controversy of Zion."

Micah 5:10-15
It shall come to pass in that day, states the Lord that I will cut off your horses from your midst. I will destroy your chariots; and I will cut off the cities of your land, and throw down all your strong holds; and I will cut off witchcrafts out of your hand, and you shall have no more soothsayers. Your graven images will also be cut off, and your standing images will be taken out of your midst. You shall no more worship the work of your hands. And I will pluck up your groves out of your midst; and will destroy your cities. I will execute vengeance in anger and fury upon the heathen, such as they have never heard.

DOCTRINE & COVENANTS 63:9a, b
I, the Lord am angry with the wicked; I am holding my Spirit from the inhabitants of the earth. I have sworn in my wrath and decreed wars upon the face of the earth, and the wicked shall slay the wicked, and fear shall come upon every man and the saints also shall hardly escape.

DOCTRINE & COVENANTS 94:5d
Vengeance is coming speedily like a whirlwind upon the ungodly and who shall escape it? The Lord's scourge shall pass over by night and day and the reports about it shall traumatize all people. Yet it shall not be stopped until the Lord comes, for the indignation of the Lord is kindled against the abominations and all the wicked works of people.

God's Seven Last Plagues or the Seven Vials of the Wrath of God

Revelation 15:1-8
And I, John, saw another sign in Heaven, for there were seven angels having the seven last plagues filled with the wrath of God.

---

[88] Bozrah-The chief city of northern Edom close to the southern frontier of Syria. Idumaea-the Greek name for Edom, occupied in part by Edomites.

And I saw what looked like a sea of glass mingled with fire; and those who had gotten victory over the beast, his image, his mark, and the number of his name, stood on the sea of glass, having the harps of God. And they sang the song of Moses, the servant of God, and the song of the Lamb, saying, "Great and marvelous are thy works, Lord God Almighty; just and true are thy ways, thou King of saints. Who shall not fear thee, O Lord, and glorify thy name? For thou only art holy; for all nations shall come and worship before thee; for thy judgments are made manifest."

Afterward I looked, and the temple of the tabernacle of the testimony in Heaven was opened; and the seven angels came out of the temple, having the seven plagues. They were clothed in pure white linen, and had their breasts girded with golden girdles. One of four beasts that guarded the throne gave the angels seven golden vials full of the wrath of God, who lives forever and ever. And the temple was filled with smoke from the glory of God, and from His power; and no man was able to enter into the temple, until the seven plagues of the seven angels were fulfilled.

Now the wrath of God is completely full. He directs seven angels to empty vials of His wrath on the earth. No one, not the Antichrist, the False Prophet or Satan can begin to imagine the horror God has prepared for those who fight against Him.

Revelation 16:1, 2
And I heard a great voice out of the temple saying to the seven angels, "Go your ways, and pour out the vials of the wrath of God upon the earth." And the first went, and poured out his vial upon the earth; and there fell a noisome and grievous sore upon the men, which had the mark of the beast and upon them, which worshipped his image.

Revelation 16:3
And the second angel poured out his vial upon the sea; and it became as the blood of a dead man; and every living soul died in the sea.

Revelation 16:4-6
And the third angel poured out his vial upon the rivers and fountains of waters; and they became blood. And I heard the angel of the waters say, "Thou art righteous, O Lord, which are, and were, and shall be, because you have judged. For they have shed the blood of saints and prophets, and you have given them blood to drink; for they are worthy." And I heard another angel who came out from the altar saying, "Even so, Lord God Almighty, true and righteous are thy judgments."

Revelation 16:8, 9
And the fourth angel poured out his vial upon the sun; and power was given him to scorch men with fire. And men were scorched with great heat, and blasphemed the name of God, which has power over these plagues; and they did not repent and give Him glory.

Revelation 16:10, 11

And the fifth angel poured out his vial upon the seat of the beast; and his kingdom was full of darkness; and they gnawed their tongues for pain, and blasphemed the God of Heaven because of their pains and their sores, and did not repent of their deeds.

Revelation 16:12-14

When the sixth angel poured out his vial upon the great river Euphrates, the water dried up so the way of the kings of the east might be prepared. And three unclean spirits like frogs came out of the mouth of the dragon, the beast and the false prophet, and they are the spirits of devils, working miracles, which go forth unto the kings of the earth and the whole world, to gather them to the battle of that great day of God Almighty.

Revelation 16:17-21

And the seventh angel poured out his vial into the air; and there came a great voice out of the temple of Heaven, from the throne, saying, "It is done." And there were voices, and thunders, and lightnings; and there was a great earthquake, such as was not since men were upon the earth, it was so mighty and so great. And the great city was divided into three parts, and the cities of the nations fell; and God remembered to give great Babylon her cup of the wine of the fierceness of His wrath.

And every island fled away, and the mountains were not found. And great hail out of Heaven fell upon men. And great hail will fall from Heaven upon men, every stone about the weight of a talent, and men will blaspheme God because of the plague of hail for it will be very great.

Revelation 17:1, 2

After the seven vials of God's wrath are poured, one of the angels spoke to John and said he would show him the judgment of the great whore that sits upon many waters, with whom the kings of the earth committed fornication, and the inhabitants of the earth have been made drunk with the wine of her fornication.

The Fall of Babylon or the Judgment of the Great Whore

Revelation 17:3-18

So he [the angel] carried me [John] away in the spirit into the wilderness; and I [John] saw a woman sitting upon a scarlet colored beast [the Antichrist], full of names of blasphemy. The beast had seven heads and ten horns. The woman was arrayed in purple and scarlet color, and decked with gold and precious stones and pearls, having a golden cup in her hand full of abominations and filthiness of her fornication; and upon her forehead was a name, Mystery, Babylon the Great, The Mother of Harlots and Abominations of the Earth.

And the woman was drunk with the blood of the saints, and with the blood of the martyrs of Jesus; and when I [John] saw her, I was astonished, but the angel with me said he would tell me [John] the mystery of the woman and the beast, which carried her. The beast, which you saw, was, and is not; and shall ascend out of the bottomless pit, and go into perdition. They that dwell on the earth, whose names were not written in the book of life from the foundation of the world, shall wonder when they behold the beast that was, and is not, and yet is.

Here is the mind, which has wisdom. The seven heads are seven mountains on which the woman sits. And there are seven kings; five are fallen, and one is, and the other has not yet come; and when he comes, he must stay for a short while. And the beast that was, and is not, is the eighth, and is part of the seven, and goes into perdition.

The ten horns, which you saw, are ten kings, which have no kingdom yet, but receive power as kings for one hour with the beast. They have one mind, and shall give their power and strength to the beast. They shall make war with the Lamb, and the Lamb shall overcome them; for He is Lord of Lords, and King of kings; and they that are with Him are called, and chosen, and faithful.

And the angel said to me [John], "The waters which you saw, where the whore sits, are people, and multitudes, and nations, and tongues. And the ten horns, which you saw upon the beast, hate the whore, and shall make her desolate and naked and shall eat her flesh, and burn her with fire. God has put in their hearts the desire to fulfill His will, and to give their kingdom to the beast, until the words of God are fulfilled. And the woman, which you saw, is the great city, which reigns over the kings of the earth [Babylon]."

Revelation 18:1-6, 24
And after these things I, [John] saw another angel coming down from Heaven, having great power. The earth was lightened with his glory, and he cried mightily with a strong voice, saying, "Babylon the great is fallen, is fallen, and has become the habitation of devils, and the hold of every foul spirit, and a cage of every unclean and hateful bird. For all nations have drunk of the wine of the wrath of her fornication, and the kings of the earth have committed fornication with her, and the merchants of the earth have become rich through the abundance of her delicacies."

And I [John] heard another voice from Heaven, saying, "Come out of her, my people, that you are not partakers of her sins, and that you do not receive her plagues. Her sins have reached Heaven, and God has remembered her iniquities. And in her was found the blood of prophets, and of saints, and of all that were slain upon the earth."

The Antichrist prepares for war.

Revelation 13:5-11
The Antichrist spoke haughty and blasphemous words and was allowed to exercise authority for forty-two months. He uttered blasphemies against God, God's name, God's dwelling and all those who dwell in heaven. He was also allowed to make war on the saints and to conquer them. He was given authority over every tribe and people, every language and nation and all the inhabitants will worship him, everyone whose name who has not been written from the foundation of the world from the book of life of the Lamb that was slaughtered.

Let anyone who has an ear listen: he who leads into captivity shall be taken captive. He who kills with the sword must be killed with the sword. Here is a call for the endurance and faith of the saints.

Revelation 16:16
And he [the Antichrist] gathered them [the kings of the earth-Rev.16:14] together into a place called in the Hebrew tongue Armageddon.

Revelation 17:12-14
And the ten horns [on the beast with seven heads] are ten kings, which have received no kingdom as yet; but receive power as kings one hour with the beast. They have one mind, and shall give their power and strength to the beast. And these shall make war with the Lamb….

As the Antichrist rushes mammoth armies to the battle, God is fully prepared for that which is to come. The Antichrist, False Prophet, and Satan command all the mighty, modern weaponry the world has ever produced. It is enough to destroy the whole world, and it is all focused on the Heavens.

The Second Coming of Jesus Christ and the First Resurrection

Matthew 24:37-40
After the tribulation of those days, the powers of Heaven will shake as the sign of the Son of Man appears. All the tribes of earth shall mourn.

I Thessalonians 4:16-17
The Lord himself shall descend from Heaven with a shout, with the voice of the archangel, and with the trump of God; and the dead in Christ shall rise first. Then, they who are alive shall be caught up together into the clouds[89] with them who remain, to meet the Lord in the air; and so we shall ever be with the Lord.

Revelation 20:6
Blessed and holy are they who have part in the first resurrection; on such the second death has no power. And they shall be priests of God and of Christ, and shall reign with Him a thousand years.

II Nephi 6:31 [9:13 LDS]
...The paradise of God must deliver up the spirits of the righteous, and the grave must deliver up the bodies of the righteous. And the spirit and the body is restored to itself again, and all men become incorruptible, and immortal, and they are living souls.

Doctrine & Covenants 108:10, 11
Now the year of my redeemed is come, and they shall mention the loving kindness of their Lord, and all that He has bestowed upon them, according to His goodness, and according to His loving kindness, forever and ever. In all their afflictions, He was afflicted. And the angel of His presence saved them; and in His love, and in His pity, He redeemed them, and bare them, and carried them all the days of old. And Enoch also, and they who were with him, and the prophets who were before him. And Noah also, and they who were before him. And Moses also, and they who were before him, and from Moses to Elijah, and from Elijah to John, who were with Christ in His resurrection. And the holy apostles, with Abraham, Isaac, and Jacob, shall be in the presence of the Lamb.

And the graves of the saints shall be opened, and they shall come forth and stand on the right hand of the Lamb, when He shall stand upon Mount Zion, and upon the city, the New Jerusalem, and they shall sing the song of the Lamb day and night forever and ever.

And for this cause, that men might be made partakers of the glories which were to be revealed, the Lord sent forth the fullness of His gospel, His everlasting covenant, reasoning in plainness and simplicity to prepare the weak for those things which are coming on the earth. And for the Lord's

---

[89] The timing of this event (caught up in the clouds to meet Christ) is debated by many Christians. Four different "rapture" scenarios are taught. RLDS Church taught that the righteous will be caught up to be with Christ when he appears at the end of the tribulation, before the war of Armageddon begins.

errand in the day when the weak shall confound the wise, and the little one become a strong nation, and two should put their tens of thousands to flight; and by the weak things of the earth, the Lord should thresh the nations by the power of His Spirit.

And for this cause these commandments were given; they were commanded to be kept from the world in the day that they were given, but now are to go forth unto all flesh. And this according to the mind and will of the Lord, who rules over all flesh; and eternal life shall be given to him that repents and sanctifies himself before the Lord.

The Lord completes His own preparation.

When the Savior rides forth on a white horse, He was, is, and always will be the Word of God. He wears a garment covered in blood. His eyes burn like flames. His sword is ready and His anger is tightly controlled. (Revelation 19:11-16) Vast armies of Heaven follow the Lord, but they have come to witness, not to fight.

Mankind will be stunned for in the midst of the world's most horrific conflict, the clouds will part, the Heavens open, and the whole world will witnesses the Second Coming of Jesus Christ. The Great Tribulation will end with Christ's triumphant return. Armies gathered to battle will fall at His appearance. Simultaneously even the faithful, who have awaited His coming, will be so overwhelmed they cannot contain their emotions.

To the utter amazement of everyone, the righteous, both living and dead, will rise in the clouds to greet their Lord. This is the first resurrection

Revelation 11:15
The seventh angel sounded; and there were great voices in heaven saying, "The kingdoms of this world are become the kingdom of our Lord, and of His Christ; and He shall reign forever and ever."

ARMAGEDDON

Revelation 19:11-16
And I saw Heaven opened, and behold a white horse; and He who sat upon him is called Faithful and True, and in righteousness He judges and makes war. His eyes as a flame of fire; and He has on His head many crowns; and a name written that no man knew, but himself. And He is clothed with a vesture dipped in blood; and His name is called, The Word of God.

And the armies, which were in Heaven, followed Him upon white horses, and they were clothed in fine linen, white and clean.

And out of His mouth proceeds the Word of God, and with it He will smite the nations; and He will rule them with the word of His mouth; and He treads the winepress in the fierceness and wrath of Almighty God. And He has on a vesture, and on His thigh a name is written: **King of Kings and Lord of Lords.**

"And He shall reign forever and ever."

<u>Revelation 11:15</u>

Although the call to battle by the Antichrist will be well known worldwide, almost no one will expect the Great Day of the Lord. When the sixth seal of God's book is opened, chaos, destruction, and horror will encompass the earth. A great earthquake will strike the planet. People, unprepared for Christ's return, will search desperately for places of safety. This will be far worse than the seals, trumps, and woes in Chapter 10. Those people still alive, Kings, mighty men, and common people will hide themselves in dens hoping mountains and falling rocks will hide them from the wrath of the Lamb. The sun will become black and the moon will look like blood. Stars will fall to the earth and the Heavens will open, moving mounts and islands out of their places. Hailstones weighing seventy-five [90] to one hundred pounds will fall. High elevations will be leveled and the entire surface of the planet will be flattened as millions die.

Matthew 24:34 [24:29 KJV]
And immediately after the tribulation of those days, the sun shall be darkened, and the moon shall not give her light, and the stars shall fall from Heaven, and the powers of Heaven shall be shaken.

Revelation 19:19
And I saw the beast, and the kings of the earth, and their armies gathered together to make war against Him that sat on the horse, and against His army.

The Book of Zephaniah portrays a terrifying picture of God's wrath.

The book of Zephaniah tells the story of the first destruction of Israel. On closer examination it also reveals and describes the Last Days. God is furious and He is letting the inhabitants of the world know it. (The following passages were taken from the *Inspired Version of the Bible*, the *HarperCollins Study Bible*; *New Revised Standard Version*, and *The Message-the Bible in Contemporary Language*.)

Zephaniah Chapter 1

Zephaniah 1:1.
The Word of the Lord that came to Zephaniah, son of Cushi during the reign of Josiah, son of Amon king of Judah: [written between 40 and 612 B.C.]

Zephaniah 1:2, 3
I will utterly consume all things from off the land, says the Lord. I will consume man and beast; I will consume the fowls of the heaven, the fish of the sea, and the stumbling blocks with the wicked; and I will cut man off from the land.

---

[90] A talent weighs between seventy-five and one hundred pounds.

Zephaniah 1:4-6
I will also stretch out my hand upon Judah, and upon all the inhabitants of Jerusalem; and I will cut off the remnant of Baal from this place, those who worship other Gods, and who turn away from the Lord; and those who have not sought the Lord nor inquired for Him.

Zephaniah 1:7, 8
Hold your peace at the presence of the Lord God; for the day of the Lord is at hand; for the Lord has prepared a sacrifice and He has called His guests. And it shall come to pass in the day of the Lord's sacrifice, that I will punish the princes, and the king's children, and all who wear foreign clothing.

Zephaniah 1:10-13
In that day, says the Lord, there shall be noise, and cries and howling in the city of Jerusalem and a great crashing in the hills. Howl, you inhabitants in the merchant section of the city. Everybody who trades for silver will be cut off. I will search Jerusalem with candles and punish the men who are settled in their places and say in their hearts, 'the Lord will not do good nor evil.' Therefore, their goods shall become booty and their houses will be desolate. They shall build houses but not inhabit them; and they shall plant vineyards but not drink the wine from the grapes.

Zephaniah 1:14-17
The great day of the Lord is near and it is coming fast. The mighty man shall cry there bitterly. That day is a day of wrath, a day of trouble and distress, a day of wasteness and desolation, a day of gloominess, a day of clouds and thick darkness. There will be trumpets and alarms against the fenced cities and against high towers. And I will bring distress upon men so that they walk like blind men, because they have sinned against the Lord; and their blood shall be poured out as dust, and their flesh as the dung.

Zephaniah 1:18
Neither their silver nor their gold shall be able to deliver them in the day of the Lord's wrath; but the whole land shall be devoured by the fire of His jealousy; for He shall quickly get rid of all them that dwell in the land.

Zephaniah Chapter 2

Zephaniah 2:1
Gather yourselves together, oh undesired nations. Do this before the decree comes forth, before the day passes and you are blown away like leaves in a windstorm, before the fierce anger of the Lord comes upon you, before the day of the Lord's anger comes upon you with full force.

Zephaniah 2:2
Seek the Lord, all humble men of the earth, who obey His commandments. Seek righteousness, seek humility so perhaps you will be sheltered in the day of the Lord's anger.

Zephaniah 2:4-5

The Lord lists Gaza, Ashkelon, Asdod, Ekron, the Kerethite people, Canaan, the land of the Philistines, as some of God's enemies that will be destroyed.

Zephaniah 2:6, 7

The seacoast shall become dwellings and cottages for shepherds and folds for flocks. It will belong to the remnant of the house of Judah and they shall have food there. They shall lie down in the houses of their enemy in the evening; for the Lord their God shall visit and restore them.

Zephaniah 2:8-10

I [the Lord] have heard the insults of Moab and the revilings of the children of Ammon, when they taunted my people and threatened their land. "Therefore, as I live," says the Lord of hosts, the God of Israel, "surely Moab shall become like Sodom and the children of Ammon like Gomorrah, a place of weeds and salt pits, and perpetual desolation. Because of their pride, they insulted and mocked the people of the Lord of hosts, but the residue of my people shall plunder them, and the survivors of my nation will inherit their land."

Zephaniah 2:11

The Lord will be terrible to these countries when He destroys all the gods of the land. The nations on every shore will worship Him, everyone in his own land.

Zephaniah 2:12-15

The Cushites and Assyrians will be destroyed, and Nineveh will be desolate because she said to herself, "I am, and there is no one besides me." She will become a lair for wild beasts and all who pass by her will scoff and shake their fists.

Zephaniah Chapter 3

Zephaniah 3:1-4

Woe to the city of oppressors who are rebellious and defiled. She obeys no one, she accepts no correction. She does not trust in the Lord, and she does not draw near to her God. Her officials are roaring lions; her rulers are evening wolves who leave nothing for the morning. Her prophets are arrogant; they are treacherous men. Her priests profane the sanctuary and do violence to the law.

Zephaniah 3:5

The just Lord is in the midst of them. He will do no wrong. Every morning He dispenses His justice, and every new day He does not fail, yet the unrighteous know no shame.

Zephaniah 3:6

I have cut off nations; their strongholds are demolished. I have left their streets deserted with no one passing through. Their cities are destroyed. No one will be left.

Zephaniah 3:7

I said to the city, "Surely you will fear me and accept correction!" Then your dwelling will not be cut off and my punishments will not come upon you. But they were still eager to act corruptly in all they did.

Zephaniah 3:8

"Therefore wait for me," declares the Lord, "for the day I will stand up to witness against you. It is my decision to gather nations, to assemble kingdoms, to pour out upon them my indignation, all the heat of my anger; for in the fire of my passion all the earth shall be consumed."

Zephaniah 3:9, 10

At that time I will give to my people a pure language, that all of them may call on the name of the Lord and serve Him with one accord. From beyond the rivers of Ethiopia, all my scattered, exiled people will bring me offerings.

Zephaniah 3:11, 12

On that day you shall not be put to shame because of all the deeds by which you have rebelled against me and I will remove from your midst, the proud and exalted so you will no longer be haughty in my holy mountain. I will leave in your presence an afflicted, lowly and humble people, and they shall seek refuge in the name of the Lord.

Zephaniah 3:13

The remnant of Israel shall do no wrong, nor speak lies. A deceitful tongue shall not be found in their mouths. Then they shall feed and lie down, and no one shall make them afraid.

Zephaniah 3:14, 15

Sing, O daughter of Zion; shout, O Israel; be glad and rejoice with all your heart, O daughter of Jerusalem. The Lord has taken away the judgments against you. He has cast out your enemy. The King of Israel, even the Lord, is in your midst; and you shall not see evil any more

Zephaniah 3:16, 17

On that day it shall be said to Jerusalem: Do not fear, O Zion; do not let your hands grow weak. The Lord, your God, is in your midst. He will save you. He will rejoice over you with joy. He will renew you in His love; He will exult over you with singing.

Zephaniah 3:18

I will gather those who are sorrowful in preparation for the solemn assembly [one of the feasts of the Lord] and remove the burden and reproach of it from you.

Zephaniah 3:19

At that time, I will deal with all who oppressed you. I will rescue the lame and gather those who have been scattered. I will give them praise and honor in every land where they were put to shame.

Zephaniah 3:20
"At that time, I will gather you; and bring you home. I will give you honor and praise among all the peoples of the earth when I restore you as my people before their very eyes," says the Lord.

The Final Battle

The armies of the Antichrist gather together into a place called Armageddon. This location will be the site of the world's last combat. It will be a cosmic struggle between the forces of good and evil, God and Satan, the powers of darkness and all the armies of Heaven. Even the great Euphrates River will dry (Revelation 16:12), allowing the armies of the east to cross and engage in the war. The major concentration of conflict will take place in the Megiddo Plain while additional troops will spread throughout Israel and the surrounding Arab countries. The world's most sophisticated weapons will target the God of the universe. God needs only one weapon: the Sword of His Spirit, His Word! By the word of his mouth His enemies are slain.

II Thessalonians 2:8
And then shall be revealed the lawless one, whom the Lord Jesus shall slay with the breath of his mouth, and bring to naught by the manifestation of his coming;

The End of Armageddon

Isaiah 34:1-3
The Lord says, "Come near to hear, you nations; and hearken, you people; let the earth hear, and all that is therein; the world, and all things that come forth of it. For the indignation of the Lord is upon all nations, and His fury upon all their armies; He has utterly destroyed them, and has delivered them for slaughter. Their slain shall be cast out, and their stink shall come up out of their carcasses, and the mountains shall be melted with their blood.

The Antichrist and false prophet are captured.

II Thessalonians 2:8-10
And then shall that wicked one be revealed, whom the Lord shall consume with the spirit of His mouth [the Sword of the Spirit, Ephesians 6:17], and shall destroy with the brightness of His coming. Yes, the Lord, even Jesus, whose coming is not until after there comes a falling away, by the working of Satan with all power, and signs and lying wonders, and with all deceptions of unrighteousness in them that perish; because they received not the love of the truth, that they might be saved.

Revelation 19:17, 18 I.V. [KJV is significantly different]

And I, John saw an angel standing in the sun. And he cried with a loud voice, saying to all the fowls that fly in the midst of Heaven, "Come and gather yourselves together to the supper of the great God. You may eat the flesh of kings, captains, and mighty men, the flesh of horses, and of them who sit on them, and the flesh of all who fight against the Lamb, both bond and free, both small and great.

Revelation 19:19-21

And I saw the Beast and the kings of the earth and their armies gathered together to make war against the Lord on horseback and against His army. And the Beast was captured and with him the false prophet who wrought miracles with which he deceived the people who worshipped his image and received the Mark of the Beast. These both were cast into a lake of fire burning with brimstone and the remnant of their armies were slain with the Word of Him that sat upon the horse, which Word proceeded out of His mouth.

Revelation 20:4, 5

And I saw thrones, and they sat upon them, and judgment was given unto them; and I saw the souls of those who were beheaded for their witness of Jesus and the Word of God. They had not worshipped the Beast or his image and did not receive his mark upon their foreheads or in their hands. They lived and reigned with Christ a thousand years. But the rest of the dead did not live again until the thousand years were over. This is the first resurrection.

Court is held for the Antichrist and the false prophet.

Daniel 7:9-11 [taken from The Complete Jewish Bible]

[This Bible version was used to clarify that Jesus Christ is the Ancient One or Ancient of Days.] "As I watched, thrones were set in place and the Ancient One took His seat. His clothing was white as snow; the hair on His head was like pure wool. His throne was fiery flames, with wheels of burning fire. A stream of fire flowed from His presence. Thousands and thousands ministered to Him. Millions and millions stood before Him. Then the court was convened and the books were opened.
I kept watching because of the arrogant words, which the horn [the Antichrist] was speaking, I watched as the beast [the Antichrist] was killed and its body destroyed. It was given over to be burned up completely. [Note: Revelation 19:19-21 indicates that the False Prophet is cast down at the same time.]

As for the other beasts [Satan and his demons], their ruler ship was taken away, but their lives were prolonged for a time and a season.

Satan is defeated and bound for a thousand years.

Shortly after the Antichrist is slain, God will totally humiliate the devil. However, He still has a purpose for the evil one. Satan will be bound for the length of the millennium, but at the end of the thousand years, the Devil will be released for a short time to tempt those born during the millennium reign. (Revelation 20:3)

Isaiah 14:12-17, 19-20

How you are fallen from Heaven, O Lucifer, son of the morning! How you are cut down to the ground, you who weakened the nations! For you said in your heart, "I will ascend into Heaven and there I will exalt my throne above the stars of God. I will also sit upon the mount of the congregation in the sides of the north. I will ascend above the heights of the clouds. I will be like the Most High." Yet, you shall be brought down to Hell, to the sides of the pit. They that see you shall look upon you and say, "Is this the man that made the earth tremble and shook the kingdoms and made the world like a wilderness and destroyed the cities and did not release his prisoners" ...

You are cast out of your grave, like an abominable branch, cast out like the remnant of those slain with the sword that lie under foot like a dead carcass at the bottom of a pit. You shall not be joined with them [the Antichrist and false prophet] in burial because you have destroyed your land and slain your people.

Revelation 20:1-3

I saw an angel come down out of Heaven, having the key of the bottomless pit and a great chain in his hand. He laid hold on the dragon, that old serpent which is the Devil and Satan, bound him a thousand years, and cast him into the bottomless pit, shutting him in there. He set a seal upon him that he could no more deceive the nations until the thousand years are fulfilled. After that, he must be loosed a little season.

Doctrine & Covenants 108:12b-f, 13

For, behold, the day will come that shall burn as an oven, and all the proud, yes, and all that do wickedly, shall become stubble, and the day that will come shall burn them up, says the Lord of hosts. It shall not leave them root or branch.

This shall be the answer of the Lord to them: "In that day when I came unto my own, none of you received me, and you were driven out. When I called again, none of you answered, yet neither my arm of redemption nor my power to deliver you was shortened at all. Behold, now at my rebuke I dry up the sea. I make the rivers a wilderness; their fish stink and die for thirst. I clothe the Heavens with blackness, and make sackcloth their covering. This is what you shall have from my hand. You shall lie down in sorrow, and there are none to deliver you, for you did not obey my voice when I called to you out of the Heavens. You did not believe my servants when they were sent to you and you did not receive them. Therefore, they sealed up their testimony and bound up the law, and you will be delivered to outer darkness, where there is weeping, and wailing and gnashing of teeth. Behold, the Lord your God has spoken it. Amen.

King of Kings and Lord of Lords

Matt Zelni

Ezekiel 39:9, 11, 12

They who dwell in the cities of Israel shall go forth and burn the weapons [left on the battlefield]. I will make a place of graves for Gog [the enemy] in the valley of passengers [Valley of Megedo] east of the sea and it shall stop the noses of those who pass by and there they shall bury Gog and his multitude and they shall call it The Valley of Hamon-gog. It will take the House of Israel seven months to bury the bodies, before the land is cleansed.

It will take seven months to clean up the land near Israel after the Great War, but the rest of the world will also need extensive restoration. This may indicate there will be a space of time between the war and the establishment of the millennium. On the other hand, this may be one of the first tasks in the millennium. (Also see Isaiah chapters 10-19 and 24 and 25.)

"It will take the House of Israel seven months to bury the bodies, before the land is cleansed."

Ezekiel 39:12

God is not kidding.
This— is for eternity!

The Last Days will test the faith of all people who call themselves Christian. Fear for their lives and for the lives of those they love will cause many people to deny the Savior. **Men and women who have a close personal relationship with Jesus must have complete trust in Him during the Tribulation, even though their own lives may be forfeited.** These Christians know that life on earth is a probationary period and real life begins when we are with the Lord. They are not deceived by false intellectualism, because the Holy Spirit resides within them, strengthening their lives and their testimony. Jesus wants this closeness with all of God's children. It is achieved through prayer, meditation, and the study of scripture. In other words, it takes time. These Christians don't just know about Jesus. They KNOW Jesus and He is the central part of their lives. He lives within them. He interacts with them. He is their best friend. He confirms the truthfulness of scripture through His still, small voice and provides unexpected insight into the ways of God. His gospel guides their lives. They know His voice. Today, these believers stand in awe as they witness His prophecies being fulfilled. They do not fear what man can do to them because they know what Jesus Christ has done for them.

In addition:

- Their study of the Old Testament confirms that prophecies about the birth and resurrection of Christ were fulfilled.
- They watch with excitement as "Lost Tribes of Israel" are returning to the Holy Land.
- They see the implementation of God's covenants with the Jews.
- They are confident that the Holy Scriptures are the Word of God, insofar as they are correctly translated.
- They trust the Old and New Testament prophecies predicting the return of Jesus Christ, and look forward to this incredible event.
- With reverence, they witness the fulfillment of last-day prophecy recorded in scripture.
- Most important, because of their personal friendship with Jesus, they can never be persuaded that God's Word is untrue. Therefore, they believe that time on earth is ending and all humanity should prepare to meet the Lord.

In contrast, there are people who pick and choose from the writings of the prophets and apostles, discarding the virgin birth, the resurrection of Christ, all admonition concerning the Last Days, a literal Satan, and an Antichrist who precedes Christ's second coming. In like manner, they consider publications on the Last Days out of touch with reality, no longer valid in an enlightened society. Such attitudes undermine God's Word, leaving little in which to believe and not much room for hope.

Jesus urges everyone to turn to Him immediately. His direction is certainly needed and it can be found in the Bible, the Book of Mormon, and the Doctrine and Covenants.

This is my everlasting covenant. When your posterity embraces the truth and looks upward, then Zion shall look downward... And the earth shall tremble with joy.

Genesis 9:21-24

This is mine everlasting covenant.

Chapter 12

What do the scriptures say about Zion and the millennium?
Note: Some scripture is paraphrased in this chapter to clarify meaning.

Enoch's City of Zion
The Bible tells us the City of Zion will return to earth shortly before Christ comes. The story of Zion is told to us in scripture.

Genesis 9:21-24 [I. V. only]
God's Everlasting Covenant
This is my everlasting covenant [with Enoch and Noah] that when your posterity embraces the truth and looks upward, then Zion shall look downward and all the Heavens shall shake with gladness and the earth shall tremble with joy. And, the general assembly of the church of the first-born shall come down out of Heaven and possess the earth and shall remain in place until the end comes.

The book of Genesis (Chapters 6 and 7 Inspired Version only) describes a righteous man named Enoch who walked and talked with God. The Lord honored Enoch's righteousness by teaching him about Christ's future birth and ministry, and the second coming of the Lord in the Last Days. He also learned of Christ's plan of salvation for humankind. With this knowledge, Enoch became a "preacher of righteousness" calling upon men to have faith in Christ and to repent of all sin. (Genesis 6:24-27, 53, 62, 65) When he spoke the words of God, his voice carried such authority that people trembled and were unable to stand in his presence.

Genesis 6:33-38 [I. V. only]
The Lord said to Enoch, "Go forth and do as I have commanded and no man will harm you. Open your mouth, and it shall be filled, and I will give you the words. Say unto this people, 'Choose this day to serve the Lord God who made you,' and behold, my Spirit is upon you. Therefore, I will justify all your words… abide in me and I in you. Walk with me…. Anoint your eyes with clay and wash them and you shall see," and Enoch did.

Thereafter, Enoch beheld spirits God had created, and he beheld other things, which were not visible to the natural eye. And, a saying spread forth in the land that the Lord raised up a seer for His people.

Genesis 6:49-51 [I. V. only]
And Enoch said, "Because Adam fell we are. By his fall came death and we are made partakers of misery and woe. Behold, Satan came among the children of men and tempted them to worship him, and men became carnal, sensual, and devilish, and are shut out from the presence of God. But, God made it known to our fathers that all men must repent."

Genesis 7:15-17 [I. V. only]
So great was Enoch's faith that he became the leader of the people of God, and when enemies came to battle against them, he spoke the Word of the Lord. The earth trembled, and rivers turned out of their course according to his command. Because the Word of God was so powerful, all nations feared Enoch and the glory of the Lord was upon His people.

Genesis 8:20, 23, 27 [I. V. only]
At that time, there were wars and much bloodshed, but the Lord came and dwelt with His people, and they dwelt in righteousness. And the fear of the Lord was upon all nations, because great was the glory of the Lord upon His people.

The Lord called His people Zion because they were of one heart and one mind and they dwelt in righteousness, and there were no poor among them.

(Summary)
Genesis 7:54, 62, 63 [I. V. only]
Enoch was shown all of the inhabitants of the earth, generation after generation. Then he said to the Lord, "Surely, Zion shall dwell in safety forever." But the Lord replied, "I have blessed Zion but I have cursed the residue of the people." In the process of time, Zion was taken up into Heaven.

From his new vantage point, Enoch was able to observe both the goodness and the sins of man. He also witnessed the crucifixion, resurrection, and ascension of Jesus Christ (Genesis 7:27, 54-64 I. V. only).

Genesis 7:65, 66 [I. V. only]
[Enoch beheld the troubles on the earth] and he wept, crying to the Lord saying, "When shall the earth rest?" And, he beheld the Son of Man ascend up to the Father, and he called unto the Lord saying, "Will you come again to earth?"

The Lord promised Enoch, "I will return again. And you and your city will return with me."

Genesis 9:21-23
This is my everlasting covenant, that when your posterity embraces the truth, and looks upward, then Zion shall look downward, and all the Heavens shall shake with gladness, and the earth shall tremble with joy; and the general assembly of the church of the first-born shall possess the earth, and shall have a place until the end. And is my everlasting covenant, which I made with Enoch.

When finally established, Zion will be the glory of Christ's Church and His people who have impatiently waited for its return.

Genesis 7:70-75
I will cause righteousness and truth to sweep the earth as a flood to gather out my elect from the four quarters of the earth to a place which I shall prepare; a holy city, that my people might be ready and be looking forward to the time of my coming. My tabernacle shall be there, and it shall be called Zion, a NEW JERUSALEM."

And, the Lord said to Enoch, "Then you and all of your city shall meet them there, and we will receive them into our bosom, and they shall see us and we will fall upon their necks, and they shall fall upon our necks, and we will kiss each other. I, the Lord will live there, and it shall be Zion which shall come forth out of all the creations which I have made; and for the space of a thousand years the earth shall rest."

And it came to pass, Enoch saw the day of the coming of the Son of Man, in the Last Days, to dwell on the earth in righteousness for the space of a thousand years.
But, before that day, he also saw Great Tribulation among the wicked. He watched as the sea was troubled and men's hearts failed them, looking with fear for the judgment of the Almighty God which would come upon the wicked.

So the Lord showed Enoch all things until the end of the world. And, he saw the day of the righteous, the hour of their redemption, and he was filled with joy. [This information is repeated in D & C 36:12 and 13.]

According to these scriptures, there is an appointed time for Enoch's city to return to earth. Zion's restoration does not depend on our response or lack of it. It will take place on God's timetable. The arrival of Enoch's city will be celebrated by the multitudes of living and resurrected saints privileged to take part in Christ's thousand-year reign.

Psalm 132:13
The Lord has chosen Zion because He desired it for His place of habitation.

Isaiah 4:1-5
In that day the branch of the Lord will be beautiful and glorious, and the fruit of the earth shall be excellent and comely to them that escaped from Israel. And it shall come to pass, they that are left in Zion, and he who remains in Jerusalem, shall be called holy, every one that is written among the living in Jerusalem. Then, when the Lord shall have washed away the filth of the daughters of Zion, and shall have purged the blood of Jerusalem from the midst thereof, by the spirit of judgment and by the spirit of burning, the Lord will create upon every dwelling-place of mount Zion, and upon her assemblies, a cloud of smoke by day and the shining of a flaming fire by night. For upon all the glory of Zion there shall be a defense. And there shall be a tabernacle for a shadow in the daytime from the heat, and for a place of refuge, and for a covert from storm and rain.

Zechariah 1:16, 17

The Lord promises, "I will return to Jerusalem with mercy. My house shall be built in it and a line shall be stretched forth upon Jerusalem. "The Lord of hosts declares, "My cities shall be prosperous and shall be spread abroad. The Lord shall yet comfort Zion and shall yet choose Jerusalem."

Doctrine & Covenants 36:2h

The Lord called His people Zion because they were of one heart and one mind and dwelt in righteousness.

Doctrine & Covenants 36:12c-g

The Lord said to Enoch, "As I live, even so I will come in the Last Days—in the days of wickedness and vengeance to fulfill the oath which I made to you, concerning the children of Noah. And, the day shall come that the earth shall rest, but before that day the Heavens shall be darkened, and a veil of darkness shall cover the earth. The Heavens shall shake and also the earth and Great Tribulations shall be among the children of men, but I will preserve my people. I will send righteousness down from Heaven, and I will send truth forth from the earth to bear testimony of my Only Begotten, His resurrection from the dead, and the resurrection of all men. And I will cause righteousness and truth to sweep the earth as with a flood, to gather out my own elect from the four quarters of the earth unto a place, which I shall prepare, a holy city. My people will gird up their loins and be looking forth for a time of my coming; for there shall be my tabernacle and shall be called Zion, a New Jerusalem." [This is the same as Genesis 7:67-69 I.V.]

Doctrine & Covenants 36:13a-b

And the Lord said to Enoch, "Then you and all your city shall meet them there. And we will receive them into our bosom, and they shall see us. And we will fall upon their necks, and they shall fall upon our necks, and we will kiss each other. And there shall be my abode, and it shall be Zion which shall come forth out of all the creations which I have made, and for the space of a thousand years the earth shall rest." [This is the same as Genesis 7:67-72 I.V.]

Doctrine & Covenants 63:13a-g

He that is faithful and endures shall overcome the world. He that sends up treasures into the land of Zion shall receive an inheritance in this world, and his works shall follow him, and he shall have a reward, in the world to come. Blessed are the dead that die in the Lord, from this time on. When the Lord comes, old things shall pass away, and all things shall become new. They shall rise from the dead, and shall not die after, and shall receive an inheritance, before the Lord in the holy city. He that lives, when the Lord shall come, and has kept the faith, is blessed. Nevertheless, he will die at the age appointed to man.

Therefore, children shall grow up, until they become old, old men shall die, but they shall not sleep in the dust. They shall be changed, in the twinkling of an eye. This is the resurrection of the dead that was preached by the apostles.

These are the things you must look for, and speaking after the manner of the Lord, they are now close at hand. In a time to come, at the day and the hour of the coming of the Son of Man, there will be foolish virgins among the wise. At that hour, there will be an entire separation of the righteous from the wicked.

Jesus Christ will soon return Zion, the New Jerusalem, to Independence, Missouri. Zionic conditions could exist for us now if people lived by God's zionic principles.

On April 7, 1947, President Israel A. Smith brought this word from the Lord:

Doctrine & Covenants 140:5c
The work of preparation and the perfection of my Saints go forward slowly, and zionic conditions are no further away or any closer than the spiritual condition of my people justifies.

II Samuel 23:5. Psalm 89:3, Psalm 89:31

"My word shall not fail; and neither will my promises. The foundation of the Lord stands sure."

If we want to live with zionic conditions, we must live zionic lives. We are responsible for our own spiritual condition. Zion begins with each of us.

Christ's early restored church prepared for Zion, the New Jerusalem.

Doctrine & Covenants 77:1a-g
The Lord spoke to Joseph Smith concerning the thing you have presented before me saying, "Listen to me, you who are ordained to the high priesthood of my church... listen to the counsel of Him who has ordained you from on high, who shall speak in your ears the words of wisdom, that salvation may be given to you. "

I say to you, "The time has come and is now at hand. There must be an organization of my people, to regulate and establish the affairs of the storehouse, for the poor. This should be done in this place [Kirtland, Ohio] and in the land of Zion [Independence, Missouri] as a permanent and everlasting establishment and order, for my church. This is to advance the cause you have chosen, the salvation of men, and the glory of your Father who is in Heaven, that all of you may be equal in the bands of Heavenly things. You must be equal in earthly things in order to obtain Heavenly things, for if you are not equal in earthly things you cannot be equal in obtaining Heavenly things. If you want me to provide a place for you in the Celestial world, you must prepare yourselves by doing the things which I have commanded and required of you."

The wisdom of D & C 77:1 exceeds the thinking of most of us today. Developing equality in earthly matters means all God's people must have their just needs and wants met, and there must be equal opportunity according to the gifts God gives each individual. This concept, which is a form of socialism, has never been successful under governments formed by man. With God as our head, it will yet be accomplished.

Scripture admonishes us to repress unnecessary wants in harmony with the law of stewardship. This is difficult, especially when we are bombarded by advertisements for things that seem necessary for modern life. However, a simpler lifestyle is achievable.

Equality in earthly matters also means that although we have different gifts and responsibilities, no office or position is more important than any other. Those who collect the trash are as essential as those who heal the sick. This requires changing attitudes and values as well as accepting greater stewardship of finances, time, energy, and other resources. However, it is never possible to give more to the Lord than He returns to us. Therefore, this concept of stewardship is designed to make all who work prosperous.

Doctrine & Covenants 64:8a
…I say to you that Zion shall flourish, and the glory of the Lord shall be upon her, and she shall be an ensign unto the people.

Early Central American inhabitants knew Zion would be established on this continent.

II Nephi 7:17-20
"This land [the Americas] shall be a land of your inheritance, and the Gentiles shall be blessed upon the land. This land shall be a land of liberty, for the Gentiles, and there shall be no kings upon the land, who shall rise up against the Gentiles. I will fortify this land against all other nations, and he that fights against Zion shall perish," says the Lord.

III Nephi 10:1
If they [the Gentiles] will repent and hearken unto my words, and not harden their hearts, I will establish my church among them. They shall come in and be part of the covenant, and be numbered among this remnant of Jacob, to whom I have given this land [the Americas] for their inheritance. They shall assist my people who are the remnant of Jacob.

Ether 6:4, 8
Ether saw the days of Christ, and he spoke concerning a New Jerusalem upon this land [the Americas]. …It shall be a land of their inheritance, and they shall build up a holy city for the Lord, like Jerusalem of old.

The Father's Promise:

II Chronicles 7:14
If my people who are called by my name, will humble themselves, and pray, and seek my face, and turn from their wicked ways; then I will hear from Heaven, and forgive their sin, and will heal their land.

Zion: Ancient Jerusalem and the New Jerusalem

Church members frequently ask, "Why are there two Jerusalems? Does the New Jerusalem in Independence, Missouri, replace the old?" The answer is unequivocally NO! The New Jerusalem exists as a place of safety for the Saints during the tribulation, and as a place of special blessing for those who live there during the Millennium. The Saints are the redeemed. They are adopted into the House of Israel and have a new and vital relationship with the Lord. Their city will include representatives from all twelve of the tribes of Israel, and this is where Enoch's city of Zion will return.

In no way does this discredit God's work in the Holy Land. The scriptures are clear: He will never break His covenants with the Twelve Tribes, nor will He abandon His ancient city. People living today are witnessing the fulfillment of His covenants with the Hebrew nations. The Jews are returning to Israel. Jerusalem and the Wailing Wall, the last remnant of the ancient Jewish temple, are now in Jewish hands. Both Israel and the old city have a strategic role in the Last Days, and Jesus Christ will return to this city, entering its eastern gate, after the war of Armageddon. Jerusalem, in Israel, will exist far beyond the end of time, and the Jews who live there will fulfill their purpose of being God's first chosen people.

Jesus will return to His temple in Old Jerusalem.

An earlier chapter of this book indicated that the temple in Jerusalem was destroyed by the Romans in 70 A. D. It was never rebuilt. However, the Bible indicates that Christ will return to this holy sanctuary in Old Jerusalem. Ezekiel Chapters 41-44 describe the prophet's vision of the temple in the Last Days. Now, Orthodox Jews are determined to rebuild their temple. They already have the building plans and all the required implements needed for worship (see the description in I Kings, Chapter 7). Even the clothing required for priests is finished. Now everyone waits for the building to begin.

The problem is the location. It must be built on the Temple Mount, which is also the site of the Dome of the Rock, Islam's sacred sanctuary. The challenges this presents are discussed at greater length in Chapter 8, Sign 24. Somehow, the difficulties must be resolved so that prophecies in the book of Ezekiel can be fulfilled. The writings of Ezekiel are filled with descriptions of things that will transpire in the Last Days (Ezekiel 38:8, 14, 16; 39:11). Chapters 41-44 describe the prophet's vision of a temple that will exist in ancient Jerusalem, during the tribulation. Several scriptures indicate Christ will return to this temple.

> ### Ezekiel 43:2, 4-6
> *I saw the glory of the God of Israel coming from the east. His voice was like the roar of rushing waters, and the earth shown with His glory…. The glory of the Lord entered the house [temple] through the gate facing east.*
>
> *Then, the Spirit lifted me up and brought me into the inner court, and the glory of the Lord filled the temple. I heard Him speaking to me from out of the temple, and a man stood by me. He said, "Son of man, this is the place of my throne and the place for the soles of my feet. THIS IS WHERE I WILL LIVE AMONG THE CHILDREN OF ISRAEL FOREVER. The House of Israel will never again defile my Holy Name.*

An unusually interesting scripture, by the same prophet, commands attention:

> **Ezekiel 44:1-3**
> *Then the Lord brought me to the gate of the outer sanctuary, which faced east, and it was shut. The Lord said to me, "This gate shall remain shut. It shall not be opened; no one may enter through it because, the Lord, the God of Israel has entered in by it. ...He shall re-enter by way of the porch, of that gate, and shall go out the same way."*

The book of Matthew (Chapter 21:1-5) describes Christ's triumphant entrance into Jerusalem before the events that led to His crucifixion. Verse 1 indicates He was near the Mount of Olives at the time He instructed His disciples to find a colt. The Mount of Olives is directly across from the Eastern or Golden Gate. Christ entered this gate while riding on the donkey.

The scriptures in Ezekiel describe a future time when "the prince" will again enter the city through the Eastern Gate, which will be reserved only for Him. Ezekiel 44 indicates the gate will not be reopened until the Second Coming. This prophetic passage predicts that Christ, upon His return, will again enter Jerusalem through the Eastern Gate. But --- an unusual event transpired in history. Several centuries after Christ's death, Moslems sealed this gate to circumvent prophecy and prevent Christ's return.

It remains sealed today. Be patient. **He hasn't come yet**!

The Millennium

When Jesus Christ returns to earth, He will establish His kingdom, which will last for a thousand years. It is impossible for us to accurately visualize such a time and place because it is totally foreign to anything we have ever experienced. We do know we will live with Him in perfect state of peace, love and harmony. If this sounds boring, I can guarantee that life with Christ will be anything but boring. We will be faced with experiences, challenges, and opportunities far beyond our imagination. But most important, we will be living with Him. We will also gradually change into His likeness as we experience His physical presence. The scriptures again provide important clues to things that will happen during these one thousand years:

> **Matthew 25:47**
> *...The righteous [both living and dead] shall go into life eternal.*

> **Revelation 20:4**
> *And I saw thrones, and judgment was given to them. And I saw the souls of them who were beheaded for their witness of Jesus, and for the Word of God, and which had not worshipped the beast, nor his image, nor received his mark upon their foreheads, or in their hands. And they lived and reigned with Christ a thousand years.*

> **Revelation 20:6**
> *Blessed and holy are they who have part in the first resurrection; on such the second death has no power, but they shall be priests of God and Christ, and shall reign with Him a thousand years.*

The millennium is described in scripture.

Isaiah 11:6-9

The wolf shall dwell with the lamb, and the leopard shall lie down with the kid; and the calf and the young lion and the fatling together; and a little child shall lead them. ...They shall not hurt nor destroy in all my holy mountain; for the earth shall be full of the knowledge of the Lord, as the waters cover the sea.

Isaiah 35:1-10

The wilderness and the solitary place shall be glad; and the desert shall rejoice, and bloom as the rose. It shall blossom abundantly, and rejoice even with joy and singing; the glory of Lebanon shall be given to it... and they shall see the glory of the Lord, and the excellence of our God.

Then the eyes of the blind shall be opened, and the ears of the deaf shall be unstopped. The lame man shall leap as a hart, and the tongue of the dumb will sing; for in the wilderness, waters shall break out, and streams will appear in the desert. The parched ground shall become a pool, and the thirsty land will have springs of water...A highway shall be there, for a way shall be cast up, and it shall be called the way of holiness. The unclean shall not pass over upon it; but it shall be cast up for those who are clean, and the wayfaring men, though they are considered fools, shall not sin there. No lion, nor any ravenous beast shall be found there, but the redeemed shall walk there, and the ransomed of the Lord shall return, and come to Zion with songs and everlasting joy upon their heads; they shall obtain joy and gladness, and sorrow and sighing shall flee away.

Jeremiah 3:16-18

...In those days, says the Lord, they shall no more talk about the Ark of the Covenant of the Lord; neither shall it come to mind; neither shall they remember it, neither shall they visit it; neither shall that be done any more. At that time, they shall call Jerusalem the throne of the Lord, and all the nations shall be gathered into it, to the name of the Lord. Neither shall they walk any more after the imagination of their evil hearts.

In those days, the House of Judah shall walk with the House of Israel, and they shall come together out of the land of the north to the land I have given for an inheritance for your fathers.

Ezekiel 34:22-31

"I [the Lord] will save my flock, and they shall no more be a prey; and I will judge between cattle and cattle, and will set up one shepherd over them, and He shall feed them , even my servant David [Jesus Christ];...and He shall be their shepherd."

"And I the Lord will be their God, and my servant David a prince among them. I the Lord have spoken it. And I will make a covenant of peace with them, and will cause the evil beast to leave the land; and they shall dwell safely in the wilderness, and sleep in the woods.... And the tree of the field shall yield her fruit, and the earth shall yield her increase. ...And I will raise up for them a plant of renown, and they shall no more be consumed with hunger or

shame…Thus they shall know that I the Lord their God am with them, and that they, even the House of Israel, are my people," says the Lord God. "And you my flock, the flock of my pasture, are men, and I am your God."

Ezekiel 36:8-11, 22-29, 33-35

O mountains of Israel, you shall sprout your branches and yield your fruit, for my people Israel, who will soon return. I am watching over you, and you shall be tilled and sown. I will multiply your population within the House of Israel, the cities will be inhabited, and your wastelands shall be recovered. Your men and beasts shall increase and bring fruit. I will enlarge your boundaries to include all the land originally given you and will bless you more than at your beginning and you shall know that I am the Lord.

I do not do this for your sakes, O House of Israel, but for My Holy Name's sake, which you have profaned among the heathen wherever you went. I will sanctify My Great Name, which was profaned among the heathen. And when I am sanctified in you, before their eyes, the heathen shall know that I am the Lord.

I will take you from among the heathen, gather you out of all countries, and bring you into your own land. Then, I will sprinkle clean water upon you and you shall be cleansed from all your filthiness and from all your idols. I will give you a new heart and a new spirit and will take away the stony heart out of your flesh. I will put my Spirit within you and cause you to walk in my statutes and you shall keep my judgments. And you shall dwell in the land that I gave to your fathers and you shall be my people and I will be your God. In the day that I have cleansed you from all your iniquities, I will also cause you to dwell in the cities and the wastelands shall be rebuilt. The desolate land shall be tilled… and they who pass by shall say, "This land which was desolate has become like the garden of Eden."

Doctrine & Covenants 98:5

In that day an infant shall not die until he is old, and his life shall be as the age of a tree, and when he dies he shall not sleep [that is to say in the earth], but shall be changed in a twinkling of an eye, and shall be caught up, and his rest shall be glorious.

God will make a new covenant with the Children of Israel.

Jeremiah 31:31-36

"Behold, the days come," says the Lord, "that I will make a new covenant with the House of Israel and with the House of Judah. It will not be according to the covenant that I made with their fathers when I took them by the hand to bring them out of the land of Egypt, for they broke that covenant although I was a husband to them."

"This shall be my new covenant with the House of Israel. After those days I will put my law into their inward parts and write it in their hearts and I will be their God and they shall be my people. And they will no longer teach each other. All of them will know me from the least to the greatest and I will forgive their iniquity and will no longer remember their sin."

Christ Will Fulfill His Old Covenants With the Children of Israel. He will establish them forever in Israel, the homeland He has given them. It will be a place of peace and righteousness forever.

Isaiah 32:17-18
The work of righteousness shall be peace and the effect of righteousness will be quiet assurance forever. My people will live in peaceful, secure dwellings and in pleasant resting places.

Isaiah 41:10, 16, 18-20
Fear not, for I am with you. Be not dismayed for I am your God. I will strengthen and help you. Yes, I will uphold you with the right hand of my righteousness…. You shall rejoice in the Lord and shall glory in the Holy One of Israel.

I will open rivers in high places and fountains in the midst of the valleys and will make in the wilderness a pool of water and place springs on the dry land. I will plant the Cedar, the Shittah tree, the Myrtle and the Oil tree in the wilderness and set the Fir tree and the Pine and the Box tree in the desert so all might see and know and consider and understand the hand of the Lord has done this and the Holy One of Israel has created it.

Jeremiah 23:5-8
"The days will come, "says the Lord, "that I will raise up a righteous branch from the house of David and a King shall reign and prosper and execute judgment and justice in the earth. In His days Judah will be saved and Israel will dwell in safety and this is the name whereby the king shall be called, The Lord Our Righteousness."

"Therefore, the days will come," says the Lord, "that they [the children of Israel] will no longer say, 'The Lord lives who brought up the children of Israel out of the land of Egypt'. But instead, they will say, 'The Lord lives who brought up and led the seed of the House of Israel out of the north country and from all countries where I had driven them.' Now they shall dwell in their own land."

Jeremiah 33:14-16
"The days will come," says the Lord, "that I will perform that good thing which I have promised the House of Israel and the House of Judah. In those days and at that time I will cause the Branch of Righteousness to grow up unto David [David is called a type and shadow of Jesus Christ]; and He shall execute judgment and righteousness in the land. In those days Judah shall be saved and Jerusalem shall dwell in safety, and this is the name it shall be called, The Lord is our Righteousness."

Jesus will live with all of His children, and fulfill His covenants with them.

When Christ returns, He intends to live with His people in Zion (Independence, Missouri) and in Old Jerusalem, Israel. Many people have more than one home, but the Lord's Spirit can be everywhere at the same time. Christ's presence will bless both places (See Chapter 6). People at each site will have special access to Him in a way we have never yet experienced. This will be an incredible experience!

Christ is going to fulfill His covenants with all of His people, including you and me. We can hold firmly to these promises for God will never leave or forsake us. We need no other guardian; we have a Savior and Redeemer!

> <u>Isaiah 2:2-4</u>
> *And it shall come to pass in the Last Days, when the mountain of the Lord's house is established on the top of the mountains, is exalted above the hills, and all nations flow into it; many people will say, "Let us go up to the mountain of the Lord, to the house of the God of Jacob. He will teach us His ways, and we will walk in His paths; for out of Zion shall go forth the law, and the word of the Lord will go out from Jerusalem."*
>
> *And He shall judge among the nations, and shall rebuke many people; and they shall beat their swords into ploughshares, and their spears into pruning hooks; nations shall not lift up swords against nations, neither shall they learn war any more. [These verses are identical to Micah 4:1-3.]*

The scriptures do not indicate this, but it is probably safe to assume that during the thousand-year reign, those who live with Christ during the Millennium, will be cleansed, taught and perfected, until they are ready to participate in God's Celestial Kingdom, following the Final Judgment. This may be the reason one thousand years are required.

"Let us go up to the
mountain of the Lord,
to the house of
the God of Jacob.
He will teach us
His ways,
and we will walk in
His paths..."

Micah 4:2

The Lord shall endure forever; He has prepared His throne for judgment and He shall judge the world in righteousness.

Psalm 9:7-8

The Lord shall endure forever.

218

Chapter 13

What do the scriptures say about the Second Resurrection and the Final Judgment?
Note: Some scripture is paraphrased in this chapter to clarify meaning.

The Second Resurrection

When the thousand years ends, all spirits living and dead, redeemed and filthy still will be called in front of God's Judgment Seat for reckoning. Those who arrive from the prison house for the wicked will receive perfect spiritual bodies just like the ones, which were given to the righteous. These bodies will never die. Their spirits must live in them forever. Where they will live is yet to be determined. Both the righteous and wicked will stand before the Lord for the final judgment of our works, each thing we chose to do in our time on earth. (Revelation 20:13).

Doctrine & Covenants 85:4a, b
The spirit and the body is the soul of man, and the resurrection from the dead is the redemption of the soul; and the redemption of the soul is through Him who quickens all things, in whose bosom it is decreed, that the poor and the meek of the earth shall inherit it. Therefore, it must be sanctified from all unrighteousness that it may be prepared for celestial glory; for after it is filled the measure of its creation, it shall be crowned with glory, even with the presence of God the Father.

The Second Resurrection will be quickly followed by the Final Judgment.

Revelation 20:11-13
And I saw a great white throne, and He who sat on it, from whose face the earth and the Heaven fled away and no place was found for them, and I saw the dead, small and great, stand before God; and the books were opened; and another book was opened, which is the book of life. And the dead were judged out of those things, which were written in those books according to their works.

And the sea gave up the dead who were in it; and death and hell delivered up the dead who were in them; and they were judged every man according to their works.

II Nephi 6:28, 29
Therefore, death and Hell must deliver up their dead, Hell must deliver up its captive spirits and the grave must deliver up its captive bodies.

Jesus Christ, Lord of Heaven and Earth, is our judge.

Psalm 9:7, 8
The Lord shall endure forever; He has prepared His throne for judgment. And He shall judge the world in righteousness; He shall minister judgment to the people in uprightness.

Psalm 96:12, 13
Let the field be joyful, and all that is therein and all of the trees of the wood rejoice before the Lord; for He comes to judge the earth; He shall judge the world with righteousness, and the people with His truth.

Isaiah 11:4
With righteousness, He shall judge the poor, and reprove with equity for the meek of the earth; and He shall smite the earth with the rod of His mouth and with the breath of His lips, He shall slay the wicked.

Malachi 3:5, 6
"I will come near to you in judgment; and I will be a swift witness against the sorcerers, and against the adulterers, and against false swearers, and against those that oppress the hireling in his wages, the widow, and the fatherless, and that turn aside the stranger from his right, and fear not me," says the Lord of hosts. For I am the Lord, I change not…

Matthew 16:30
For the Son of man shall come in the glory of His Father, with His angels; and then He shall reward every man according to his works.

Matthew 25:32-35
When the Son of man shall come in His glory, and all the holy angels with Him, then He shall sit upon the throne with His glory. And before Him shall be gathered all nations; and He shall separate them from one another, as a shepherd divides sheep from the goats; the sheep on His right hand, but the goats on His left.

John 5:22
The Father judges no man but He has committed all judgment to His Son; that all should honor the Son, even as they honor the Father. He, who does not honor the Son, does not honor the Father who sent Him.

John 12:48
He that rejects me, and does not receive my words, as one who judges him; the word that I have spoken shall judge him in the last day.

Ecclesiastes 3:16, 17
And I saw under the sun the place of judgment, that wickedness was there; and the place of righteousness, that iniquity was there. I said in my heart, God shall judge the righteous and the wicked; for there is a time for every purpose and for every work.

Ecclesiastes 12:14
God shall bring every work into judgment with every secret thing, whether it is good, or whether it is evil.

Micah 4:3, 4
And He shall judge among many people, and rebuke strong nations afar off; and they shall beat their swords into ploughshares, and their spears into pruning hooks; nations shall not lift up swords against nations, neither shall they learn war any more. But they shall sit every man under His vine and under His fig tree; and none shall make them afraid; for the mouth of the Lord of hosts has spoken it. All people will walk in the name of their God, and we will all walk in the name of the Lord our God forever and ever.

I Corinthians 3:13
Every man's work shall be revealed; for the day shall declare it, because it shall be revealed by fire; and the fire shall try every man's work to discover what sort it is.

Mormon 4:57-65
I speak now concerning those who do not believe in Christ. Will you believe in the day when the Lord shall return? Or in that great day when the earth shall be rolled together as a scroll and the elements melt with fervent heat? Or will you believe in that great day when you are brought to stand before the Lamb of God? Can you then say there is no God or deny the Christ when you behold the Lamb of God?

Do you suppose that you could dwell with Him, being conscious of your guilt? Do you think that you could be happy to dwell with that Holy Being when your souls are racked with a consciousness of your guilt and your abuse of His laws?

I tell you that you would be more miserable to dwell with a holy and a just God under a consciousness of your filthiness before Him, than you would be to dwell with the damned souls in hell. For behold, when you are brought to see your nakedness before God, and also, the glory of God and the holiness of Jesus Christ, it will kindle a flame of unquenchable fire upon you. Oh then, you unbelieving, turn to the Lord!

Cry mightily unto the Father in the name of Jesus, that perhaps you may be found spotless, pure, fair and white, having been cleansed by the blood of the Lamb at that great and last day.

Doctrine & Covenants 85:29
When the third trump sounds, the spirits of men who are to be judged, and are found under condemnation; these are the rest of the dead who did not live again until the thousand years ended, neither again until the end of the earth.

The final judgment will determine where each soul will spend eternity.

Alma 19:56-59

...There is a space between death and the resurrection of the body, and a state of the soul in happiness or in misery [the Millennium or Hell]. Until the time which is appointed of God that the dead shall come forth and be reunited, both soul and body, and be brought to stand before God, and be judged according to their works.

This brings about the restoration of those things, which have been spoken by the prophets. The soul shall be restored to the body, and the body to the soul; yes, and every limb and joint shall be restored to its body; yes, even a hair of the head shall not be lost, but all things shall be restored to their proper frame.... And then shall the righteous shine forth in the kingdom of God. But behold, an awful death will come upon the wicked; for they die without righteousness, and they are unclean, and no unclean thing can inherit the kingdom of God. They are cast out, and consigned to partake of the fruits of their labors or their works, which have been evil; and they drink the dregs of a bitter cup.

Alma 19:64-68, 70, 71

...My son, the plan of restoration is requisite and just, according to the power and resurrection of Christ. The soul of man shall be restored to its body, and every part of the body shall be restored to itself. And it is requisite with the justice of God, that men should be judged according to their works; and if their works were good in this life, and the desires of their hearts were good, they should also, at the last day, be restored to that which is good.

If their works were evil, they shall be restored for evil. Therefore, all things shall be restored to their proper order; everything to its natural frame; mortality raised to immortality; corruption to incorruption; raised to endless happiness, to inherit the kingdom of God, or to endless misery, to inherit the kingdom of the devil. ...

Thus they stand or fall; for behold, they are their own judges, whether to do good or do evil. Now the decrees of God are unalterable; therefore, the way is prepared, and whosoever will may walk therein, and be saved.

Acts 17:31

...God commands all men everywhere to repent, because He has appointed a day, in which He will judge the world in righteousness by Him [Christ] whom He has ordained; and He has given assurance of this to all men, in that He raised Him from the dead.

Men are saved by the grace of Jesus Christ, but judged by their own works.

By His grace, we are saved.

Acts 15:11
We believe that through the grace of the Lord Jesus Christ we shall be saved.

Romans 4:23-25
All have sinned, and come short of the glory of God; therefore, we are justified only by His grace through the redemption that is in Christ Jesus. God has provided Him to atone for our sins by our faith in His blood. ...

Ephesians 2:5
God, who is rich in mercy and His great love wherewith He loved us, even when we were dead in sins, has quickened us together with Christ, (by grace ye are saved;) and has raised us up together, and made us to sit together in Heavenly places in Christ Jesus.

We will be judged and rewarded by our works.

I Corinthians 3:11-15
According to the grace of God, which is given to me, as a wise master builder, I have laid the foundation and another will build thereon. But let every man take heed how he builds on it, for no other foundation can man lay than Jesus Christ. Now if any man builds on this foundation using gold, silver, precious stones, wood, hay, or stubble, his work will be known; for the day shall declare it, because it shall be revealed by fire, and the fire shall try every man's work and reveal what sort it is. If any man's work remains which he has built, he shall receive a reward. If any man's work shall be burned, he shall suffer loss; but he himself may be saved, yet by fire.

I Peter 1:16-19
It is written, "Be holy for I am holy. "And if you call on the Father, who without respect of persons, judges according to every man's work, pass the time of your sojourning here in fear; for you know that you were not redeemed with corruptible things, such as silver and gold ..., but with the precious blood of Christ, a lamb without blemish and without spot.

Revelation 14:13
And I heard a voice from Heaven saying to me, Write, Blessed are the dead which die in the Lord from henceforth, that they may rest from their labors; and their works do follow them.

Revelation 20:12, 13
And I saw the dead, small and great, stand before God; and the books were opened; and another book was opened, which is the book of life; and the dead were judged out of those things which were written in the books, according to their works.

Revelation 22:12

Behold, I come quickly; and my reward is with me to give every man according as his work shall be.

I Nephi 4:52

The day shall come that they [all men] must be judged for their works, yes, even the works, which were done by their temporal body in the days of probation. Wherefore, if they should die in their wickedness, they must be cast off concerning the things, which are spiritual, which are pertaining to righteousness.

They must be brought to stand before God to be judged by their works, and if their works have been filthy, they are filthy. And if they are filthy, they cannot dwell in the kingdom of God.

II Nephi 12:66

Out of the books, which shall be written, I will judge the world, every man according to their works [deeds].

Alma 19:56

Until the time which is appointed by God that the dead shall come forth and be reunited, both soul and body, and be brought to stand before God, and be judged according to their works.

Doctrine & Covenants 59:1

Blessed are they who have come up to this land [Zion] with an eye single to my glory, according to my commandments. For they that live shall inherit the earth, and they that die shall rest from all their labors, and their works shall follow them. And they shall receive a crown in the mansions of my Father, which I have prepared for them.

Doctrine & Covenants 76:7v

They [humanity] shall be judged according to their works; and every man shall receive according to his own works, and his own dominion, in the mansions which are prepared, and they shall be servant of the Most High.

Hell, Satan and the Lake of Fire

Hell, and all who follow Satan will be cast into the Lake of Fire and will be there for eternity (Revelation 20:14). Those who spend eternity in the Lake of Fire choose this destination for themselves. Unrepentant pride, guilt, or a desire to be God are a few of the reasons they turn their backs on the Salvation of Jesus Christ.

Revelation 20:14

And death and hell were cast into the lake of fire. This is the second death. And whosoever was not found written into the book of life was cast into the lake of fire.

Mosiah 1:125-129
The Lord said, "At judgment day, the words of Mosiah shall stand as a bright testimony against these people for every man will be judged according to his works, whether they are good or whether they are evil. And if they are evil they are consigned to an awful view of their own guilt and abominations which causes them to shrink from the presence of the Lord into a state of misery and endless torment from which they cannot return; Therefore, they have drunk damnation to their own souls.

Therefore, they have drunk out of the cup of the wrath of God, which justice cannot deny them any more than it could deny that Adam should fall because of his partaking of the forbidden fruit. Therefore, mercy could have no claim on them forever. And their torment is as a lake of fire and brimstone whose flames are unquenchable and whose smoke ascends up forever and ever."

Mosiah 8:61-65
Behold and fear and tremble before God, for you ought to tremble. The Lord does not redeem any that rebel against Him and die in their sins. All those who perished in their sins ever since the world began, and have willfully rebelled against God, knowing but not keeping His commandments, have no part in the first resurrection. Therefore, you ought to tremble. Salvation will not come to any who do this, for the Lord cannot redeem them. He cannot deny himself. Therefore, justice must be fulfilled.

Mosiah 8:77-89
Remember that he who persists in his own carnal nature and goes on in the ways of sin and rebellion against God, remains in his fallen state and the devil has all power over him. Therefore, it is as though there was no redemption made for him because he is an enemy to God. The devil is also an enemy to God.

And now, if Christ had not come into the world, speaking of things to come as though they were already here, there could have been no redemption. And if Christ had not risen from the dead, or broken the bands of death so that the grave should have no victory and death should have no sting, there could have been no resurrection. But there is a resurrection; therefore, the grave has no victory, and the sting of death is swallowed up in Christ. He is the light and the life of the world; yes, a light that is endless, that can never be darkened and a life, which is endless, that there can be no more death.

Even this mortal [body] shall put on immortality. This corruption [human bodies] shall put on incorruption and shall be brought to stand before the bar of God to be judged of Him, according to their good or evil works. If they are good, they receive the resurrection of endless life and happiness, but if they are evil, they will go to the resurrection of endless damnation.

Doctrine & Covenants 76:4a-e
I, the Lord say, concerning all those who know my power, and have taken part in it, but suffered themselves, through the power of the Devil, to be overcome, deny the truth, and defy my power; they are the sons of perdition, of whom I say it was better for them never to have been born. They are

vessels of wrath, doomed to suffer the wrath of God, with the Devil and his angels, in eternity. I have said there is no forgiveness for them in this world or in the world to come. They have denied the Holy Spirit, after having received it, and have denied the only begotten Son of the Father; and crucified Him to themselves, putting Him to open shame. These are the ones who shall go away, into the lake of fire and brimstone, with the Devil and his angels. They are the only ones on whom the second death shall have any power; yes, the only ones who shall not be redeemed in the due time of the Lord, after the sufferings of His wrath. All the rest shall be brought forth by the resurrection of the dead, through the triumph and the glory of the Lamb, who was slain, who was in the bosom of the Father before the worlds were made.

Doctrine & Covenants 76:7n-s
Last of all, these are all they who will not be gathered with the saints, to be caught up unto the church of the Firstborn, and received into the cloud. These are they who are liars, and sorcerers, and adulterers, and whoremongers, and whosoever loves and makes a lie. These are they who suffer the wrath of God, on the earth. These are they who suffer the vengeance of eternal fire. These are they who are cast down to hell and suffer the wrath of Almighty God until the fullness of times, when Christ shall have subdued all enemies under His feet, and shall have perfected His work, when He shall deliver up the kingdom and present it to the Father spotless. Saying: "I have overcome and have trodden the winepress alone, even the winepress of the fierceness of the wrath of Almighty God; then shall He be crowned with the crown of His glory, to sit on the throne of His power to reign forever and ever."

Doctrine & Covenants 85:6g, 7,8a
[They who do not receive one of the glories] and remain [after the glories are awarded] shall also be quickened; nevertheless, they shall return again to their own place, to enjoy that which they are willing to receive, because they were not willing to enjoy that which they might have received.

For what does it profit a man if a gift is bestowed upon him, and he does not receive the gift? Behold, he does not rejoice in that which is given to him, nor does he rejoice in the giver of the gift.

I say to you, "That which is governed by law, is also preserved by law, and perfected and sanctified by the same. That which breaks a law, and does not abide by the law, but seeks to become a law unto itself, and wills to abide in sin, and altogether lives in sin, cannot be sanctified by law, neither by mercy, justice, or judgment; therefore, they must remain filthy still."

Doctrine & Covenants 85:30
And the fourth trump sounds saying these are found who are to remain until that great and last day, even the end, and they shall remain filthy still.

The Book of Life:

"The redemption of the soul is through Him who quickens all things, in whose bosom it is decreed, that the poor and the meek of the earth shall inherit it."

D&C 88:17

The kingdoms of this world are become the kingdom of our Lord and of His Christ; and He shall reign forever and ever. Amen

<u>Revelation 11:15</u>

For thine is the kingdom and the power and the glory forever.

Chapter 14

What do the scriptures say about the Kingdom of Heaven?

Note: Some scripture is paraphrased in this chapter to clarify meaning.

Many of us have wondered about the Kingdom of Heaven. We hear lovely stories and myths, many of which are not accurate. The scriptures, again, provide the clearest picture of that time and place to come.

What is Heaven like?

Psalms 145:13
Your [Christ's] kingdom is an everlasting kingdom, and your dominion endures throughout all generations.

Isaiah 9:7
There shall be no end to the increase of His government and peace.

Daniel 7:13, 14, 18
One like the Son of man came with the clouds of Heaven…And there was given Him dominion, and glory, and a kingdom, that all people, nations, and languages, should serve Him. His dominion is an everlasting dominion, which shall not pass away, and His kingdom that which shall not be destroyed.

Micah 4:7, 8
The Lord shall reign over them in mount Zion from henceforth, even forever.

Matthew 5:5
Blessed are the poor in spirit, who come unto me; for theirs is the kingdom of Heaven.

Matthew 25:35
The king shall say to them on His right hand, "Come ye blessed of my Father, inherit the kingdom prepared for you from the foundation of the world."

Mark 4:21
If a man should cast seed into the ground; and should sleep and rise, night and day, and the seed should spring up and grow, he doesn't know how; so is the kingdom of God.

Mark 10:12, 13
Suffer the little children to come unto me, and forbid them not; for of such is the kingdom of God. I say to you, "Whoever does not receive the kingdom of God as a little child, shall not enter in."

Luke 13:21
I shall liken the kingdom of God to a bit of leaven, which a woman took and hid in three measures of meal, till all of it was leavened.

John 3:5
Except a man be born of water, and the Spirit, he cannot enter into the kingdom of God.

Romans 8:16, 17
The Spirit bears witness with our spirit, that we are the children of God; and if children, then heirs; heirs of God, and joint heirs with Christ… that we may be glorified together.

Romans 24:17
The kingdom of God is not meat and drink; but righteousness, and peace, and joy in the Holy Ghost.

Acts 20:32
I commend you to God, and to the word of His grace, which is able to build you up and to give you an inheritance among all who are sanctified.

I Corinthians 4:20
The kingdom of God is not in word, but in power.

Titus 3:7
Being justified by His grace, we are made heirs according to the hope of eternal life.

I Peter 1:4
An inheritance incorruptible, and undefiled, that does not fade away, is reserved in Heaven for you.

Revelation 11:15
The kingdoms of this world are become the kingdom of our Lord, and of His Christ; and He shall reign forever and ever.

II Nephi 6:42
The righteous, the saints of the Holy One of Israel who have believed in the Holy One of Israel…shall inherit the kingdom of God, which was prepared for them from the foundation of the world: and their joy shall be full forever.

Doctrine & Covenants 72:1
He who is faithful and wise in time is accounted worthy to inherit the mansions prepared for them by my Father.

Doctrine & Covenants 76:8a-c
But great and marvelous are the works of the Lord and the mysteries of His kingdom, which He showed to us, [Celestial, Terrestrial, Telestial] which surpasses all understanding in glory, and in might, and in dominion, which He commanded us we should not write, while we were yet in the Spirit, and are not lawful for man to utter. Neither is man capable to make them known.

They are only to be seen and understood by the power of the Holy Spirit, which God bestows on those who love Him and purify themselves before Him; to whom He grants this privilege of seeing and knowing for themselves; that through the power and manifestation of the Spirit, while in the flesh, they may be able to bear His presence in the world of glory. And to God and the Lamb be glory, and honor, and dominion forever and ever. Amen.

Doctrine & Covenants 85:9, 10a, b, c,
All kingdoms have a law given: and there are many kingdoms: for there is no space, in which there is no kingdom: and there is no kingdom in which there is no space, either a greater or lesser kingdom. And to every kingdom is given a law; and there are certain bounds and conditions in every law.

All beings who do not abide by those conditions are not justified; for intelligence cleaves to intelligence; wisdom receives wisdom; truth embraces truth; virtue loves virtue; and light cleaves to light. Mercy has compassion on mercy and claims her own; justice continues its course, and claims its own; judgment goes before the face of Him who sits upon the throne, and governs and executes all things. He comprehends all things, and all things are before Him, and all things are round about Him; and He is above all things, and in all things, and is through all things, and is round about all things: and all things are by Him, and of Him; even God, forever and ever.

Doctrine & Covenants 85:11a-b
And again, I say to you, "He has given a law to all things by which they move in their times, and their seasons. Their courses are fixed; even the courses of the Heavens, and the earth; which comprehend the earth and all the planets. They give light to each other in their times, and in their seasons, in their minutes, in their hours, in their days, in their weeks, in their months, in their years: all these are one year with God, but not with man.

Doctrine & Covenants 85:12a-f
The earth rotates around the sun, and the sun gives his light by day, and the moon gives her light by night; and the stars give their light and their glory as they follow their paths in the Heavens, in the midst of the power of God.

To what shall I liken these kingdoms that you may understand? All these are kingdoms, and any man who has seen any or the least of these, has seen God moving in His majesty and power. I say to you, Christ has seen Him. Nevertheless, He came unto His own and was not comprehended. The light shown in darkness, and the darkness did not understand. Nevertheless, the day shall come when you shall comprehend even God, being quickened in Him, and by Him. Then you shall know that you have seen me, that I am, that I am the true light that is in you, and that you are in me, otherwise you could not be filled to overflowing.

Doctrine & Covenants 85:13a-d, 14a-d, 15
Behold, I will liken these kingdoms to a man having a field, and he sent forth his servants into the field, to dig in the field; and he said to the first, Go and labor in the field, and in the first hour I will come to you and you shall see the joy of my countenance. And he said to the second, Go also into the field, and

in the second hour I will visit you with joy on my face; and also to the third, saying, I will visit you; and to the fourth, and so on unto the twelfth.

And the lord of the field went unto the first in the first hour, and tarried with him all that hour, and he was made glad with the light and joy on the face of his lord. Then he withdrew from the first that he might visit the second also, and the third, and the fourth, and so on unto the twelfth. In this way they all received the light of the countenance of their lord; every man in his hour, and in his time, and in his season; beginning at the first, and so on until the last. From the last to the first, and from the first to the last, every man in his own order, until his hour was finished, even as his lord had commanded him, that his lord might be glorified in him, and be in him, that they all might be glorified.

Therefore, I will liken all these kingdoms, and the inhabitants thereof to this parable; every kingdom in its hour, and in its time, and in its season; even according to the decree which God has made.

Christ is King of Heaven.

Isaiah 9:7
Of the increase of His government and peace there is no end, upon the throne of David, and upon His kingdom, to order it, and to establish it with judgment and with justice from henceforth even forever.

Isaiah 65:17-25
Behold, I create new Heavens and a new earth; and the former shall not be remembered, nor come to mind. But be glad and rejoice forever in that which I create; for, behold, I create Jerusalem a rejoicing, and her people a joy. And I will rejoice in Jerusalem, and joy in my people; and the voice of weeping shall no more be heard in her, nor the voice of crying.

In those days, there shall be no more an infant of days, nor an old man that has not filled his days; for the child shall not die, but shall live to be a hundred years old; but the sinner, living to be a hundred years old, shall be accursed.

And they shall build houses, and inhabit them; and they shall plant vineyards, and eat the fruit of them. They shall not build, and another inhabit; they shall not plant, and another eat; for as the days of a tree are the days of my people, and my elect shall long enjoy the work of their hands. They shall not labor in vain, nor bring forth for trouble, for they are the seed of the blessed of the Lord, and their offspring with them.

And it shall come to pass, that before they call, I will answer; and while they are yet speaking, I will hear.

The wolf and the lamb shall feed together, and the lion shall eat straw like the bullock; and the dust shall be the serpent's meat. They shall not hurt nor destroy in all my holy mountain, states the Lord.

<u>**Zechariah 14:9**</u>
And the Lord shall be King over all the earth; in that day, there shall be one Lord, and His name one.

<u>**Matthew 25:32**</u>
When the Son of man shall come in His glory, and all the holy angels with Him, then He shall sit upon the throne of His glory.

<u>**Luke 1:32, 33**</u>
He shall be great and shall be called the Son of the Highest; and the Lord God shall give to Him the throne of His father David; and He shall reign over the house of Jacob forever, and of His kingdom, there shall be no end.

<u>**Revelation 11:15**</u>
And the seventh angel sounded; and there were great voices in Heaven, saying, the kingdoms of this world are become the kingdom of our Lord, and of His Christ; and He shall reign forever and ever. [Isaiah 9:7; Daniel 7:13, 14; Zechariah 14:9; Matthew 27:11, 12; Mark 15:3, 4]

The Glories or the-Final Rewards for Mankind

<u>**I Corinthians 15:35-57**</u>
Some men will say, "How are the dead raised up? And with what body do they come?" Don't you know, the seed, which you sow, does not begin to grow until it dies? And that seed which you sow is not the body, which it shall be, but a piece of grain; it may be wheat, or some other. But God gives it a body that pleases Him and every seed has its own body.

*All flesh is not the same flesh. There is one kind of flesh of men, another flesh of beasts, another of fish, and another of birds. Some [people's] bodies are **Celestial bodies**, and some [people's] bodies are **Terrestrial bodies**, and some [people's] bodies are **Telestial bodies**. . There is one glory of the sun [Celestial], and another glory of the moon [Terrestrial], and another glory of the stars [Telestial], and as one star differs from another star in glory, so also is the resurrection of the dead. It [the body] is sown [buried] in corruption, but it is raised in incorruption, sown in dishonor but raised in glory, sown in weakness, raised in power, sown in a natural body but raised as a spiritual body.*

And so it is written, the first man Adam was made a living soul; the last Adam [Jesus Christ] was made a quickening spirit. That which is natural is first and not that which is spiritual, but afterward, that which is spiritual. The first man is of the earth, [earthy]; the second man is the Lord from Heaven. As the earthy is, so also are they who are of the earth; and as the Heavenly is, so also are they that are Heavenly. And as we have borne the image of the earthy, we shall also bear the image of the Heavenly.

Now I say this, brothers, that flesh and blood cannot inherit the kingdom of God; neither can corruption inherit incorruption, but I will show you a mystery. We shall not all sleep, but we shall all be changed in a moment, in the twinkling of an eye, at the sound of the last trump. For the trumpet shall sound, and the dead shall be raised incorruptible, and we shall be changed, for this corruptible body must put on incorruption, and this mortal body must put on immortality.

So when this corruptible body puts on incorruption and this mortal body shall have put on immortality, then the saying that is written, 'Death is swallowed up in victory. O death, where is your sting? O grave, where is your victory?'

'The sting of death is sin; and the strength of sin is the law. But thanks be to God, who gives us the victory through our Lord Jesus Christ. '

Doctrine & Covenants 85: 1c, 2a-f

I now send you another Comforter my friends so that it may abide in your hearts; even the Holy Spirit of promise which is the same that I promised to my disciples as is recorded in the testimony of John. This Comforter is the promise which I give you of eternal life; even the glory of the Celestial kingdom which glory is that of the church of the Firstborn, even of God the holiest of all through Jesus Christ His Son. He [is] that ascended up on high as He also descended below; in that He comprehends all things, that He might be the light of truth in all and through all things, which truth shines: this is the light of Christ.

He is in the sun, and the light of the sun, and the power by which it was made. He is also in the moon, and is the light of the moon, and the power by which it was made. He is also in the stars, and the power thereof by which they were made. And He is in the earth also, and the power thereof; even the earth, upon which you stand.

And the light which now shines, which gives you light, is through Him who enlightened your eyes, which is the same light that quickens your understandings; which light proceeds forth from the presence of God, to fill the immensity of space. The light which is in all things; which gives life to all things; which is the law by which all things are governed; even the power of God who sits upon His throne, who is in the bosom of eternity, who is in the midst of all things.

In order to make it possible for men to take part in the glories to be revealed, the Lord sent forth the fullness of His gospel and His everlasting covenant, in simple and plain language, to prepare the weak for those things which are coming on earth. It will also prepare them for the Lord's errand, in the day when the weak shall confound the wise, and the little one [Israel] shall become a strong nation and two will put tens of thousands to flight. The Lord will thresh the nations by the power of His Spirit and by the weak things of the earth. And for this cause, these commandments were given. They were commanded to be kept from the world in the day that they were given, but now they are to go forth to all flesh. This is according to the mind and will of the Lord, who rules over all flesh; and he who repents and sanctifies himself before the Lord, shall be given eternal life.

Celestial Bodies

Doctrine & Covenants 76:5 a-r

And again, we bear record for we saw and heard, and this is the testimony of the gospel of Christ, concerning them who come forth in the resurrection of the just.

These are they who received the testimony of Jesus, and believed on His name, and were baptized after the manner of His burial, being buried in water in His name, and this according to the commandment which He has given. That by keeping the commandments, they might be washed and cleansed from all their sin, and receive the Holy Spirit by the laying on of the hands of him who is ordained and sealed unto this power; and who overcome by faith, and are sealed by that Holy Spirit of promise, which the Father sheds forth upon all those who are just and true. These are they who are the church of the Firstborn; these are they into whose hands the Father has given all things. These are they who are priests and kings, who have received of His fullness, and of His glory, and are priests of the Most High after the order of Melchisedec, which was after the order of Enoch, which was after the order of the only begotten Son. Wherefore, as it is written, they are gods, even the sons of God; wherefore all things are theirs, whether life or death, or things present, or things to come, all are theirs, and they are Christ's, and Christ is God's; and they shall overcome all things. These are they whom He shall bring with Him, when He shall come in the clouds of Heaven, to reign on earth over His people. These are they who shall have part in the first resurrection. These are they who shall come forth in the resurrection of the just. These are they who are come unto Mount Zion, and unto the city of the living God, the Heavenly place, the holiest of all. These are they who have come to an innumerable company of angels; to the general assembly and church of Enoch, and of the Firstborn. These are they whose names are written in Heaven, where God and Christ are the judge of all. These are they who are just men made perfect through Jesus the mediator of the new covenant, who wrought out this perfect atonement through the shedding of His own blood. These are they whose bodies are Celestial, whose glory is that of the sun, even the glory of God the highest of all; whose glory the sun of the firmament is written of as being typical.

Doctrine & Covenants 76:i-k

And thus we saw the glory of the Celestial, which excels in all things; where God, even the Father, reigns upon His throne forever and ever, before whose throne all things bow in humble reverence and give Him glory forever and ever. They who dwell in His presence are the church of the Firstborn; and they are as they are seen, and know as they are known, having received of His fullness and of His grace; and He makes them equal in power, and in might, and in dominion. And the glory of the Celestial is one, even as the glory of the sun is one.

Doctrine & Covenants 85:4a-d

Now I say to you, that through the redemption, which is made for you, comes the resurrection from the dead. And the spirit and the body is the soul of man. And the resurrection from the dead is the redemption of the soul; and *the redemption of the soul is through Him who quickens all things, in whose breast it is decreed, that the poor and the meek of the earth shall inherit it. Therefore, It must be sanctified from all unrighteousness, that It may be prepared for the Celestial glory. For after it has filled the measure of its creation, it shall be crowned with glory, even with the presence of God the Father, so that bodies who are of the Celestial kingdom may possess it forever and ever. And for this intent, it was made and created; and for this intent, they are sanctified.*

Doctrine & Covenants 85:6c, d
When they die, they shall rise again in a spiritual body. They who are of a Celestial spirit shall receive the same body, which was a natural body; and their glory shall be that glory by which their bodies are quickened. You, who are quickened by a portion of the Celestial glory, shall then receive of the same, even a fullness.

Terrestrial Bodies

Doctrine & Covenants 76:6a
And again, we saw the Terrestrial world, and these are they who are of the Terrestrial, whose glory differs from that of the church of the Firstborn, who have received the fullness of the Father, even as that of the moon differs from the sun of the firmament.

Behold, these are they who died without law; and also they who are the spirits of men kept in prison, whom the Son visited, and preached the gospel unto them, that they might be judged according to men in the flesh, who received not the testimony of Jesus in the flesh, but afterward received it.

These are they who are honorable men of the earth, who were blinded by the craftiness of men. These are they who receive of His glory, but not of His fullness. These are they who receive of the presence of the Son, but not of the fullness of the Father; wherefore they are Terrestrial bodies, and not Celestial bodies, and differ in glory as the moon differs from the sun. These are they who are not valiant in the testimony of Jesus; wherefore they obtained not the crown over the kingdom of our God.

And now this is the end of the vision, which we saw of the Terrestrial, that the Lord commanded us to write while we were yet in the Spirit.

Doctrine & Covenants 76:7h
And we saw the glory of the Terrestrial, which excels in all things the glory of the Telestial, even in glory, and in power, and in might, and in dominion.

Doctrine & Covenants 76:7k
And the glory of the Terrestrial is one, even as the glory of the moon is one.

Doctrine & Covenants 85:5a, b

They who are not sanctified through the law which I have given to you, even the law of Christ, must inherit another kingdom, even that of a Terrestrial kingdom or that of a Telestial kingdom. For he who is not able to abide the law of a Celestial kingdom, cannot abide a Celestial glory.

Doctrine & Covenants 85:6e

They who are quickened by a portion of the Terrestrial glory shall then receive of the same, even a fullness.

Telestial Bodies

Doctrine & Covenants 76:7a-g

And again, we saw the glory of the Telestial, which glory is that of the lesser, even as the glory of the stars differs from that of the glory of the moon in the firmament; these are they who received not the gospel of Christ, neither the testimony of Jesus. These are they who do not deny the Holy Spirit; these are they who are thrust down to hell; these are they who shall not be redeemed from the Devil, until the last resurrection, until the Lord, even Christ the Lamb, shall have finished His work; these are they who receive not of His fullness in the eternal world, but of the Holy Spirit through the ministration of the Terrestrial; and the Terrestrial through the ministration of the Celestial; and also the Telestial receive it of the administering of angels, who are appointed to minister for them, or who are appointed to be ministering spirits for them, for they shall be heirs of salvation. And thus, we saw in the Heavenly vision, the glory of the Telestial, which surpasses all understanding; and no man knows it except him to who God has revealed it.

Doctrine & Covenants 76:7l, 7m

And the glory of the Telestial is one, even as the glory of the stars is one, for as one star differs from another star in glory, even so each one differs from another in the Telestial world. For these are they who are of Paul, and of Apollos, and of Cephias. These are they who say they are some of one and some of another, some of Christ, and some of John, and some of Moses, and some of Elias; and some of Enoch, but did not receive the gospel or the testimony of Jesus, neither the testimony of the prophets; neither the everlasting covenant.

Doctrine & Covenants 76:7t-v

But behold, we saw the glory and the inhabitants of the Telestial world. They were as innumerable as the stars in the firmament of Heaven, or as the sand upon the seashore, and heard the voice of the Lord saying: These all shall bow the knee, and every tongue shall confess to Him who sits upon the throne forever and ever; for they shall be judged according to their works. Every man shall receive according to his own works, and his own dominion, in the mansions, which are prepared. They shall be servants of the Most High, but where God and Christ dwell they cannot come, worlds without end.

And they, who are quickened by a portion of the Telestial glory, shall then receive of the same, even a fullness.

The New Heaven and New Earth, the New Jerusalem

Revelation 21:1-17

And I saw a new Heaven and a new earth; for the first Heaven and the first earth were passed away; and there was no more sea. And I John saw the holy city, New Jerusalem, coming down from God out of Heaven, prepared as a bride adorned for her husband. And I heard a great voice out of Heaven saying, "Behold, the tabernacle of God is with men, and He will dwell with them, and they shall be His people, and God himself shall be with them, and be their God."

And God shall wipe away all tears from their eyes; and there shall be no more death, neither sorrow, nor crying, neither shall there be any more pain; for the former things are passed away. And He that sat upon the throne said, "Behold I make all things new." And He said to me, "Write; for these words are true and faithful. "And He said to me, "It is done. I am Alpha and Omega, the beginning and the end. I will freely give to him that is thirsty the fountain of the water of life. He that overcomes shall inherit all things; and I will be his God, and he shall be my son. But the fearful, and unbelieving, and the abominable, and murderers, and whoremongers, and sorcerers, and idolaters, and all liars, shall have their part in the lake, which burns with fire and brimstone, which is the second death.

Then there came to me one of the seven angels which had the seven vials of the seven last plagues, and talked with me, saying, "Come with me. I will show you the bride, the Lamb's wife. "And he carried me away in Spirit to a great and high mountain, and showed me that great city, the holy Jerusalem, descending out of Heaven from God, having the glory of God; and her light was like a precious stone, even like jasper, and clear as crystal. It had a great and high wall with twelve gates, and at the gates were twelve angels, and the names written on the gates were the names of the twelve tribes of the children of Israel.

On the east, there were three gates; on the north three gates; on the south three gates; and on the west three gates. And the wall of the city had twelve foundations, and in them, the names of the twelve apostles of the Lamb were written. And he that talked with me had a golden reed to measure the city, and the gates and wall thereof. And the city lay foursquare, and he measured the city with the reed, twelve thousand furlongs. The length and breadth and the height of it are equal. And he measured the wall thereof, a hundred and forty and four cubits, according to the measure of the angel. And the wall of the building was of jasper; and the city was pure gold, like clear glass. And the foundations of the wall of the city were garnished with all manner of precious stones. The first foundation was jasper; the second, sapphire; the third, a chalcedony; the fourth, an emerald; the fifth, sardonyx; the sixth, sardius, the seventh, chrysolite, the eighth, beryl; the ninth, a topaz; the tenth, a chrysoprasus; the eleventh, a jacinth; and the twelfth, an

238

amethyst. And the twelve gates were twelve pearls; every several gate was one pearl; and the street of the city was pure gold, as it were transparent glass.

I saw no temple there; for the Lord God Almighty and the Lamb are the temple of it. And the city had no need of the sun, neither of the moon, to shine in it; for the glory of God did lighten it, and the Lamb is the light thereof. And the nations of them that are saved shall walk in the light of it; and the kings of the earth bring their glory and honor into it.

And there shall in no wise enter into it anything that defiles, nor works abominations, or lies; but it is for those who are written in the Lamb's book of life.

Revelation 22:1-17
And he showed me a pure river of water of life, clear as crystal proceeding out of the thrown of God and of the Lamb. In the midst of the street of it, and on either side of the river, was the tree of life, which bore twelve kinds of fruits, and yielded her fruit every month; and the leaves of the tree were for the healing of the nations.

And there shall be no more curse but the throne of God and of the Lamb shall be In it; and His servants shall serve Him; and they shall see His face; and His name shall be in their foreheads. And their shall be no night there; and they need no candle, neither light of the sun; for the Lord God gives them light and they shall reign forever and ever.

And he said unto me these sayings are faithful and true; and the Lord God of the holy prophets sent His angel to show unto His servants the things which must shortly be done.

Behold I come quickly; blessed is he that keeps the sayings of this prophecy of this book.

And John saw these things, and heard them. And when he had heard and seen he fell down to worship before the feet of the angel, which showed him these things. Then the angel said to him, see that you do not worship me for I am your fellow servant, and of your brothers, the prophets, and of them, which keep the sayings of this book. Worship God.

Then the angel said to John, do not seal the sayings of the prophecy of this book; for the time is at hand. He that is unjust let him be unjust still; and he which is filthy, let him be filthy still; and he that is righteous, let him be righteous still; and he that is holy, let him be holy still. And behold, I come quickly; and my reward is with me to give every man according, as his works shall be. I am Alpha and Omega, the beginning and the end, the first and the last. Blessed are they who do His commandments that they may have right to the tree of life, and may enter in through the gates into the city. For outside are dogs, and sorcerers and whoremongers, and murderers, and idolaters, and those who love to lie.

I Jesus have sent my angel to testify to you these things in the churches.

I am the root and the offspring of David, and the bright and morning star.

And the spirit and the bride say come. And let him that hears say, come. And let him who is thirsty come. And whosoever will, let him take the water of life freely.

Revelation 22:16, 17

Blessed are they which are called
to the marriage supper of the Lamb.

Rev. 19:9

Matt Zelnik

An afterthought, I am certain some of my readers will be disturbed because I left out verses 18 and 19 in the above scriptures from the book of Revelation. The verses say:

Revelation 22:18, 19
For I testify to every man that hears the words of the prophecy of this book, if any man shall add to these things, God shall add to him the plagues that are written in this book. And if any man shall take away from the words of the prophecy of this book, God shall take away his part out of the book of life, and out of the holy city, and from the things, which are written in this book.

The reasons these verses are relegated to an afterthought:

- Many people believe Revelation 22:18, 19 indicate there can be no continuing revelation. They assume that biblical scriptures were assembled in the order in which prophets and apostles wrote them and that these scriptures (Revelation 22:18, 19) indicate it is God's will that no more be added. This is a misunderstanding of historical fact. Biblical scholars document that the Book of Revelation was not the last book to be written in the Bible. The council, which assembled the 66 books in their present order, CHOSE to put the Book of Revelation last. This created the dilemma, which made it sound as though God would never again reveal himself (continuing revelation).
- There are other verses in the Bible and one in the Doctrine and Covenants which say the same thing as Revelation 22:18, 19. <u>If interpreted as above in #1, nothing which follows Deuteronomy 4:2 is, or could possibly be, the revealed word of God.</u>

Deuteronomy 4:2
You shall not add to the word, which I command you, neither shall you diminish anything from it, that you may keep the commandments of the Lord your God, which I command you. [Read also Proverbs 30:6 and D & C 17:6d-g. Malachi 3:6 says, "I am the Lord. I change not."]

Deuteronomy 12:32
What thing so ever I command you, observe to do it; you shall not add thereto, nor diminish from it.

Proverbs 30:6
Do not add to His words lest He reprove you, and you are found to be a liar.

Doctrine & Covenants 17:6a, f, g
We know that all men must repent and believe on the name of Jesus Christ and worship the Father in His name. ...And we know that these things are true, and according to the revelations of John, neither adding to nor diminishing from the prophecy of His book, the Holy Scriptures, or the revelations of God which shall come hereafter by the gift and power of the Holy Ghost, the voice of God, or the ministering of angels. And the Lord God has spoken it. And honor, power, and glory be surrendered to His holy name, both now and forever. Amen.

All these verses indicate that MAN CANNOT add or take away from God's word. This does not prevent God from continuing to reveal himself through additional scripture. He can also correct mistakes that men have made in recording or translating His word.

I am Alpha and Omega, the beginning and the end, the first and the last.

Blessed are they who do my commandments that they may have right to the tree of life, and may enter in through the gates into the holy city.

Revelation 22:13, 14

The Lord God can do anything He wants, when He wants, how He wants.

And the Lord God has spoken it. And honor, power, and glory be surrendered to His holy name, both now and forever. Amen.

Doctrine & Covenants 17:6g

LIFE AFTER DEATH CHART

STEP 1	STEP 2		STEP 3	STEP 4	STEP 5	STEP 6
END OF LIFE OR TEMPORAL DEATH	SOULS OF THOSE WHO DIE GO TO PARADISE OR HELL		THE RETURN OF JESUS CHRIST AND THE FIRST RESURRECTION	SECOND RESURRECTION	FINAL JUDGEMENT	GOD'S NEW HEAVEN AND EARTH- ETERNITY
The body dies and is put in a grave. The Spirit returns to God for temporary placement in Paradise or Hell.	(A) Paradise is a resting place for righteous spirits.	Great Tribulation (about 7 years) + War of Armageddon	(A) Saints, living and dead, will rise in the air to meet Him. The resurrected dead will receive spiritual bodies that will never die.	Souls that resided in Hell are resurrected to stand before Christ's Judgment Bar.	Christ will Judge all people who ever lived.	All souls will be given a place to live for Eternity. (See the 3 Glories And the Lake of Fire below)
Alma 19:56-71	(B) Hell or the Prison House is a place of learning and correction for the spirits of the amoral and immoral human beings: some will receive Christ while in Hell. The Wicked remain filthy still.		Matthew 25:32 / I Thess. 4:14-17 / Revelation 20:4 / D & C 76:7n-s	Rev. 20:11, 12 / D & C 85:29	John 5:22 / Eccles. 12-14	
	Alma 19:42-47		THE MILLENNIUM 1000 years			
			Gen. 7:70-75 / Gen. 9:21-23 / Isaiah 4:1-5			

The Glories
See I Cor. 15:35-56

1. *Celestial* - (Glory of the Sun) Life in the presence of The Father and Son. D & C 76:5a-r; 85:4a-d

2. *Terrestrial* - (Glory of the Moon) Life in the presence of Jesus Christ. D & C 76:7a-f; 85:6e

3. *Telestial* - (Glory of the Stars) Those redeemed from Hell at the 2nd Resurrection will receive the ministry of Holy Spirit & Angels. Life in eternity will be tolerable for them, but far removed from rewards received by the faithful. D & C 76:7g, l

4. *The Lake of Fire, or Second Death:* This is the spiritual death for those who remain filthy still. D & C 76:n-r

If you have faith as big as a grain of mustard seed, you shall say to this mountain, move... and nothing shall be impossible for you

Matthew 17:20

You have been saved by grace through faith.

Ephesians 2:8

Chapter 15

What do the scriptures say about God's promises and Christian preparation?

Note: Some scripture is paraphrased in this chapter to clarify meaning.

There is only one who will save this world. His name is Jesus Christ.

Christ provided for mankind's salvation by dying in our place. Those who look for peace can find it in Him. But, it is not enough merely to accept Jesus. It is not enough just to be baptized. Our lives must change. Our hearts must be broken and our spirits contrite, knowing we are unworthy and yet of great value to our Lord and Savior. We must become obedient followers, committed to Him until He takes us home.

Jesus says, "Hear my voice," Matthew 17:4 I. V. That means pay attention! Listen to everything I say. Follow my guidance. Obey my commands. Hold on until the end. In other words, do what you are told! Be fully prepared for His return.

Doctrine & Covenants 85:16-18
My friends, I leave these sayings with you, to ponder in your hearts with this commandment, which I give to you; that you shall call upon me while I am near.

- Draw near to me, and I will draw near to you.
- Seek me diligently and you shall find me.
- Ask and you shall receive.
- Knock and it shall be opened to you.
- Whatsoever you ask the Father in my name that is expedient for you, it shall be given to you; and if you ask anything that is not expedient for you, it shall be turned unto your condemnation.

> *Behold, that which you hear is as the voice of one crying in the wilderness; in the wilderness because you cannot see him. My voice is Spirit; my Spirit is truth. Truth abides and has no end; and if it be in you it shall abound. [See Isaiah 40:3, Matthew 3:3, Luke 3:4, John 1:23]*

> *And if your eye is single to my glory, your whole body shall be filled with light, and there shall be no darkness in you, and that body which is filled with light comprehends all things. Therefore, sanctify yourselves that your minds become single to God, and the days will come that you shall see Him: for He will unveil His face to you, and it shall be in His own time, and in His own way, and according to His own will. [See Matthew 6:22, Luke 11:34.]*

OUR FATHER REQUIRES OBEDIENCE.

Jeremiah 11:4
…"Obey my voice and do according to all which I command you. You shall be my people and I will be your God."

Hebrews 5:8-9
Although He was the Son, yet He learned obedience by the things, which He suffered. And being made perfect He became the author of eternal salvation to all who obey Him.

GOD'S PURPOSE

Revelation 22:13-14
Christ said, "I am Alpha and Omega, the beginning and the end, the first and the last. Blessed are they who do my commandments that they may have the right to the tree of life and may enter in through the gates into the city."

Doctrine & Covenants 22:23b
"There is no end to my works, neither to my words; for this is my work and my glory to bring to pass the immortality and the eternal life of man."

These words of assurance are very important, especially for times of grave difficulty. Christ will return, but His Second Coming will be preceded by a time of fear, hatred, war, murder, and death. Most people will not welcome Him. Instead, many will blaspheme in His presence, refusing to acknowledge Him as Lord. They will take up weapons and fight against Him in league with the armies of Satan and the Antichrist. IF YOU HAVE NOT YET DEVELOPED A PERSONAL TESTIMONY OF JESUS CHRIST, IT IS ESSENTIAL THAT YOU DO SO. Faith and repentance are the two first steps. Then, be baptized in His name. Spend time getting to know the Lord, asking that He become more real in your life each day. Pray throughout your daily activities. Meditate on His Word and on things you have learned about Him. Persist, persist, persist until you know God is your personal friend. Having this confidence is one of the greatest things that will ever happen to you.

The rest of this chapter examines the promises of God and the preparations expected of those who wait for the bridegroom to come.

CHRISTIANS MUST HAVE A STRONG FAITH.

We pray, "Lord, my faith is weak."
God's Word says:

Matthew 17:20
If you have faith as big as a grain of mustard seed, you shall say to this mountain, move to another place and it shall be moved and nothing shall be impossible for you.

II Corinthians 5:7
We walk by faith and not by sight.

Ephesians 2:8
You have been saved by grace through faith. You are unable to do this for yourself. It is the gift of God.

Hebrews 11:1
Faith is the assurance of things hoped for, the evidence of things not seen.

Hebrews 11:6
Without faith, it is impossible to please Him for he who comes to God must believe that He is and that He rewards all those who diligently seek Him.

James 1:5, 6
If any of you lack wisdom, ask of God that gives to all people liberally and does not find fault, and it shall be given to you. But, ask in faith, nothing wavering, for he that wavers is like a wave of the sea driven and tossed with the wind.

I Peter 1:7-9
The trial of your faith is much more precious than gold, which perishes when tried by fire. Your faith will be found worthy of praise, honor and glory when Jesus Christ, whom you love, though you have never seen Him, appears. Though you have not seen Him, yet you believe and rejoice with unspeakable joy, and receive the object of your faith [Jesus Christ] who is the salvation of your soul.

I Nephi 4:38-39 [15:23, 24 LDS]
Nephi's brothers asked, "What is the meaning of the rod of iron that Lehi saw, which led to the tree?" And Nephi said, "That is the Word of God; and whoever listens to the Word of God, and holds fast to it, will never perish, neither will temptations and the fiery darts of the adversary overpower them, or make them blind, and lead them away to destruction."

III Nephi 10:19-23 [22:11-15 LDS]
O you afflicted, tossed by the tempest and not comforted; behold …all your children shall be taught of the Lord, and they shall have great peace. You shall be established in righteousness. You shall be far from oppression and terror, and you shall not fear, because it will not come near you. Those who gather together against you shall fall for your sake…. No weapon that is formed against you shall prosper; and you shall condemn every tongue that reviles against you, to judge you.

"This is the heritage of the servants of the Lord, and their righteousness is of me," says the Lord. [See I Nephi 7:34-64.]

Alma 3:27-32, 36 [5:14-15; 19 LDS]
And now, I ask of you, my brothers of the church, "Have you been born spiritually of God? Have you received His image in your countenances? Have you experienced this mighty change in your hearts? Do you exercise faith in the redemption provided by your creator? Do you look forward with an eye of faith, and view this mortal body raised in immortality, and this

corruption raised in incorruption, to stand before God, to be judged according to the deeds, which have been done, in the mortal body? Can you imagine you hear the voice of the Lord saying to you in that day, Come to me you blessed, for behold, your works have been the works of righteousness upon the face of the earth? ...Can you look up to God at that day with a pure heart and clean hands?"

REPENTANCE IS REQUIRED OF ALL GOD'S CHILDREN.

We pray, "Lord, I am a sinner."
God's Word says:

Ezekiel 18:21, 22
If the wicked will turn from all the sins that he has committed, and keep all my statutes, and do those things, which are right, they will surely live, and not die. All their transgressions will never again be mentioned. In God's righteousness they shall live.

Matthew 9:13, 14; and Mark 2:14, 15
Jesus said, "Those who are whole don't need a physician, only those who are ill... I did not come to call the righteous, but sinners to repentance."

Mark 1:13 [Mark 1:15 KJV]
The time is fulfilled, and the kingdom of God is at hand. Repent and believe in the gospel of Jesus Christ.

Luke 15:4-7
Jesus told this parable: "Suppose one of you has a hundred sheep and loses one of them. Does he not leave the ninety-nine in the open country and go after the lost sheep until he finds it? And, when he finds it, he joyfully puts it on his shoulders and goes home. Then, he calls his friends and neighbors together and says, 'Rejoice with me; I have found my lost sheep. ' I tell you, that in the same way there will be more rejoicing in Heaven over one sinner who repents than over ninety-nine righteous persons who do not need to repent."

II Peter 3:9
The Lord is neither slow in keeping His promise nor His coming, as some understand slowness. He is patient with us, not wanting anyone to perish, but everyone to come to repentance.

Mosiah 1:122 [3:21 LDS]
The time shall come when the knowledge of the Savior shall spread throughout every nation, kindred, tongue, and people. And, when that time comes, no one except little children will be found blameless before God, unless they repent and have faith in the name of the Lord, God, Omnipotent.

THOSE WHO WANT TO BE PART OF CHRIST'S HOUSEHOLD MUST BE BAPTIZED IN HIS NAME.

We pray, "Lord, I want to be part of your family."
God's Word says:

Genesis 6:62 [I. V. only]

You must be born again, into the kingdom of Heaven, of water, and of the Spirit, and be cleansed by the blood of my Only Begotten, so you may be sanctified from all sin, and enjoy the words of eternal life in this world and in the world to come; even immortal glory. For, by the water you keep the commandment, by the Spirit you are justified [declared righteous, forgiven of all sin], and by the blood you are sanctified [made holy].

II Nephi 13:7-17 [II Nephi 31:5-13 LDS]

If the Lamb of God, who is holy, needed to be baptized by water to fulfill all righteousness, how much more do we, being unholy, need to be baptized by water …And, after He was baptized with water, the Holy Ghost descended upon Him, in the form of a dove. This was Christ's example of the straight path and the narrow gate, by which we should enter [His kingdom]. And, He said to the children of men, "Follow me."

It is not possible to follow Jesus, unless we are willing to keep the commandments of the Father who said, "Repent, repent and be baptized in the name of my beloved Son. "

And the voice of the Son said, "He that is baptized in my name will receive the Holy Ghost from the Father just like I did. Therefore, follow me, and do the things which you have seen me do… Then, you will receive the baptism of fire and the Holy Ghost, and can speak with the tongues of angels, and shout praises unto the Holy One of Israel."

Alma 5:24-28 [7:14-16 LDS]

Now, I say to you, that you must repent and be born again. The Spirit says, "If you are not born again, you cannot inherit the kingdom of Heaven. "Therefore, come and be baptized unto repentance, so that you may be washed free of sin, and so that you may have faith on the Lamb of God, who takes away the sins of the world, who is mighty to save and to cleanse from all unrighteousness …

III Nephi 5:23-24 [11:22-23 LDS direction for authorized priesthood]

So there is no dispute among you, whoever repents of his sins… and desires to be baptized in my name, baptize them in this way: You shall go down and stand in the water, and you shall baptize them in my name. These are the words, which you shall use. Call them by name saying, "Having authority given me of Jesus Christ, I baptize you in the name of the Father, and of the Son, and of the Holy Ghost. Amen. "Then you shall immerse them in the water and bring them up out of the water. This is the manner that you will baptize in my name, for I say to you, that the Father, and the Son, and the Holy Ghost are one; and I am in the Father, and the Father is in me, and the Father and I are one. [See III Nephi 5:22-27, 33-37; Mormon 4:86-89, 95; Moroni 6:2-4].

Mormon 4:95 [9:29 LDS]
See that you are not baptized unworthily; see that you do not partake of the sacrament of Christ unworthily, but do all things in worthiness, and do it in the name of Jesus Christ, the Son of the living God; and if you do this and endure to the end, you will not be cast out.

Moroni 8:29 [8:26 LDS]
The first-fruit of repentance is baptism, and baptism comes by faith, to fulfill the commandments. The fulfilling of commandments brings remission of sins, and the remission of sins brings meekness and lowliness of heart. Then, because of meekness and lowliness of heart, the visitation of the Holy Ghost comes. He is the comforter, who is filled with hope and perfect love, which love endures by diligence in prayer, until the end comes when all the saints shall dwell with God.

Come forth and show your God that you are willing to repent of your sins, and enter into a covenant with Him to keep His commandments. Witness to Him, this day, by going into the waters of baptism. And, whoever does this and keeps the commandments of God, from that time on will have eternal life, according to the testimony of the Holy Spirit.

THE HOLY SPIRIT IS WITH GOD'S REBORN CHILDREN

We pray, "Lord, how can a man be born again?"
God's Word says:

John 3:3-5
Jesus said, "Unless a man is born again, he cannot see the kingdom of God. "Nicodemus asked, "How can a man be born when he is old? Can he enter his mother's womb a second time?" And Jesus answered, "Unless a man is born of water and of the Spirit, he cannot enter into the kingdom of God. That, which is born of the flesh, is flesh; and that which is born of the Spirit, is spirit."

Acts 8:17
Then they laid their hands on them, and they received the Holy Ghost.

Acts 19:6
When Paul laid his hands on them, the Holy Ghost came upon them.

Timothy 4:14
Do not neglect the gift that is in you, which was given you by prophecy, with the laying on of hands by the elders.

Moroni 2:1, 2 [2:1, 2 LDS]
The words of Christ, which He spoke to His disciples, "...Ye shall call on the Father in my name, in mighty prayer; and after you have done this, you shall have power, that whoever you lay your hands upon shall receive the Holy Ghost."

Doctrine & Covenants 34:2
You shall baptize by water, and they shall receive the Holy Ghost by the laying on of the hands.

Doctrine & Covenants 49:2g
Believe on the name of the Lord Jesus, who was on the earth, and is to come, the beginning and the end; repent and be baptized in the name of Jesus Christ, according to the holy commandment, for the remission of sins. And whosoever does this, shall receive the gift of the Holy Ghost, by the laying on of the hands of the elders of this church.

PRAISE GOD! He adopted YOU into His household.

You are God's child, created by Him and saved by His grace because Jesus Christ died in your place. It is your privilege, as a baptized member of Christ's church, to be both sanctified [made holy) and justified (declared righteous and able to stand in the presence of the Almighty God). As a believer, you have been ADOPTED into the House of Israel. You are a joint heir, entitled to all the rights and privileges in God's covenant with His chosen people. How can this be? Scriptures provide the answer.

Romans 8:15
You have not received the spirit of bondage to fear but you have received the Spirit of ADOPTION that permits you to call God, Father. The Spirit itself bears witness with our spirit that we are the children of God. And if we are His children, then we are the heirs of God and joint heirs with Christ. So if we suffer with Him, we may also be glorified together.

Galatians 4:4-7
When the fullness of time had fully come, God sent His Son, born of a woman, born under the law, to redeem those who were under the law so we might be ADOPTED as His children. Because you are now His sons and daughters, God sent the Spirit of His Son into your hearts and the Spirit calls out, "Abba, Father. "Therefore, you are no longer a servant but His child and if you are His child, you are an heir of God through Jesus Christ.

Ephesians 1:3-8
Praise to God and Father of our Lord Jesus Christ who through Christ blessed us in the Heavenly places with all spiritual blessings. He chose us before the creation of the world to be holy and blameless before Him in love. In this love, He predetermined that we would be ADOPTED as His children through Jesus, according to His pleasure and will. Because of His grace and His wonderful glory, He has made us acceptable through Jesus Christ in whom we have redemption through His blood and His forgiveness of our sins.

I Nephi 3:197-203 [13:41-14:2 LDS]
There is one God and one Shepherd over all the earth and the time will come that He shall make himself known to all nations, both the Jews and also the Gentiles... and the last shall be first, and the first shall be last. And it shall come to pass, if the Gentiles listen to the Lamb of God in that day, He shall make himself known to them in word and also in power and in deed, taking

away their stumbling blocks and softening their hearts toward the Lamb of God. They shall be numbered among the children of your father and also among the House of Israel. They shall be a blessed people upon the Promised Land forever.

"He shall make himself known to them in word and also in power..."

I Nephi 3:198-199

Preparation for Warfare

There will be a war (Revelation Chapters 16, 17, 18) before Christ's wedding (Revelation Chapters 20, 21) and Christ's people must be prepared. We will be faced by major physical threats but our most important battle is spiritual. Our Heavenly Father is concerned that we have adequate protection to withstand spiritual warfare. Therefore, He provides the armor and the weapons we will need to stand fast under enemy attacks. It is our responsibility to make full use of them.

YOU ARE NOT CORRECTLY DRESSED WITHOUT YOUR FULL ARMORMON

Ephesians 6:10-18
Be strong in the Lord and in the power of His might. Put on the whole armor of God that you may be able to stand against the wiles of the devil, for we wrestle not against flesh and blood, but against principalities, against powers, against the rulers of darkness of this world, and against spiritual wickedness in high places.

Therefore, take the whole armor of God that you may be able to withstand the evil day that is coming, and having done all this, you will stand. Stand therefore, having your body surrounded by truth, and having on the breastplate of righteousness, and your feet covered with the gospel of peace. Above all, take the shield of faith that is used to defend you against all the fiery darts of the wicked, and take the helmet of salvation, and the sword of the Spirit, which is the Word of God, and pray always in the Spirit with perseverance, earnestness, and humbleness for all of the saints.

If this verse is too long to memorize, concentrate on the pieces of armor that God is giving to you. Visualize yourself being fully clothed in this armor.

Christ places the Helmet of Salvation upon your head. You cannot do this for yourself. Jesus covers you with His Breastplate of Righteousness. Again, this is His job, not yours. You must buckle on the Belt of His Truth and always seek and speak truth. He covers your feet with His Peace. You must walk in it. Faith is your Shield, but you must pick it up and carry it at all times.

Your only defensive weapon is the Sword of the Spirit, which is God's Word in the scriptures. You must know His word and have it in your heart to make use of it. This (His word) is the weapon Jesus will use to defeat His enemies before He ushers in His Kingdom on earth. Nothing can stand against it.

When you pray, request that His Holy Spirit be your constant companion.

THE LORD IS OUR HELP IN TIMES OF TROUBLE.

We pray, "Lord, I'm in trouble."
God's Word says:

Psalm 31:33
You [Lord] are my rock and my fortress; therefore, for your name's sake, lead me and guide me.

Psalm 48:14
This God is our God forever and ever: He will be our guide even to death.

Psalm 119:105
Your word is a lamp unto my feet, and a light unto my path.

Proverbs 3:5, 6
Trust in the Lord with all your heart, and do not trust your own understanding. In all your ways acknowledge Him, and He shall direct your paths.

Proverbs 6:20, 23
"My son, keep your father's commandments and your mother's teaching. Bind them upon your heart forever. Fasten them around your neck. When you walk, they will guide you. When you sleep, they will watch over you; when you awake, they will speak to you. These commandments are a lamp, and this teaching is a light."

Isaiah 30:21
Your ears shall hear a word behind you, saying, "This is the way, walk in it. It will direct you to the right and to the left."

GOD'S HELP WHEN WE ARE AFRAID

We pray, "Lord, I am afraid."
God's Word says:

Psalm 23:4, 5
Though I walk through the valley of the shadow of death, I will not be afraid, for you are with me. Your rod and staff comfort me. You prepare a table before me in the presence of my enemies. You anoint my head with oil. My cup runs over.

Psalm 27:1

The Lord is my light and my salvation; whom shall I fear? The Lord is the strength of my life; of whom shall I be afraid?

Psalm 46:1, 2

God is our refuge and strength, a very present help in trouble. Therefore, we will not fear, though the earth is removed, and though the mountains are carried into the midst of the sea.

Isaiah 41:13

I the Lord, your God, will hold your right hand, saying to you, Fear not; I will help you.

Isaiah 43:1-3

Fear not, for I have redeemed you, I have called you by your name. You are mine. When you pass through the waters, I will be with you, and through the rivers, they will not overflow you. When you walk through the fire, you shall not be burned; neither shall the flame kindle upon you. For I am the Lord your God, the Holy One of Israel, your Savior.

Matthew 10:25 [10:28 KJV]

Do not be afraid of those who kill the body but are unable to kill the soul.

II Timothy 1:7

God has not given us the spirit of fear, but of power, and of love, and of a sound mind.

Hebrews 13:6

We may boldly say, "The Lord is my helper, and I will not fear what man shall do to me."

I John 4:18

There is no fear in love; but perfect love casts out fear, because fear causes torment. He that is afraid is not made perfect in love.

Therefore:

- Our faith in His Word must be unwavering.
- Our repentance must be complete and continuous.
- Our concern for one another must be absolute.
- Our love of God and His son Jesus Christ must never fail.
- We must hold on to the rod of iron until the very end, and move out with His strength and courage, as we face unprecedented times that will prepare us for Christ's return to earth.

Is this humanly possible? No! We need to cry to Christ for help.

THE LORD IS OUR GUARDIAN AND SECURITY.

We pray, "Lord, please protect me."
God's Word says:

Exodus 23:22
The Lord says, "If you shall obey my voice, and do all that I say, then I will be an enemy to your enemies and an adversary to your adversaries.

Deuteronomy 33:27
The eternal God is your refuge, underneath are the everlasting arms. He shall thrust out the enemy from before you and shall say, "Destroy them."

Psalm 3:3
You, O Lord, are a shield for me. You are my glory and the one who lifts my head.

Psalm 7:1
O Lord my God, in you do I put my trust; save me from all who persecute me, and deliver me.

Psalm 9:9
The Lord will be a refuge for the oppressed, a refuge in times of trouble.

Psalm 23
The Lord is my shepherd; I shall not want [for anything]. He makes me lie down in green pastures. He leads me beside the still waters. He restores my soul. He leads me in the paths of righteousness for His name's sake. Yea, though I walk through the valley of the shadow of death, I WILL FEAR NO EVIL for thou art with me. Thy rod and thy staff comfort me. You prepare a table for me [food for me to eat, or a banquet of wisdom and blessing] in the presence of my enemies. You anoint my head with oil; my cup runs over. Surely, goodness and mercy shall follow me all the days of my life; and I will dwell in the house of the Lord forever.

Psalm 31:1-5
In you, O Lord I put my trust. Let me never be ashamed. Deliver me in thy righteousness. Bow down your ear [to my prayers], and deliver me speedily. Be my strong rock and a house of defense to save me. For you are my rock and my fortress. Therefore, for your name's sake, lead me and guide me. Pull me out of the net that they have laid for me, for you are my strength. Into your hand, I commit my spirit; you have redeemed me, O Lord God of truth.

Psalm 32:7
You are my hiding place. You shall preserve me from trouble; you shall cover me with songs of deliverance.

Psalm 34:19
Many are the afflictions of the righteous, but the Lord delivers them from all of their troubles.

Psalm 59:16, 17

I will sing of your power; yes, I will sing aloud of your mercy in the morning, for you have been my defense and refuge in the day of my trouble. Unto you, O my strength, I will sing; for God is my defense and the God who covers me with mercy.

Psalm 61:3

You have been a shelter for me and a strong tower from my enemy.

Psalm 62:1, 5-8

Truly, my soul waits on God; from Him comes my salvation…. My soul; wait only on God, for my expectation is from Him. Only He is my rock and my salvation; He is my defense. I shall not be moved. In God is my salvation and my glory; the rock of my strength and my refuge is in God. Trust in Him at all times, all you people. Pour out your heart before Him. God is a refuge for us.

Psalm 91:7, 10, 11

A thousand shall fall at your side and ten thousand at your right hand, but they shall not come near you. There shall no evil befall you, neither shall any plague come near your home, because He gives His angels charge over you, to keep you in all your ways.

Proverbs 3:25

Do not be afraid of sudden fear, neither of the desolation of the wicked, when it comes. The Lord shall be your confidence and shall keep your foot from being snared.

Isaiah 43:2

When you pass through the waters, I will be with you; and the rivers will not overflow you. When you walk through fire, you shall not be burned; neither shall the flame touch you.

Isaiah 54:17

"No weapon that is formed against you shall prosper, and every tongue that rises against you in judgment you shall condemn. This is the heritage of the servants of the Lord, and their righteousness is of me," says the Lord.

Nahum 1:7

The Lord is good, a stronghold in the day of trouble; and He knows them that trust in Him.

Zephaniah 3:17

The Lord, thy God in the midst of thee, is mighty, He will save, He will rejoice over you with joy. He will rest in His love. He will joy over you with singing.

John 6:37

Jesus said, "All that the Father gives me shall come to me, and I will never cast out any who come to me."

John 10:27

Jesus said, "My sheep hear my voice, and I know them, and they follow me. I give them eternal life, and they shall never perish, neither shall any man take them from me. My Father, who gave them to me, is greater than all, and no man will take them out of my Father's hand."

John 14:18

Jesus said, "I will not leave you comfortless. I will come to you."

John 16:33

Jesus said, "These things I have spoken to you so in me you shall have peace. In the world you shall have tribulation, but be of good cheer; I have overcome the world."

Romans 8:38, 39

For I am persuaded, that neither death, nor life, nor angels, nor principalities, nor powers, nor things present, nor things to come; not height, nor depth, nor any other creature shall be able to separate us from the love of God which is in Christ Jesus our Lord.

II Thessalonians 3:3

But the Lord is faithful. He shall establish you and keep you from evil.

Hebrews 6:11-12, 18-20

We desire that every one of you show diligence and full assurance of hope until the end, so that you are not slothful, remaining followers of those who through faith and patience inherit God's promises. It is impossible for God to lie; therefore, we have a strong consolation and can lay hold of the hope set before us. We have hope, as an anchor of our souls, both sure and steadfast, that our prayers have entered under the veil to the mercy seat of God. There, the forerunner, Jesus Christ has already entered for us, yes, Jesus who was made a High Priest forever after the order of Melchisedec."

I Peter 3:12-14

The eyes of the Lord are over the righteous, and His ears are open to their prayers: but the face of the Lord is against them that do evil. And, who is he that will harm you, if you are followers of that which is good? If you suffer for the sake of righteousness, be happy and not afraid or troubled.

I Peter 4:12, 13

Friends, don't think of the fiery trial as something strange that is happening to you. Its purpose is to try you or strengthen you. Rejoice when you suffer for you are taking part in Christ's suffering, and when His glory is revealed, you will be filled with gladness and overwhelming joy.

Jude 1:24, 25

Now, to Him that is able to keep you from falling, and to present you faultless before the presence of His glory with exceeding joy; To the only wise God our Savior, be glory and majesty, dominion and power, both now and forever. Amen.

THE LORD WILL SUPPLY OUR COURAGE.

We pray, "I have no courage."
God's Word says:

Psalm 27:14
Wait on the Lord: Be of good courage, and He shall strengthen your heart. Wait, I say, on the Lord.

Isaiah 40:29
He gives power to the faint; and to them who have no might He increases strength.

Isaiah 40:31
They who wait upon the Lord shall renew their strength. They shall mount up with wings as eagles. They shall run and not be weary, and they shall walk and not faint.

Isaiah 41:10
Do not be afraid for I am with you. Be not dismayed, for I am your God. I will strengthen you. Yes, I will help you. I will hold you up with the right hand of my righteousness.

Philippians 4:13
I can do all things through Christ who strengthens me.

THE PEACE OF GOD IN TIMES OF TROUBLE

We pray, "Father, I need the peace that comes only from you."
God's Word says:

Psalm 4:8
I will lie down in peace and sleep, for you keep me in safety, Lord.

Psalm 29:11
The Lord will give strength to His people. The Lord will bless His people with peace.

Psalm 37:11
The meek shall inherit the earth and shall delight themselves in the abundance of peace.

Psalm 85:8
I will hear what God, the Lord will speak, for He will speak peace to His people and to His saints.
Isaiah 26:3
You will keep Him in perfect peace, whose mind is centered on you, because He trusts in you.

Isaiah 26:12
Lord, you will ordain peace for us; for you have created all our works in us.

Isaiah 32:17
The work of righteousness shall be peace; and the effect of righteousness is quietness and assurance forever.

Isaiah 52:7 [Mosiah 8:47-52 RLDS; 15:14-18 LDS]
How beautiful upon the mountains are the feet of Him that brings good news, that publishes peace, that tells the good news, that publishes salvation, that says to Zion, thy God reigns!

Isaiah 55:12
You shall go out with joy and be led forth with peace. The mountains and the hills shall break forth before you in singing, and all the trees of the field shall clap their hands.

Habakkuk 3:17-19
Although, the fig tree shall not blossom, neither shall fruit be in the vines; the labor of the olive shall fail, and the fields shall yield no meat; the flocks shall be cut off from the fold and there shall be no herd in the stalls. Yet shall I rejoice in the Lord, I will joy in the God of my salvation. The Lord God is my strength, and He will make my feet like hinds' feet, and He will make me to walk upon mine high places.

Mark 4:31
Peace, be still.

Luke 7:50
Your faith has saved you. Go in peace.

John 14:27
Peace I leave with you. I give to you my peace in a different way than the world gives peace. Don't let your heart be troubled, and don't let it be afraid.

Romans 5:1
Therefore, being justified by faith, we have peace with God through our Lord, Jesus Christ.

Philippians 4:7
And the peace of God, which passes all understanding, shall keep your hearts and minds through Christ Jesus.

Colossians 3:15
Let the peace of God rule in your hearts, and be thankful.

WHAT MORE IS EXPECTED OF CHRISTIANS IN THE LAST DAYS?

WE MUST TRUST IN THE LORD!

We pray, "Lord, I place my trust in you."
God's Word says:

Psalm 46:1, 2
God is our refuge and strength, a very present help in times of trouble. Therefore, we will not fear, though the earth be removed, and though the mountains be carried into the midst of the sea.

Psalm 103:2-4
Bless the Lord, O my soul, and forget not all His benefits. He has forgiven all your sins and healed all your diseases. He has redeemed your life from destruction and crowned you with loving kindness and tender mercies.

Proverbs 3:5, 6
Trust in the Lord with all your heart, and do not lean on your own understanding. In all your ways acknowledge Him, and He shall direct your paths.

Matthew 6:28, 29
Take no thought for your life saying, what shall we eat? Or what shall we drink? Or how shall we be clothed? Life is more than meat and the body more than clothing …Your Heavenly Father knows your needs and will provide for you.

John 6:35
Jesus said, "I am the bread of life. He that comes to me shall never hunger, and he that believes in me shall never thirst."

Romans 8:32
He did not spare His own Son, but delivered Him up for all of us. Therefore, through Him, shall he not freely give us all things?

Philippians 4:19
My God shall supply all your needs, according to His riches in glory, by Christ Jesus.

WE MUST RETAIN OUR HOPE IN JESUS CHRIST.

We pray, "I have lost my hope."
God's Word says:

Psalm 121:1-3
I will lift up my eyes to the hills. Where does my help come from? My help comes from the Lord, the maker of Heaven and earth. Behold, He that keeps Israel will neither slumber nor sleep.

Proverbs 3:25, 26
Have no fear of sudden disaster or of the ruin that overtakes the wicked, for the Lord will be your confidence and will keep you from falling.

Zechariah 4:6
"Not by might, nor by power, but by my spirit," says the Lord of hosts.

John 14:12
Jesus said, "I tell you the truth, anyone who has faith in me will do what I have been doing. He will do even greater things than these, because I am going to the Father. And I will do whatever you ask in my name, so that I [God's Son] may bring glory to My Father. You may ask me for anything in my name, and I will do it."

Romans 8:28
We know ALL THINGS work together for good for those who love God and are called according to His purposes.

Philippians 1:6
Be confident, He who has begun a good work in you will continue helping you grow in Him, until Jesus Christ returns.

Hebrews 10:35, 36
Do not throw away your confidence; it will be richly rewarded. You need to persevere so, when you have done the will of God, you will receive what He has promised. In just a very little while, He who is coming will come and will not delay. My righteous ones must live by faith, and if they shrink back, I will not be pleased with them. But, we are not among those who shrink back and are destroyed. We are those who believe and are saved.

Jacob 2:22-24 RLDS [2:17-19 LDS]
Think of your brothers as much as you think of your selves. Be friendly with everyone and free with your substance, so they may be rich just like you. But, before you seek for riches, seek the kingdom of God. And, after you have obtained a hope in Christ, you shall obtain riches, if you seek them; and, you will seek them intending to do good; to clothe the naked, and to feed the hungry, and to liberate the captive, and administer relief to the sick and afflicted.

DOCTRINE & COVENANTS 142:5
The hopes of My people and the goals of My church, while not yet realized, and at times seem distant, are closer to realization than many recognize. It is yet day when all can work. The night will come when, for many of my people, the opportunity to assist will have passed.

WE MUST WAIT PATIENTLY FOR HIM.

We pray, "Lord, please give me patience."
God's Word says:

Psalm 27:14
Wait on the Lord. Be of good courage, and He shall strengthen your heart.

Psalm 37:7
Rest in the Lord and wait patiently for Him. Do not be disturbed when men prosper by carrying out wicked schemes. Refrain from anger and turn from wrath. Do not fret. It only leads to evil, and evil men will be cut off.

Psalm 40:1
I waited patiently for the Lord, and He listened to me and heard my cry.

Isaiah 40:31
But they that wait upon the Lord shall renew their strength. They shall mount up with wings as eagles. They shall run and not be weary; they shall walk and not faint.

Romans 5:3, 4
We glory in tribulations, knowing that tribulation teaches patience, and patience provides experience, and experience gives us hope. And hope does not make us ashamed, because the love of God is shed abroad in our hearts, by the Holy Ghost, which is given to us.

Romans 8:25
If we hope for that which we do not see, then we must wait with patience for it.

Romans 15:4, 5
The things that were written before now were written for our learning, that we through patience and comfort of the Scriptures might have hope. Now, the God of patience and consolation grant you to be likeminded toward each other, according to Christ Jesus.

Galatians 5:22
The fruit of the Spirit is love, joy, peace, longsuffering, gentleness, goodness, faith. There is no law against these things.

Hebrews 6:12
Do not be lazy, but follow those who through faith develop patience and inherit the promises [of God].

Hebrews 10:36
You have need of patience, so after you have done the will of God, you will receive His promise.

<u>**James 1:2-4**</u>
Brothers and sisters, count it all joy when you fall into many temptations, knowing this: the trying of your faith increases patience. Let patience have her perfect work, so you may become perfect and entire, wanting for nothing.

<u>**James 5:7, 8**</u>
Be patient therefore, brothers and sisters, until the coming of the Lord. Behold, the farmer waits for the precious fruit of the earth and has patience for a long time, until he receives the early and latter rain. You must also be patient. Establish your hearts, for the coming of the Lord draws near.

WE MUST BLESS THOSE WHO PERSECUTE US.

One of the purposes of trials and problems is learning to give them to the Lord, allowing Him, in His time, to overcome them. This builds faith. If we are unable to do this, how can we prepare for that which is ahead? Practice builds confidence in His ability to care for ALL of our needs. It prepares us for the greater challenges that lie ahead.

We pray, "How shall we handle persecution, Jesus?"
God's Word says:

<u>**John 15:20**</u>
Jesus said, "The servant is not greater than his lord. If they have persecuted me, they will also persecute you."

<u>**Romans 12:14**</u>
Bless them that persecute you; bless, and curse not.

<u>**II Corinthians 4:9**</u>
We are troubled on every side, yet not distressed: we are perplexed, but not in despair; persecuted, but not forsaken; cast down but not destroyed; always carrying within us the death of the Lord Jesus, that the life of Jesus might be manifest inside us. For we who live are always delivered to death for Jesus' sake, that the life of Jesus might be made whole in our mortal flesh.

<u>**Colossians 3:12-17**</u>
Put on, as the holy and beloved elect of God, all mercy, kindness, humbleness of mind, meekness, long-suffering, forbearing one another, and forgiving one another. If any of you have a quarrel against another, you must forgive the other, even as Christ forgave you,

Above all these things, put on charity which is the bond of perfection. And, let the peace of God rule in your hearts... and be thankful. Let the word of Christ dwell in you richly, with all wisdom; teaching and admonishing one another in psalms and hymns and spiritual songs, singing with grace in your hearts to the Lord.

And whatsoever you do in word or deed, do all in the name of the Lord Jesus, giving thanks to God and the Father by Him.

II Timothy 3:12
Everyone who lives a godly life, in Christ Jesus, will suffer persecution. Evil men and seducers will become much worse, deceiving and being deceived. But continue in the things, which you have learned and have been assured, knowing from whom you have learned them. From a child you have known the Holy Scriptures, which are able to make you wise unto salvation, through faith, which is in Jesus Christ.

I Peter 4:12, 13
Beloved, do not think it strange when you have a fiery ordeal, which tries you, as though something unusual has happened. Instead, rejoice because you are taking part in Christ's sufferings, so that when His glory is revealed, you may be glad also, with exceeding joy. Those who reproach you for your belief in Christ are speaking evil of Him. Be happy and glory in the spirit God gives you; for you are glorifying Him.

WE WILL STRENGTHEN OUR TESTIMONY.

During the Last Days, it will be essential to maintain our testimony of Christ, in the hope of bringing others to Him. If we are able to do this, He will open many doors. He is our courage, strength, and hope. Our firm confidence in Him allows His spirit to sustain us, in every possible situation.

We pray, "Please strengthen my testimony, Lord."
God's word says:

Psalm 118:17
I shall not die but live and declare the works of the Lord.

Luke 21:13, 14
I will give you a mouth and wisdom, which all your adversaries shall not be able to speak against. And, it shall become a testimony for you.

II Timothy 1:8
Do not be ashamed of the testimony of our Lord... but take part in the afflictions of the gospel according to the power of God who has saved us, and called us with a holy calling, not according to our works, but according to His own purpose and grace, which was given us in Christ Jesus before the world began.

Alma 12:18-20
The Lord said to them, "Go forth to your brothers, and establish my word. Be patient and long suffering in afflictions so that you may be good examples for them in me, and I will make you an instrument in my hands to bring about the salvation of many souls. "And it came to pass that the hearts of the sons of Mosiah, and also those who were with them, took courage to go forth to their enemies and declare the Word of God, to them.

WE WILL TRUST GOD'S WISDOM.

Romans 8:28
We know ALL THINGS WORK TOGETHER FOR GOOD TO THOSE WHO LOVE GOD, to those who are called according to His purpose.

Proverbs 2:6
The Lord gives wisdom; knowledge and understanding come out of His mouth. He lays up sound wisdom for the righteous. He is a buckler for them that walk uprightly.

Proverbs 3:19-23
The Lord by wisdom has founded the earth; by understanding, He has established the Heavens. By His knowledge, the depths are broken up and the clouds drop down the dew. My son, do not let these things depart from your eyes. Keep sound wisdom and discretion, so they shall be life to your soul and grace to your neck. Then you shall walk safely in your way, and your foot shall not stumble.

WE WILL REJOICE IN THE LORD.

Philippians 4:4, 6, 7
Rejoice in the Lord always; again I say rejoice. Let your moderation be known to all men for the Lord is at hand. Be afflicted for nothing, but in everything by prayer and supplication, with thanksgiving, let your requests be made known to God. And, the peace of God, which passes all understanding, shall keep your hearts and minds through Christ Jesus.

I Thessalonians 5:16-24
Rejoice always. Pray without ceasing. In everything, give thanks, for this is the will of God in Christ Jesus, concerning you. Quench not the Spirit. Do not despise prophecy. Prove all things; hold fast to that which is good. Abstain from all appearances of evil. And may the God of peace sanctify you: and I pray God your whole spirit and soul and body be preserved blameless until the coming of our Lord Jesus Christ. Faithful is He that calls you.

Doctrine & Covenants 110:22
Brothers, shall we not go on in so great a cause? Go forward and not backward. Courage brothers, and on to the victory! Let your hearts rejoice and be glad. Let the earth break forth into singing. Let the dead speak forth anthems of eternal praise to the King Immanuel, who ordained before the world existed, that which would enable us to redeem men out of their prisons; and for the prisoners to go free.

WE WILL PRAISE THE LORD OUR GOD.

I Chronicles 16:25-29

Great is the Lord, and greatly to be praised; He also is to be feared above all gods, for the gods of the people are idols; but the Lord made the Heavens. Glory and honor are in His presence; strength and gladness are in His place. Give unto the Lord all you kindreds of the people. I give unto the Lord glory and strength. Give unto the Lord the glory due His name. Bring an offering, and come before Him. Worship the Lord in the beauty of holiness.

Psalm 8:1, 3-5

O Lord our Lord, how excellent is thy name in all the earth! You have set your glory above the Heavens.... When I consider your Heavens, the work of your fingers, the moon and the stars which you have ordained; what is man that you are mindful of him, and the son of man that you visit him? You have made him a little lower than the angels, and have crowned him with glory and honor.

Psalm 18:46

The Lord lives, and blessed be my Rock. And, let the God of my salvation be exalted.

Psalm 34:1-3

I will bless the Lord at all times. His praise shall continually be in my mouth. My soul shall make her boast in the Lord; the humble shall hear of it and be glad. O magnify the Lord with me, and let us exalt His name together.

Psalm 96:1-13

O sing unto the Lord a new song; sing unto the Lord, all the earth. Sing unto the Lord, bless His name; show forth His salvation from day to day. Declare His glory among those who don't know Him, His wonders among all people. For the Lord is great and greatly to be praised. He is to be feared above all other gods. For all the gods of the nations are idols; but the Lord made the Heavens. Honor and majesty are before Him; strength and beauty are in His sanctuary. Give unto the Lord the glory due His name. Bring an offering and come into His courts.

O worship the Lord in the beauty of holiness; fear before Him, all the earth. Tell those who don't know Him that the Lord reigns; the world shall be established and it shall not be moved. He shall judge the people righteously. Let the Heavens rejoice and the earth be glad. Let the sea roar and the fullness of it. Let the field be joyful and all that is in it; then all the trees of the wood will rejoice before the Lord; for He comes. He comes to judge the earth. He shall judge the world with righteousness and the people with His truth.

WE WILL BE THANKFUL.

Psalm 100:1-5
Make a joyful noise unto the Lord, all you lands. Serve the Lord with gladness; come before His presence with singing. You know that the Lord is God. It is He who has made us and not we ourselves. We are His people and the sheep of His pasture. Enter into His gates with thanksgiving and into His courts with praise. Be thankful to Him, and bless His name, for the Lord is good; His mercy is everlasting, and His truth endures to all generations.

Colossians 3:15
Let the peace of God rule in your hearts... and be thankful.

Colossians 3:17
Whatsoever you do in word or deed, do it all in the name of the Lord Jesus, giving thanks to God and the Father by Him.

I Thessalonians 5:18
In everything, give thanks, for this is the will of God in Christ, concerning you.

Mosiah 9:56 [18:23 LDS]
...Observe the Sabbath day and keep it holy, and every day give thanks to the Lord your God.

Doctrine & Covenants 59:2d
You shall thank the Lord your God IN ALL THINGS.

The scriptures tell us to expect very difficult times in the future. As challenging as these times may become, Christ expects us to be faithful until the very end.

WE WILL ENDURE TO THE END.

We pray, "Lord, help me to endure."
God's Word says:

Matthew 10:19
And you shall be hated by all the world for my name's sake; but s/he who endures to the end will be saved.

Matthew 24:10, 11
Iniquity will be everywhere, and the love of many will grow cold. But s/he who remains steadfast, and is not overcome will be saved.

Mark 13:13
And because iniquity shall be everywhere, the love of many shall grow cold; but he that endures to the end will be saved.

Hebrews 3:14
For we are made partakers of Christ, if we hold the beginning of our confidence steadfast, unto the end.

269

I Nephi 3:187-189 [I Nephi 13:37 LDS]

Blessed are they who shall seek to bring forth my Zion at that day, for they shall have the gift and the power of the Holy Ghost. And if they endure to the end, they shall be lifted up at the last day, and shall be saved in the everlasting kingdom of the Lamb; and whoever shall publish peace, yes, tidings of great joy, how beautiful upon the mountains they shall be.

I Nephi 7:69 [22:31 LDS]

If you shall be obedient to the commandments and endure to the end, you shall be saved at the last day.

II Nephi 7:10 [10:6 LDS]

Behold, I am the law, and the light; look to me and endure to the end, and you shall live, for I will give eternal life to him who endures to the end.

II Nephi 13:30 [31:20 LDS]

If you shall press forward, feasting upon the word of Christ, and endure to the end, the Father says, "You shall have eternal life."

Omni 1:47 [1:26 LDS]

Come unto Him and continue in fasting and praying, and endure to the end; and as the Lord lives, you will be saved.

Mosiah 2:10 [4:6 LDS]

The atonement has been prepared from the foundation of the world, so salvation might come to those who puts their trust in the Lord and are diligent in keeping His commandments, continuing in faith even to the end of the life of their mortal bodies. [See I Nephi 3:188; II Nephi 13:20, 21, 30; Alma 16:135, 137; Alma 18:2; III Nephi 12:18, 29; Mormon 4:95; Moroni 6:3; 8:3.]

Doctrine & Covenants 12:3

Seek to bring forth and establish my Zion. Keep my commandments in all things; and if you keep my commandments and endure to the end, you shall have eternal life, which is the greatest of all the gifts of God.

Doctrine & Covenants 16:4e

Take upon you the name of Christ, and speak the truth in soberness; and as many as repent and are baptized in my name, which is Jesus Christ, and endure to the end, shall be saved.

Doctrine & Covenants 50:2

Behold, I the Lord have looked upon you and have seen abominations in the church that professes my name; but blessed are they who are faithful and endure, whether in life or in death, for they shall inherit eternal life. [See D & C 17:5d, 6a].

REMINDERS FROM THE LORD

We pray, "What else do you want us to know, Lord?"
God's Word says:

Matthew 5:10-15
Blessed are the pure in heart, for they shall see God. Blessed are all the peacemakers, for they shall be called the children of God. Blessed are all they who are persecuted for my name's sake, for theirs is the kingdom of Heaven. And, blessed are you when men shall revile you, and persecute you, and shall say all manner of evil against you falsely for my name's sake. You shall have great joy and be exceedingly glad; for great shall be your reward in Heaven; for they also persecuted the prophets who were before you.

Matthew 10:14 I. V.
Behold, I send you forth as sheep in the midst of wolves; therefore, be wise servants, and harmless as doves. [KJV 10:16 says, "Be as wise as serpents."]

Doctrine & Covenants 49:2d
Therefore, I say to you, that I have sent you my everlasting covenant, even that which was from the beginning, and that which I have promised I have fulfilled, and the nations of the earth shall bow to it.

Ezekiel 34:23-30
"I will set up one Shepherd over them and He shall feed them, and He shall be their shepherd. And, I the Lord will be their God, and my servant David, a prince among them; I the Lord have spoken it. And I will make a covenant of peace, and will cause the evil Beast [the Antichrist] to be removed from the land; and they shall dwell safely in the wilderness, and sleep in the wood. And I will make them and the places round about my hill a blessing; and I will cause the shower to come down in its season; there shall be showers of blessing.

And, the tree of the field shall yield her fruit, and the earth shall yield her increase, and they shall be safe in their land. And, when I have broken the bands of their yoke and delivered them from those who used them, they shall know that I am the Lord. They shall no longer be prey to the heathen, and the beasts of the land shall not devour them, but they shall dwell in safety, and no one shall make them afraid. And, I will raise up a remarkable plant, so they will never again be consumed with hunger or bear the shame of the heathen any longer. Then they will know that I, the Lord their God am with them and that they, the House of Israel, are my people, "says the Lord.

Revelation 22:14
Blessed are they who keep His commandments so that they may have right to the tree of life, and may enter in through the gates into the holy city.

More Ways to Prepare Spiritually

- Speak with God through prayer, fasting, and meditation.
- Study the scriptures and other good books.
- Live a lifestyle of Holiness.
- Serve others.
- Use your talents, time, finances, and material possessions wisely.
- Spend time fellowshipping with other believers.
- Take part in social actions.
- Evangelism
- Endure loyally for Christ until the end.

©P.S.Blain Photography and Graphics

"And, the tree of the field shall yield her fruit, and the earth shall yield her increase, and they shall be safe in their land."

Ezekiel 34:27

You must take upon you the name of Christ which is my name, for by this name you shall be called at the last day; and whoso taketh upon him my name and endureth till the end, the same shall be saved at the last day. Whatsoever you shall do, you shall do it in my name; therefore, ye shall call the church in my name and you shall call upon the Father in my name and He shall bless the church for my sake.

III Nephi 12:18-19

You shall take upon you the name of Christ.

274

Appendix

The Boy Scout Motto: Be Prepared!

Physical Preparations for Prolonged Power Failure

Individual households should always be prepared for unexpected emergencies such as flooding, loss of power, and so on. Preparation will not guarantee your well-being during the tribulation or any major disaster, but if these items are available, they may mean the difference between life and death. Every home should have an emergency center where emergency necessities are kept. Consider making one or two emergency purchases with each paycheck to stock it. The single storage location should be near your means of transportation and with the ability to be packaged and ready to go in a moment's notice.

The four basic needs to sustain life are food, water, shelter, and adequate warmth. The following is recommended for short-term emergency preparation to sustain you at home for seven to ten days.

Heat Source for Warmth and Cooking

- Large kerosene or propane heater and adequate amount of fuel (smaller rooms need less heat). However, you may need to keep water pipes from freezing also. Place a heater in the room where it will do the most good. Purchase as many as you can. Buy heaters with flat tops that can be used for cooking, if necessary. VENTILATE ROOMS WHERE HEATERS ARE USED.
- Wood-burning heat/cook stove (the best you can afford)
- Firewood or pellets (for fireplace or wood-burning stove)
- On a sunny day, a mirror or magnifying glass can direct sunbeams to a pile of dry twigs, thereby starting a small fire. Mirrors or aluminum foil can also be used to cook meals by directing the sun's rays toward the cook pot or baking dish. Start early, and prepare for a long wait. See a good Boy Scout handbook for directions.
- Handmade fire starters: Wrap small pieces of broken candle tapers in two- or three-inch squares of wax paper. Twist paper at both ends of candle. Put under dry twigs. Light the twisted end of the wax paper. Add heavier twigs when a small fire has started. Larger pieces of wood should wait until it is clear that a good fire is burning. DO NOT BURN PINE IN AN INDOOR FIREPLACE. It forms creosote in chimneys and may start a house fire.
- Gasoline generator and adequate fuel, depending on its size, can temporarily power a furnace or refrigerator and even a TV if necessary. However, unless you own a gas station, it is possible your generator will have no fuel.
- Cover windows/doors with sheet plastic, carpet, tarps, or blankets. Use towels or caulking to plug any spot where cold air enters. Don't caulk or cover every little crack as ventilation is needed.
- Dress appropriately in winter so you stay warm without another source of heat. Wear several layers of loose warm clothing. Discard a few layers if you get too

hot. Choose shoes and boots a size too large and wear several pairs of socks inside them. Change wet clothing immediately.

- Use heavy work gloves with lighter-weight gloves beneath them. Cover your head with a ski mask and warm hat. Remember a warm scarf for your neck. Keep a poncho or light rain gear available.
- Commercial foot and hand warmers, survival socks, and gloves
- Fire starters, lighters, matches (Waterproof your matches by dipping them in melted candle wax.)
- Fire starters: visit this website to research and purchase reliable fire starters. www.motherearthnews.com/blogs/blog.aspx?blogid=1510&tag=firestarter
- Arctic wear and survival equipment, visit www.wilderness-survival.net

For emergency cooking: use your grill outdoors. Use your camping skills and cook over an open fire with a stick from a tree. Put fire out with a quantity of water or soil. Smothering with dirt is preferable as it prevents smoke that may be seen, drifting into the air and it conserves your water supply.

EMERGENCY NOTICE: Do not heat or cook with charcoal inside closed buildings, charcoal fumes are deadly.

COOKING SURFACE:

- Fireplace grill
- Wood-burning stove
- Coleman camping stove and fuel—use in ventilated area
- Outside grill or open fire
- Homemade Candle Burner: Save and clean used tuna fish cans, or other small metal cans. Cut corrugated cardboard strips the height of the can, making sure the columns in the cardboard are vertical. Wrap the cardboard so it fits tightly inside the can. Lint from dryers can also be saved for packing the tins. Melt old candles in a double boiler (this prevents the wax from catching fire). Salvage a candlewick or small candle and put it inside the center of the can. Pour wax over the top. Trim the wick to the height of the can when the wax has hardened. For use: place the candle burner between bricks or under a non-flammable stands, which will hold the pot or skillet above the flame.

WATER SOURCE: Each family member, pets included, will need an average of one gallon of water a day. Store as much as you possibly can. Dehydration is a killer. Do not allow yourselves to become dehydrated. (Note: Commercial water bottles do not keep for any length of time. Put water in heavier containers and recycle them periodically.)

Your home water heater can provide some needed water, if tap water is unavailable. Reserve a clean hose to drain the water heater. Purify water by boiling or by using water purification tablets or Clorox. Purify the hose with a mix of Clorox and water, regularly.

Obtain large water container(s). Barrels that held items such as cooking oils and olives may be available locally and converted into rain barrels. These are inexpensive. We paid $5 plus the cost of conversion materials for used barrels. Commercial rain barrels are also available to capture rainwater from roofs. They cost about $90–$150 each. This water can be used for gardens, bathing, washing clothes, and other needs. DO NOT ALLOW WATER TO FREEZE IN THESE BARRELS. EMPTY ANY BARREL THAT MUST REMAIN OUTSIDE IN THE WINTER.

Boil any impure water before drinking for 1 MINUTE AT A FULL BOIL. At higher elevations for 3 to 5 minutes as it boils at a lower temperature.

Clorox: Keep liquid bleach on hand to purify water, to add to dishwater, or to use in water for cleaning. To purify water for drinking: using a WATER DROPPER or MEDICINE DROPPER, 2 <u>DROPS</u> of liquid bleach per quart or ½ tsp per 5 gallons of water, stir with a clean utensil. If water is cloudy, you can double the amount. Let the water sit for 30 minutes to an hour. For more information, go to http://www.doh.wa.gov/phepr/handbook/purify.htm   Also, a printable PDF file here: http://www.doh.wa.gov/phepr/handbook/hbk_pdf/purify.pdf   **Water purification tablets** are available at camping stores, follow directions on the package.

HEAT
If you lose your heat in the coldest part of winter:

- Keep working water lines from freezing by allowing faucets to run constantly at the lowest pressure (smallest stream).
- If water lines are not working properly, be sure to drain them so that the water inside does not freeze and burst the metal.
- As a preventive measure, wrap water pipes with commercial foam to prevent them from freezing in the winter.
- If possible, keep hot water on your heat source throughout cold months. The steam will prevent dry air, and water will be available for foods, beverages, and dishwashing.
-

FOOD: Think simple! For emergencies, make your food preparation as easy as possible. Buy and store nutritious foods that have a long shelf life. With a marking pen, date your purchases and rotate the food at least twice a year. Work towards storing foods for 6 months to a year. Possible choices include the following:

- Canned or boxed foods, including beverages, sugar, flour, powdered milk
- Canned meat, fruit, juice, etc., that can be eaten without cooking
- Nutrition bars and canned liquids such as Ensure
- Canned ready-to-eat soups, vegetables
- Instant tea and coffee
- Dried or dehydrated foods
- Other according to individual preferences
- Explore sources for canned and dried foods for long term storage. Some of these have a known shelf life of 10 or more years. Check camping stores and catalogs and online sources for food for long term storage. Internet link: http://foodstoragemadeeasy.net/
-

Learn about wild food sources. Numerous books are available in libraries and bookstores. Many people already recognize wild day lilies and cattails. Many of their parts (root, stem, and flower) are edible. Early dandelions are nutritious, but become bitter as they age. Some plants are poisonous. Obtain a good book on wild, edible foods so your knowledge will be up to the challenge. Avoid mushrooms and toadstools unless you are an expert.

KITCHEN NEEDS

- Clorox, hand soap, waterless body wash, dish soap, and water
- GOOD HAND-OPERATED CAN OPENER—try to find one that is dependable.
- Good knives/kitchen scissors
- Camping pots and skillets for on top of fire or other fuel source
- Spatulas, large cooking spoons
- Hot pads or gloves
- Paper towels (after first use, dry and save for fire starter or other uses)
- Plastic zip-close bags, large and small (check into the green storage bags and plastic containers that remove ethylene gases the produce gives off so keeps the fresh foods fresher longer.)
- Wax paper, foil, plastic wrap, plastic bags, and paper bags
- Large supply of paper plates, bowls, hot and cold cups, paper towels to help when it's difficult to wash dishes. Plastic forks and spoons are okay, but regular tableware carefully cleaned works better unless you plan to discard the plastic utensils. Wipe all tableware clean with damp paper towels and dip in solution of bleach or vinegar and water.
- Heavy-duty plastic trash bags in several sizes

HYGIENE AND SANITATION

- Keep clean with plenty of soap and water. If this is not available:
- Use baby wipes in plastic containers to clean your body. The baby wipes are less expensive than personal wipes and are especially helpful in emergencies. Keep one box in the kitchen to clean hands and another in bathroom for washing purposes. Keep a third box in the car. Although regular towels and washcloths can be used, you may not have a way to launder them, and they will harbor germs.
- Store bath soap, liquid bath, and no-rinse liquid shampoo
- Store a large supply of toilet tissue so it isn't necessary to resort to things such as plant leaves. My son is saving phone books and old books for this emergency.
- First-aid kit, well stocked
- Vitamins and medications, at least three months' supply, more if possible
- Keep extra toothbrushes and toothpaste on hand. Baking soda or salt can substitute for toothpaste.

DISHWASHING: In emergency situations, it is very important to avoid spreading germs and viruses that may develop on dirty dishes. Paper plates and cups may be the best alternative for short-term use. If regular dishes must be used, assign a specific set

278

(plate, cup, glass, and utensils) to each family member. It is important to keep them as clean as possible. To avoid more work, wipe food off plates immediately. Use a paper towel, newspaper, or even green leaves (be sure you do not pull or use poison ivy, oak, or sumac). If you are unable to heat water to wash dishes, or if water is limited, place a small amount of dish soap into a squirt bottle. Fill with water and shake to dissolve soap. Squirt a small amount of soapy water on a paper towel and use to wash your own dishes. Vinegar, bleach, or salt may be added to bottled water for rinsing.

SUPPLIES TO STORE: Liquid dishwashing soap: keep a small amount of dish soap pre-mixed in a bottle of water from your storage supply. Use this judiciously to keep from running out of your water supply.

TOOLS: (Purchase the best quality hand tools you can afford to buy.)

- Sharp pocketknife and other work knives
- Knife-sharpening stone
- Shovels, rakes, hoes
- Ax and hatchet
- Hammer and nails
- Heavy-duty wood saw
- Pitchfork
- Gasoline-powered equipment IF you have a supply of gasoline power saw etc.

LIGHT SOURCE

- Flashlights and batteries (get best flashlight you can afford). Buy two or more packages of each size battery needed. Rotate batteries that are kept in your storage so they stay charged.
- Look for solar lights that can be moved indoors at night.
- Kerosene lanterns or camping lamps and fuel (Buy fuel at gas station or use lamp fuel from stores.)
- Big block-type candles that don't tip easily. When burning, put them inside large, clear glass jars or vases for extra fire protection and for additional light reflection. A mirror or aluminum wrap behind a candle will reflect more light.
- Buy candlewicks (available at craft stores) for repairing messed up block candles. Use a long nail or ice pick to make new holes in candles.
- Commercial lighters and wooden matches; keep these in a waterproof container.

Warning: Do Not Leave Candles Burning in Empty Rooms or where Children of Pets can Reach them.

BEDDING

- Metallic reflective heat sheets for bedding warmth
- The best, lightweight sleeping bags (with washable liners) you can afford. You can make your own washable liner using a twin-size flannel or fleece sheet. Fold it in half lengthwise. Sew one end closed, and sew the open side about halfway up. Stuff sewn sheet inside sleeping bag and sleep inside this liner.

- Blankets, sheets, pillowcases and pillows (In cold weather you can't beat fleece bedding and satin comforters to wrap up in.)

COMMUNICATION:

- Cell phone, these may not work if the communication towers are affected.
- Obtain a hand-operated device to charge the cell phone.
- Battery-operated radio, short-wave radio, crank-radio, ham-radio operator station, etc.
- In an emergency, local lines may be tied up. Obtain the number of an out-of-state friend or relative that family members should call if separated locally and phones are not working. That person can let the local family know the location and status of each member.

EMERGENCY TOILET

This is usually a disagreeable task since most of us like our indoor plumbing. However, if the toilet isn't working, some ingenuity is required. To protect the plumbing and to take care of immediate emergency needs, the following can be done:

- In the winter, if water lines are inoperative, put RV and marine antifreeze in toilet bowls and drains for sink, shower, and tub (available at camping and marine and RV stores). Use 1 or 2 cups as necessary.
- If you can't use the toilet, at least you can have the comfort of the toilet seat. Drain the toilet and place a large, heavy-duty plastic trash bag into the toilet bowl. Wrap the edge over toilet bowl, allowing the excess to hang loosely over the side. Place the toilet seat over the bag. Add one cup of deodorizing cat litter. After each use, cover excrement with more cat litter. Change bag often. Dispose by placing used bag inside a second one. Place outside in covered container until trash can be picked up again.
- In a long-term situation, human waste can be composted for use around shrubs and flowers. Information on do-it-yourself composting toilets and commercial composting toilets is available online at Wikipedia, www.wikipedia.org; search for composting toilet. If raw (not-composted) human waste is buried, care must be taken to prevent the runoff from seeping into any water source needed for drinking.
- Do not trust human waste compost on vegetable or fruit gardens. Some bad bacteria may enter the edibles and make those who eat them deathly ill.

OTHER HELPFUL ITEMS FOR STORAGE

- Clothesline and clothespins
- Salt, sand, or cat litter to sprinkle on ice so it is safe to walk on
- Pocket knife, heavy duty kitchen scissors
- Hack saw
- Duct tape
- Salve, lotion, lip balm
- Hatchet or ax to chop wood
- Power saw and fuel

- Matches and/or fire starters

EMERGENCY EVACUATION: In preparation for possible local, regional, or national emergency evacuation, the following things should be purchased and packed now. Store them in a location where they can be retrieved at a moment's notice.

BACKPACKS: Obtain a good-quality backpack for each member of the family.

Supplies for each backpack:
- Clothing, basic minimum: a change of underwear, jeans, two T-shirts, sweatshirt, heavy jacket, hat, gloves, sturdy shoes, extra socks, lightweight plastic boots; more if room is available
- Warm sleeping bag: Buy the best lightweight bag you can afford.
- Box of food that requires no preparation: Energy bars, cheese, canned meats and soups, dark chocolate, etc., to last for several days
- Adequate bottled water for every member of the family
- Camp cooking kit: plate, cup, tableware, and a good can opener for each family member.
- Small cooking heater: commercial or homemade candle burner described earlier
- Fire source: automatic lighter, waterproof matches, and fire starter
- Soap, two washcloths, and towels
- Flashlight or battery-operated lanterns. Have good batteries on hand.
- Good, sharp pocketknife
- Good-quality tent, with attached bottom and preferably winter ready

A Personal Experience During an at-Home Emergency

During Christmas of 2005, an ice storm dropped a tree branch on our roof, cutting our power lines. We were without the use of our furnace, electricity, tap water, or toilet. Using techniques in this chapter, we were able to stay in our home while others, having similar trouble, moved to motels. Some of these ideas are primitive, but they worked. We survived five days with a fair amount of comfort, until the power was restored. If necessary, the ideas above would have worked indefinitely.

Powerful suggestions, some possibly discussed in previous chapters.

- Prayerfully ask that Christ help you develop strong/stronger faith in Him.
- Think about things in your life you know are wrong. Talk to Him about them and repent.
- Be baptized in His name.
- Have Elders of the church lay their hands upon you to confer the Holy Ghost.
- Continue in prayer. Study the scriptures and other good books.
- Associate with others who are growing in their faith.
- Attend a scripture-based church in order to grow and help others grow.
- Seek out a scripture study group.
- Practice tithing and give offerings. Remember, you can never give more to God than He will give to you.
- Practice fasting.

- Repent of sin in your life as often as you recognize it.
- Hold on to your new/renewed faith until God calls you home.

Have I interpreted everything in this book correctly? Probably not. I am not a theologian, just an independent student of scripture. Please check theological concepts with your own scriptures before forming unbreakable conclusions.

My computer spell and grammar-check caught many of the glaring errors in this manuscript. Three friends also went over and over this book looking for omissions, inconsistencies and other mistakes. I was astonished when my publisher's editor later went through the manuscript and found MULTIPLE errors still on each page. Thank God for professionals. **Now, if it does not affect important content, please overlook anything else that is wrong**

If you disagree with any conclusions in this book, and can back up your opinion with two or more scriptures, let me hear from you. I will collect suggestions and if the opportunity arises, revise the book at a later date. My G-Mail Address is djeanneroberts@gmail.com

With respect and prayers for all my readers,

Jeanne Roberts

REFERENCE MATERIALS

Christians should educate themselves about the coming tribulation. The following reference books were used to compile all information in this manuscript. They are recommended as excellent sources for your study.

BASIC BOOKS FOR EVERY RLDS HOME STUDY LIBRARY

The Inspired Version of the Bible, Herald Publishing House, Independence, Mo., www.heraldhouse.org/

The Book of Mormon, Herald Publishing House, Independence, Mo., www.heraldhouse.org/

The Doctrine and Covenants—Herald Publishing House, Independence, Mo., www.heraldhouse.org/

Strong's Concordance of the Bible—Thomas Nelson Publishers Nashville, Tenn. 1985 www.thomasnelson.com

OR

Cruden's Complete Concordance:
Zondervan Publishing House, Grand Rapids, Michigan. http://www.zondervan.com/

Combined Concordances for the Scriptures: Herald Publishing House, Independence, Mo., www.heraldhouse.org/ (Note: This concordance for the Bible is not complete. It includes only the Latter Day Saint additions.)

Joseph Smith's New Translation of the Bible: Herald Publishing House, Independence, Mo., www.heraldhouse.org/ This helpful book prints the text of the Inspired Version of the Bible next to the King James Version, clearly showing the changes made by God through Joseph Smith.

Compendium of the Scriptures: Herald Publishing House, Independence, Mo., (out of print)*, www.heraldhouse.org/

A Compendium of the Faith and Doctrine of the Reorganized Church of Jesus Christ of Latter Day Saints: Herald Publishing House, Independence, Mo., (out of print)*, www.heraldhouse.org/ *NOTE: Herald House no longer publishes these two compendiums. However, they are very important books for Latter Day Saints who study the scriptures. Try to find old copies.

POSSIBLE RESOURCES FOR OLD RLDS PUBLICATIONS

Richard Price Publishing (Restoration Book Store), Independence, Mo., (816) 461-5659 www.restorationbookstore.org/

The Old Book Man www.oldbookman.us/rare.html

Amazon: http://www.amazon.com

E-Bay: http://www.ebay.com/

STUDY MATERIALS

- The New King James Version of the Bible, Word Publishing, Minneapolis, Mn.
- The New International Version of the Bible, Kenneth Barker, general editor
- Zondervan Publishing House, Grand Rapids, Mi, www.zondervan.com/
- *The Complete Jewish Bible*, David H. Stern, Jewish New Testament Publications, Jerusalem, Israel, http://www.messianicjewish.net/jntp/
- Harper Collins Bible Dictionary, Paul J. Achtemeier, general editor, Harper Collins Publishers, San Francisco, http://www.harpercollins.com/
- *The Bible Reader's Companion*, Lawrence O. Richards, Chariot Victor Publishing, a Division of Cook Communications, http://www.cookministries.org/
- *Illustrated Bible Handbook*, Lawrence O. Richards, Thomas Nelson Publishers, Nashville, TN, http://www.thomasnelson.com
- *The Bible Timeline*, by Thomas Robinson, Thomas Nelson Publishers, Nashville, TN, http://www.thomasnelson.com
- *The Wall Chart of World History from Earliest Times to the Present*, Professor Edward Hull, M.A., L.L.D., F.R.S., Barnes and Noble Publishing, London. http://www.barnesandnoble.com/
- *Josephus, The Complete Works*, Translated by William Whiston, A. M. Thomas Nelson Publishers, Nashville, TN, http://www.thomasnelson.com

BOOKS ON THE LAST DAYS

I have also read many of the Last Days books published since 1970. Their ideas vary widely, and some follow the scriptures more closely than others. Something of importance can be learned from most of them, but many also contain scriptural errors. Some that have been very helpful to me are the following:

Prophecy and Today, Norma Anne Holik, Th.D., Independence, Mo., 1978. This self-published book, which may be out of print, is by an RLDS author and scholar who incorporates a sound understanding of our Three Standard Books. Check Richard Price Publications, Independence, Mo., (816) 461-5659.

The Sign, a Biblical Study of End-Time Events, by Robert Van Kampen, Crossway Books, Wheaton, Ill. This scholarly manuscript may be heavy reading for some people. However, the author has done a masterful job of searching the scriptures and understanding the times that are to come. He explores the various rapture theories and agrees with the Doctrine & Covenants on this matter. www.crossway.org/home/books

The *Left Behind* Series by Tim LaHaye and Jerry Jenkins, Tyndale Publishing, www.tyndale.com/ combine interesting fiction with a somewhat accurate account of Bible prophecy. If the reader can sort fact from fiction, these books provide an interesting interpretation about the time to come, even though they support the pre-tribulation version of the rapture. This is a popular adventure series for those who enjoy fiction based on scripture.

The Late Great Planet Earth, Hal Lindsey, Zondervan, Grand Rapids, Mi., http://www.zondervan.com/
Satan Is Alive and Well on Planet Earth, Hal Lindsey, Zondervan, Grand Rapids, MI, http://www.zondervan.com/

There's a New World Coming: An In-Depth Analysis of the Book of Revelation, Hal Lindsey, Harvest House Publishers, Eugene, www.harvesthousepublishers.com/

Scriptural Parables for the Latter Days, Andrew C. Skinner and W. Jeffery Marsh, Deseret Book Company, Salt Lake City, Utah http://deseretbook.com/

The Second Coming, by David Pawson, of Sovereign World Limited, Kent, England, http://www.sovereignworld.com/

Many well-known ministers have also written on this subject. Their books may provide helpful insights, but most support the pre-rapture theory.

For Dummies Books, http://www.dummies.com

- Camping for Dummies
- Carpentry for Dummies
- Woodworking for Dummies
- Household Repair for Dummies

(Research the above internet site for a variety of "For Dummies" books with other helpful survival information.)

Doctrine and Covenants 36:12-14

Enoch beheld the Son of Man ascend up to the Father, and he called to the Lord saying, "Will you not come again upon the earth?"... And the Lord said to Enoch, "As I live, even so I will come in the last days.... And I will cause righteousness and truth to sweep the earth as a flood, and gather out my own elect from the four quarters of the earth to a place which I shall prepare; a holy city, that my people may gird up their loins, and be looking forth for the time of my coming; for there shall be my tabernacle, and it shall be called Zion, a New Jerusalem."

And the Lord said to Enoch, "Then you and all your city will meet them there, and we will receive them into our bosom, and they shall see us, and we will fall upon their necks, and they shall fall upon our necks, and we will kiss each other. And there shall be my abode, and it shall be Zion which shall come forth out of all the creations which I have made; and for the space of a thousand years the earth shall rest." And it came to pass that Enoch saw the days of the coming of the Son of Man, in the last days, to dwell on the earth in righteousness, for the space of a thousand years.

CPSIA information can be obtained
at www.ICGtesting.com
Printed in the USA
BVOW04s2154290317

479819BV00002B/90/P